ABOUT SSNs AND TINs ON GOVERNMENT FORMS AND CORRESPONDENCE

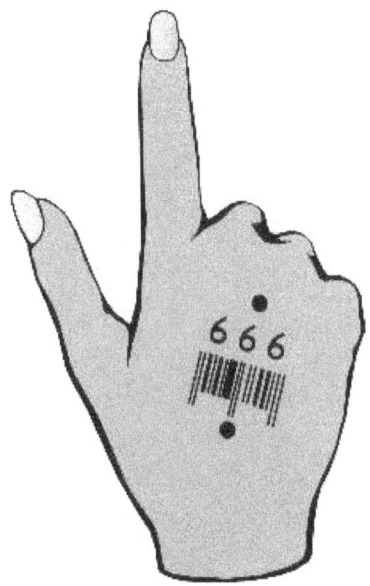

DEDICATION

"He [the Beast, meaning civil government, Rev. 19:19] causes all, both small and great, rich and poor, free and slave, to receive a mark on their right hand or on their foreheads, and that no one may buy or sell except one who has the mark or the name of the beast, or the number of his name."
[Rev. 13:16-17, Bible, NKJV]

"First Bowl: Loathsome Sores

"So the first went and poured out his bowl upon the earth, and a foul and loathsome sore came upon the men who had the mark of the beast and those who worshiped his image."
[Rev. 16:2, Bible, NKJV]

"And the smoke of their torment ascends forever and ever; and they have no rest day or night, who worship the beast and his image, and whoever receives the mark of his name."
[Rev. 14:11, Bible, NKJV]

"And I saw the beast, the kings of the earth, and their armies, gathered together to make war against Him who sat on the horse and against His army. Then the beast was captured, and with him the false prophet who worked signs in his presence, by which he deceived those who received the mark of the beast and those who worshiped his image. These two were cast alive into the lake of fire burning with brimstone."
[Rev. 19:19-20, Bible, NKJV]

"The Saints [Christians] Reign with Christ 1,000 Years

And I saw thrones, and they sat on them, and judgment was committed to them. Then I saw the souls of those who had been beheaded for their witness to Jesus and for the word of God, who had not worshiped the beast or his image, and had not received his mark on their foreheads or on their hands. And they lived and reigned with Christ for a thousand years."
[Rev. 20:4, Bible, NKJV]

Resources on what the Mark of the Beast is and the spiritual effects of taking the Mark:

1. *Property and Privacy Protection Topic*, Section 7: Numerical Identification and Automated Tracking (OFFSITE LINK) – Family Guardian Fellowship
   http://famguardian.org/Subjects/PropertyPrivacy/PropertyPrivacy.htm#NUMERICAL_IDENTIFICATION_AND_AUTOMATED_TRACKING:
2. *Social Security: Mark of the Beast*, Form #11.407
   http://famguardian.org/Publications/SocialSecurity/TOC.htm
3. *Socialism: The New American Civil Religion*, Form #05.016
   http://sedm.org/Forms/FormIndex.htm
4. *666 and the Mark of the Beast*-Amazing Facts
   http://www.amazingfacts.org/media-library/media/e/364/t/666-and-the-mark-of-the-beast
5. *Satan's Mark and God's Seal*-Amazing Facts
   http://www.amazingfacts.org/media-library/media/e/14118/t/satans-mark---gods-seal
6. *The Mark of the Beast*-Amazing Facts
   http://www.amazingfacts.org/media-library/media/e/419/t/the-mark-of-the-beast
7. *The Mark of the Beast*-Amazing Facts
   http://www.amazingfacts.org/media-library/study-guide/e/4997/t/the-mark-of-the-beast

TABLE OF CONTENTS

DEDICATION 2
TABLE OF CONTENTS 3
LIST OF TABLES 5
TABLE OF AUTHORITIES 5
1 Introduction 18
2 What We SPECIFICALLY Object to about Social Security Numbers and Taxpayer Identification Numbers 18
3 Social Security Numbers (SSNs) and Taxpayer Identification Numbers (TINs) are what the FTC calls a "franchise mark" 22
4 Why Knowing about SSNs and TINs is VERY important 30
5 Types of Numbers 33
   5.1 Tabular comparison of different types of numbers 33
   5.2 Social Security Numbers 36
   5.3 Individual Taxpayer Identification Numbers (ITINs) 36
   5.4 What kind of identifying number must Members use when corresponding with the IRS and for PRIVATE purposes then? 37
6 Interchangeability of SSNs with TINs 38
7 You were Never Lawfully Issued a "Social Security Number" 39
   7.1 Introduction 39
   7.2 The Delineation: Lower Case vs. Upper Case 40
   7.3 2. The SSA-3000 Discrepancy 40
   7.4 DHS Form I-9 and I-9 Instructions 41
   7.5 NRA Status and the "Brand Name" 41
   7.6 The Reality of Involuntary Servitude 41
   7.7 Conclusion: A Number Never Assigned and Labor Mischaracterized 42
8 SSN Numerical Identifier Origin Map 42
   8.1 The Application Bifurcation 42
      8.1.1 The U.S. Person Instrument: 43
      8.1.2 The Nonresident Alien Instrument: 43
   8.2 SS-5 to U.S. Persons Map 43
   8.3 SS-5 to Withholding Certificate Map 44
   8.4 Trade or Business Withholding Map 44
   8.5 The Statutory Conflict (42 U.S.C. §405(c)) 44
      8.5.1 Why the CONTEXT of "United States" Matters 45
      8.5.2 Connection to this Map 45
   8.6 The 26 U.S.C. 864(b) "Personal Services" Scam 46
      8.6.1 What § 864(b) actually defines 46
      8.6.2 Why the "physical presence = U.S. source" interpretation collapses 47
      8.6.3 Why this interpretation is the only one consistent with the statutes 47
   8.7 Summary 48
   8.8 Unified Summary Table WITH Capitalization Distinctions 48
9 Who owns the CARD, the NUMBER, and the LABEL and why you don't "have" a STATUTORY number unless you can control government with it 50
   9.1 Social Security CARD as PROPERTY 50
   9.2 Social Security NUMBER as PROPERTY 52
   9.3 "Social Security Number" LABEL as PROPERTY 52
   9.4 VOLUNTARY and LAWFUL USE of a STATUTORY NUMBER and a STATUTORY LABEL in connection with the franchise contract is what incurs legal obligations 53
   9.5 Consequences of using the SSN ONLY when there is LAWFUL participation 55

	9.6 Why you can't "HAVE" a STATUTORY number but CAN "HAVE" a NON-STATUTORY number	55
10	Social Security Trust	56
11	Who can lawfully be issued a "Social Security Number"?	58
12	Social Security Numbers assigned to or used by Nonresident Aliens (Members)	61
13	How to terminate or change the status of the number	63
14	State citizens or nationals cannot use numbers	65
15	Authorities on why nonresidents don't need SSNs/TINs to open bank accounts or for private employment	66
16	Mandatory Use of SSNs/TINs	69
	16.1 Compelled use forbidden by Privacy Act	69
	16.2 Burden of Proof on Those Compelling Use	70
	16.3 Penalties for compelled use	70
	16.4 When is it mandatory under the I.R.C. to provide government issued numbers?	71
	16.5 Mandatory use by ALIENS on the W-9 form	78
17	Penalties for failure to disclose numbers	80
	17.1 Failure to provide TIN on information returns	80
	17.2 Foreign Investment in Real Property Transfer Act (FIRPTA) penalties	81
18	Getting Rid of SSNs/TINs in your IRS or other government record	81
19	Quitting Social Security and living without SSNs or TINs	83
20	Changing the status of the SSN from U.S. person to Foreign Person	83
21	How to use "substitute numbers" to avoid being privileged	88
	21.1 DOD ID Numbers for Military Members	88
	21.2 Using all zeros	90
	21.3 Defining "Social Security Number" with your own definition	90
	21.4 Useful forms	91
22	Banking and Financial Industry Policy and Guidance on Use of SSN's and TINs	92
23	How to respond to requests for SSNs or TINs	96
	23.1 Avoiding confrontations in responding to requests for SSN/TIN from business associates	96
	23.1.1 Legal constraints for requesting an SSN/TIN	96
	23.1.2 Best strategy	98
	23.1.3 Socratic questions in response to the request for "the number"	99
	23.2 Dealing with Requests by Withholding Agents for an SSN/TIN to "U.S. Persons" on a W-9	100
	23.3 Financial Institutions	102
	23.4 Private Employer Job or Contract Applications	102
	23.5 Government applications for an account or benefit	104
	23.6 Dealing with "public servants" who demand a number at an audit or examination	105
	23.7 Submitting legal evidence as a non-resident indicating that "you" were never issued or applied for a "Social Security Number" or "Taxpayer Identification Number"	110
	23.8 Proving to federal agencies that they are FORBIDDEN by the Privacy Act from compelling the use of an SSN	119
	23.8.1 Forcing the agency to satisfy their burden or proof	119
	23.8.2 Proving that the TAX LAWS at least DO NOT require the use of an SSN in your case	121
	23.8.3 Conclusion and summary	123
24	Rebutted False Arguments About Government Identifying Numbers	125
	24.1 California DMV: We have a right to ask for Social Security Numbers as part of driver license applications	125
25	Summary and Conclusions	128
26	Resources for Further Study and Rebuttal	132
27	Questions that Readers, Grand Jurors, and Petit Jurors Should be Asking the Government	133
	27.1 Interrogatories	133
	27.2 Admissions	137

LIST OF TABLES

Table 1: Types of identifying numbers 34
Table 2: I.R.C. Statutory "Benefits" 74

TABLE OF AUTHORITIES

Constitutional Provisions

Article 1, Section 8, Clause 3 45
Article 4, Section 3, Clause 2 .... 25, 89
Article 4, Section 3, Clause 2 of the Constitution 20, 52
Article I or Article IV 20
Article III 20
Bill of Rights 125, 128
Declaration of Independence 19, 54, 110, 118
Federalist Paper No 45 (Jan. 1788) 127
Fifth Amendment 115, 116
First Amendment 19, 21, 36, 56, 61, 97, 98, 109, 116, 118, 124
Fourteenth Amendment 122, 128
Fourth Amendment 91
Sixteenth Amendment 122
Tenth Amendment 56
The Federalist No. 51 (1788), James Madison 21
Thirteenth Amendment 58, 66, 77, 99, 103, 107, 110, 116
U.S. Constitution, Article IV § 3 (2) 23

Statutes

1 Stat. 1 118
1 U.S.C. §204 36
18 U.S.C. §§911 and 912 124
18 U.S.C. §1001 .... 115, 116, 117
18 U.S.C. §1002 137
18 U.S.C. §1003 117
18 U.S.C. §1028 117
18 U.S.C. §1030 .... 64, 117
18 U.S.C. §1512 114
18 U.S.C. §1581 .... 90, 103
18 U.S.C. §1583 90
18 U.S.C. §1621 .... 115, 116
18 U.S.C. §208 .... 116, 138
18 U.S.C. §208(a) 55
18 U.S.C. §210 115
18 U.S.C. §211 90
18 U.S.C. §241 56
18 U.S.C. §247 98
18 U.S.C. §3 .... 64, 90, 137
18 U.S.C. §4 .... 65, 90, 137
18 U.S.C. §641 .... 55, 108
18 U.S.C. §654 98
18 U.S.C. §872 90

Reference	Pages
18 U.S.C. §911	64, 122, 123, 129
18 U.S.C. §912	54, 55, 61, 64, 90, 102, 108, 112, 114, 124, 129, 136, 137
18 U.S.C. §912	103
20 C.F.R. §422.103(b)(3)	46, 49
22 U.S.C. §2721	115, 118
26 U.S. Code §7701(a)(30)	101
26 U.S.C. § 3402(f)	49
26 U.S.C. §§6039 or 6039E	70
26 U.S.C. §§671 to 679	75
26 U.S.C. §§6721 - 6723	101
26 U.S.C. §§7701(a)(26), 6041A, 6041, 3406(a),(b),(h)(4),(h)(10), 31, 3402	49
26 U.S.C. §1	60, 74
26 U.S.C. §1(h)(11)(C)(i)(II)	74
26 U.S.C. §1.1441-1(c)(3)	84
26 U.S.C. §1402(b)	103
26 U.S.C. §1441	79, 80
26 U.S.C. §1445(b)(2)	81
26 U.S.C. §1445(f)(1)	81
26 U.S.C. §162	33, 60, 122
26 U.S.C. §170(b)(1)(A)(v)	44
26 U.S.C. §170(c)	44
26 U.S.C. §3121	30
26 U.S.C. §32	60
26 U.S.C. §321(d)	57
26 U.S.C. §3401(a)	109
26 U.S.C. §3401(c)	59, 99
26 U.S.C. §3402	44, 49
26 U.S.C. §3402(d)	99
26 U.S.C. §3402(f)	44
26 U.S.C. §3402(p)	97
26 U.S.C. §3406	98, 109
26 U.S.C. §3406(a)	44
26 U.S.C. §3406(b)	44
26 U.S.C. §3406(h)(10)	44
26 U.S.C. §3406(h)(4)	44
26 U.S.C. §501(c)	74, 76
26 U.S.C. §6001	59
26 U.S.C. §6011(b)	39, 128
26 U.S.C. §6013(g) and (h)	122
26 U.S.C. §6041	44, 79
26 U.S.C. §6041(a)	108
26 U.S.C. §6041A	44
26 U.S.C. §6109	34, 37, 38, 43, 61, 65, 71, 101, 116, 128
26 U.S.C. §6109(a)	128
26 U.S.C. §6109(a)(1)	37
26 U.S.C. §6109(a)(2) and (3)	66
26 U.S.C. §6109(a)(4)	66
26 U.S.C. §6109(d)	37, 38
26 U.S.C. §6109(g)	62, 63
26 U.S.C. §6109(i)	63
26 U.S.C. §6114	74
26 U.S.C. §6331	31
26 U.S.C. §6331(a)	57
26 U.S.C. §643(b)	75
26 U.S.C. §6671(b)	56
26 U.S.C. §6712	74
26 U.S.C. §6721(a)	80, 132

Reference	Pages
26 U.S.C. §6724(a)	101
26 U.S.C. §6901	56, 57
26 U.S.C. §6903	56, 57
26 U.S.C. §7207	124
26 U.S.C. §7343	56, 103
26 U.S.C. §7701(a)(1)	79, 80
26 U.S.C. §7701(a)(14)	70
26 U.S.C. §7701(a)(16)	121
26 U.S.C. §7701(a)(26)	22, 26, 32, 44, 60, 74, 76, 79, 103, 108, 126
26 U.S.C. §7701(a)(30)	34, 42, 70, 75, 76, 79, 95, 97, 120, 122, 128
26 U.S.C. §7701(a)(30).	66
26 U.S.C. §7701(a)(31)	91, 108
26 U.S.C. §7701(a)(41)	39
26 U.S.C. §7701(a)(9)	30
26 U.S.C. §7701(a)(9) and (a)(10)	66, 68, 72, 81, 96, 108, 109, 121, 122
26 U.S.C. §7701(b)(1)(B)	42, 67, 79, 91, 99
26 U.S.C. §83	122
26 U.S.C. §861(a)(3)(C)(i)	108
26 U.S.C. §861(a)(8)	122
26 U.S.C. §864(b)	46
26 U.S.C. §864(b)(1)(A)	75
26 U.S.C. §871	108
26 U.S.C. §871(a)	45
26 U.S.C. §871(b)	45, 46, 74
26 U.S.C. §871(f)	74, 76
26 U.S.C. §872	108, 122
26 U.S.C. §894	74
26 U.S.C. §897	81
26 U.S.C. §911(d)(1)	79
26 U.S.C. Section 6109	100
26 U.S.C.§ 871(b)	45
28 U.S.C. §1605(a)	127
28 U.S.C. §1605(a)(2)	106
28 U.S.C. §1746(1)	114, 116
28 U.S.C. §3001(15)(A)	53
28 U.S.C. §3002(15)(A)	56
31 U.S.C. §3701(a)(8)	42
31 U.S.C. §3720(a)	42
4 U.S.C. §110	66
4 U.S.C. §110(d)	86, 127
4 U.S.C. §72	54, 57, 76, 108
42 U.S.C. §1301	139
42 U.S.C. §1301(a)	86
42 U.S.C. §1301(a)(1)	87, 112
42 U.S.C. §1994	103
42 U.S.C. §2000d	28
42 U.S.C. §405	50
42 U.S.C. §405(c)	49
42 U.S.C. §405(c)(2)	48
42 U.S.C. §405(c)(2)(B)(i)(I)	45
42 U.S.C. §405(c)(2)(B)(i)(I),(III)	49
42 U.S.C. §405(c)(2)(B)(i)(III)	45
42 U.S.C. §405(c)(2)(C)(i)	126
42 U.S.C. §408	102, 130, 142
42 U.S.C. §408(a)(8)	90, 97
42 U.S.C. §602(a)(25)	28
42 U.S.C. §901	41

Citation	Page(s)
44 U.S.C. §1505(a)(1)	57
5 U.S.C. §2105	50, 54, 59, 135
5 U.S.C. §2105(a)	71, 112, 134
5 U.S.C. §301	100, 132
5 U.S.C. §301 (federal employees)	71, 72, 81
5 U.S.C. §552a Legislative Notes	69, 70, 119, 120
5 U.S.C. §552a(b)	105
5 U.S.C. §552a(g)(4)	70
5 U.S.C. §553a(a)(2)	120
7 U.S.C. §2011	28
7 U.S.C. §2025(e)	28
8 U.S.C. §1101	86
8 U.S.C. §1101(a)(21)	79, 85, 96, 142
8 U.S.C. §1101(a)(3)	34
8 U.S.C. §1401	122, 140, 142
Buck Act, 4 U.S.C. §110(d)	127
California Revenue and Taxation §17018	125
California Revenue and Taxation §6017	125
California Vehicle Code	125
Chapter 61 of the Internal Revenue Code	79
Copyright Act, 17 U.S.C. §105	52
Federal Crop Insurance Act	62
Foreign Sovereign Immunities Act, 28 U.S.C. Chapter 97	117
Freedom of Information Act (FOIA)	62
HIPAA	89
I.R.C. §§3121, 3401	42
I.R.C. §6041	100, 101
I.R.C. §6109	101
I.R.C. §6109(a)(2)	101
I.R.C. §6109(a)(3)	101
I.R.C. Subtitle A	31, 126
Internal Revenue Code	122, 132
Internal Revenue Code Subtitle A	63
Internal Revenue Code Subtitles A and C	22, 29
Internal Revenue Code, Section 6109	63
Privacy Act	100, 101
Privacy Act of 1974	122, 124
Privacy Act of 1974, 5 U.S.C. §552a(a)(1)	123, 124
Privacy Act, 5 U.S.C. §552a	60
Privacy Act, 5 U.S.C. §552a(b)	55, 91
Religious Freedom Restoration Act (R.F.R.A.)	118
Religious Freedom Restoration Act (RFRA), 42 U.S.C. Chapter 21B	19
Section 7(b) of the Privacy Act, Pub.L. 93-579	70
Sherman Anti-Trust Act	118
Social Security Act	39, 54, 56, 63, 112, 129, 132, 139, 140
Social Security Act as of 2005, Section 1101	140
Social Security Act at 42 U.S.C. 1301(a)(1)	126
Social Security Act of 1935	56
Social Security Act, 42 U.S.C. §405	46
Social Security Act, 42 U.S.C. §405(c)(2)(B)(i) and (ii)	45
Social Security Act, Section 1101(a)(1)	139
Social Security Act, Section 1101(a)(2)	139
Social Security Act, Title 42, Chapter 7	132
Title 26 of the U.S. Code	36
Title 42	36, 54, 56, 106, 139
Title 42 of the U.S. Code	56, 126
Title 5 of the U.S. Code	61, 134

U.C.C. §2.103(1)(a) 19
U.C.C. §2.104(1) 19
U.C.C. §2-103(1) 117
U.C.C. §2-103(1)(a) 23
U.C.C. §2-103(l)(a) 98
U.C.C. §2-104(1) 23, 98, 117
Uniform Commercial Code (U.C.C.) 117

Regulations

20 C.F.R. §402.1 .... 43, 44, 48, 49
20 C.F.R. §422. 103 through 422.107 41
20 C.F.R. §422.103 .... 34, 42, 50, 116, 135, 137
20 C.F.R. §422.103 through 20 C.F.R. §422.107 41
20 C.F.R. §422.103 through 422.107 41
20 C.F.R. §422.103(a) 48, 49
20 C.F.R. §422.103(a),(b)(3) 48
20 C.F.R. §422.103(b) 43
20 C.F.R. §422.103(b)(3) 43, 49
20 C.F.R. §422.103(d) 52, 90, 91, 96, 102, 106, 109, 112, 129, 135, 136
20 C.F.R. §422.104 .... 34, 58, 63, 64, 67, 76, 85, 128, 139
20 C.F.R. §422.104(a) 139
20 C.F.R. §422.401 42
20 C.F.R. §422.402(e) 41
20 C.F.R. Subpart E 41
26 C.F.R. §§1.864-2, 1.861-4, 1.1441-4 49
26 C.F.R. §1.1-1 .... 59, 87
26 C.F.R. §1.1-1(a)(2)(ii) 103
26 C.F.R. §1.1-1(c) 99, 116
26 C.F.R. §1.1441-1 .... 66, 78, 80, 97
26 C.F.R. §1.1441-1(b)(5)(i) 109
26 C.F.R. §1.1441-1(c)(14) 74
26 C.F.R. §1.1441-1(c)(26) 75
26 C.F.R. §1.1441-1(c)(3) 37, 76, 79
26 C.F.R. §1.1441-1(d) 79, 121
26 C.F.R. §1.1441-1(d)(3) 79
26 C.F.R. §1.1441-1(e)(1)(ii)(A)(1) 109
26 C.F.R. §1.1441-1(e)(5) 74
26 C.F.R. §1.1441-1(e)(5)(ii) 74
26 C.F.R. §1.1441-4 .... 45, 75
26 C.F.R. §1.1441-4(b)(4) 75
26 C.F.R. §1.1441-5(c) 75
26 C.F.R. §1.1441-5(e) 75
26 C.F.R. §1.1441-6(g)(1) 75
26 C.F.R. §1.1461-1(c)(2)(i) 75
26 C.F.R. §1.469-9(b)(4) 75
26 C.F.R. §1.6012-1(a)(6) 84
26 C.F.R. §1.6041-4(a)(1) 109
26 C.F.R. §1.6041-6 101
26 C.F.R. §1.6721-1(a)(1) 132
26 C.F.R. §1.861-4 45
26 C.F.R. §1.864-2 .... 45, 47, 49
26 C.F.R. §1.871-1(b)(i) 91
26 C.F.R. §1.871-7(a)(4) 108
26 C.F.R. §1.872-2(f) 103, 108
26 C.F.R. §301.6109-1 .... 62, 63, 70, 84, 100, 121

26 C.F.R. §301.6109-1(a)	97
26 C.F.R. §301.6109-1(b)	32, 35, 40, 43, 71, 97, 106, 122, 131
26 C.F.R. §301.6109-1(b)(1)	121
26 C.F.R. §301.6109-1(b)(2)	121, 123, 124
26 C.F.R. §301.6109-1(b)(2)(iv)	37
26 C.F.R. §301.6109-1(d)	43
26 C.F.R. §301.6109-1(d)(3)	34, 36, 104, 128
26 C.F.R. §301.6109-1(d)(3)(i)	85, 87
26 C.F.R. §301.6109-1(d)(4)	61
26 C.F.R. §301.6109-1(g)(1)(i)	43, 64, 83, 90
26 C.F.R. §301.6109-1(g)(2)	84
26 C.F.R. §301.6721-1(a)(1)	80
26 C.F.R. §301.7701-11	39, 43, 48, 128
26 C.F.R. §301.7701-7	30
26 C.F.R. §301.7701-7(b)	121
26 C.F.R. §31.3401(a)(6)-1(b)	109
26 C.F.R. §31.3401(a)-3	57
26 C.F.R. §31.3401(c)-1	59, 99
26 C.F.R. §31.3406(g)-1(e)	109
26 C.F.R. §31.6011(b)-2	43, 48
26 C.F.R. §31.6011(b)-2(b)	43, 44, 49
31 C.F.R. §1010.100	95
31 C.F.R. §1020.220	92
31 C.F.R. §1020.410	67
31 C.F.R. §1020.410(b)(3)(x)	102, 123
31 C.F.R. §306.10	68, 123
80 FR 47833	48
Social Security Regulations, Social Security Administration	132
Title 20 of the Code of Federal Regulations	59, 86
Treasury Regulations	36

Rules

Federal Rule of Civil Procedure 17(b)	26, 59
Federal Rule of Civil Procedure 8(b)(6)	137

Cases

Ashton v. Cameron County Water Improvement District No. 1, 298 U.S. 513, 56 S.Ct. 892 (1936)	59, 140
Ashwander v. T.V.A., 297 U.S. 288, 56 S.Ct. 466, 80 L.Ed. 688 (1936)	29
Ashwander v. Tennessee Valley Auth., 297 U.S. 288 (1936)	129
Bowen v. Roy, 476 U.S. 693 (1986)	28, 133
Broadrick v. Oklahoma, 413 U.S. 601, 616 -617 (1973)	106
Budd v. People of State of New York, 143 U.S. 517 (1892)	32, 57, 78
Burgin v. Forbes, 293 Ky. 456, 169 S.W.2d. 321, 325	140
Burton v. Wilmington Parking Authority, 365 U.S. 715 (1961)	27
C.I.R. v. Trustees of L. Inv. Ass'n, 100 F.2d. 18 (1939)	70
Camden v. Allen, 2 Dutch., 398	20, 28, 77, 114, 131
Carter v. Carter Coal Co., 298 U.S. 238, 56 S.Ct. 855 (1936)	59, 125, 140
Civil Service Comm'n v. Letter Carriers, 413 U.S. 548, 556 (1973)	106
Clearfield Trust Co. v. United States, 318 U.S. 363, 369 (1943)	21
Cleveland Bed. of Ed. v. LaFleur, 414 U.S. 632, 639-640, 94 S.Ct. 1208, 1215 (1974)	113
Connick v. Myers, 461 U.S. 138, 147 (1983)	105
Cooke v. United States, 91 U.S. 389, 398 (1875)	21
Curtin v. State, 61 Cal.App. 377, 214 P. 1030, 1035	112, 120

Doe v. Chao, 540 U.S. 614 (2004) 71
Dollar Savings Bank v. United States, 19 Wall. 227 22
Downes v. Bidwell, 182 U.S. 244 (1901) 31
Economy Plumbing & Heating v. U.S., 470 F.2d. 585 (1972) 70
Edmonson v. Leesville Concrete Company, 500 U.S. 614 (1991) 27
Electric Co. v. Dow, 166 U.S. 489, 17 S.Ct. 645, 41 L.Ed. 1088 .... 29, 64
Elliott v. City of Eugene, 135 Or. 108, 294 P. 358, 360 134
Fauntleroy v. Lum, 210 U.S. 230 , 28 S.Ct. 641 22
Flemming v. Nestor, 363 U.S. 603 (1960) 20, 55, 56, 138
Flemming v. Nestor, 363 U.S. 603, 610, 80 S.Ct. 1367 (1960) 139
Flesch v. Circle City Excavating & Rental Corp., 137 Ind.App. 695, 210 N.E.2d. 865 53
Freeman v. Alderson, 119 U.S. 185, 7 S.Ct. 165, 30 L.Ed. 372 53
Frost v. Corporation Commission, 278 U.S. 515, 49 S.Ct. 235 (U.S., 1929) 29
Gardner v. Broderick, 392 U.S. 273, 277 -278 (1968) 105
Gomillion v. Lightfoot, 364 U.S. 339, 345 125
Great Falls Manufacturing Co. v. Attorney General, 124 U.S. 581 129
Great Falls Manufacturing Co. v. Attorney General, 124 U.S. 581, 8 S.Ct. 631, 31 L.Ed. 527 .... 29, 63
Great Falls Mfg. Co. v. Attorney General, 124 U.S. 581, 8 S.Ct. 631, 31 L.Ed. 527 .... 29, 63
Gulf, C. & S. F. R. Co. v. Ellis, 165 U.S. 150 (1897) 107
Haig v. Agee, 453 U.S. 280 (1981) 142
Hammer v. Dagenhart, 247 U.S. 251, 275, 38 S.Ct. 529, 3 A.L.R. 649, Ann.Cas.1918E 724 .... 59, 125
Hanson v. Vernon, 27 Ia., 47 .... 20, 28, 77, 114, 131
Harman v. Forssenius, 380 U.S. 528 at 540, 85 S.Ct. 1177, 1185 (1965) 125
Hurley v. Commission of Fisheries, 257 U.S. 223, 225, 42 S.Ct. 83, 66 L.Ed. 206. 29
In re Riggle's Will, 11 A.D.2d. 51 205 N.Y.S.2d. 19, 21, 22 52
Insanity. State v. Haner, 186 Iowa, 1259,173 N.W. 225 116
Jones v. Commonwealth, 154 Ky. 752,159 S.W. 568, 569 116
Kaiser Aetna v. United States, 444 U.S. 164 (1979) 134
Kelley v. Johnson, 425 U.S. 238, 247 (1976) 105
Lacey v. State, 13 Ala.App. 212, 68 So. 706, 710 .... 112, 120
Leonard v. Vicksburg, etc., R. Co., 198 U.S. 416, 422, 25 S.Ct. 750, 49 L.Ed. 1108 .... 29, 64
License Tax Cases, 72 U.S. 462, 18 L.Ed. 497, 5 Wall. 462, 2 A.F.T.R. 2224 (1866) 25, 77, 126, 129
Loan Association v. Topeka, 20 Wall. 655 (1874) 20, 28, 77, 114, 131
Long v. Rasmussen, 281 F. 236 (1922) 70
Loughborough v. Blake, 5 Wheat. 317, 5 L.Ed. 98 31
Marsh v. Alabama, 326 U.S. 501 (1946) 27
Matter of Mayor of N.Y., 11 Johns., 77 .... 20, 28, 77, 114, 131
Meredith v. United States, 13 Pet. 486, 493 22
Milwaukee v. White, 296 U.S. 268 (1935) 22
Munn v. Illinois, 94 U.S. 113 (1876) 23
Newblock v. Bowles, 170 Okl. 487, 40 P.2d. 1097, 1100 140
Northern Liberties v. St. John's Church, 13 Pa.St. 104 .... 20, 28, 77, 114, 131
Norton v. Shelby County, 118 U.S. 425 (1885) 141
O'Connor v. Ortega, 480 U.S. 709, 723 (1987) 105
O'Neill v. United States, 231 Ct.Cl. 823, 826 (1982) 21
Pack v. Southwestern Bell Tel. & Tel. Co., 215 Tenn. 503, 387 S.W.2d. 789, 794 .... 51, 138
Pannoyer v. Neff, 95 U.S. 714, 24 L.Ed. 565 53
Perry v. United States, supra at 352 (1935) 21
Pierce v. Somerset Ry., 171 U.S. 641, 648, 19 S.Ct. 64, 43 L.Ed. 316 .... 29, 64
Poindexter v. Greenhow, 114 U.S. 270, 5 S.Ct. 903 (1885) 141
Pray v. Northern Liberties, 31 Pa.St. 69 .... 20, 28, 77, 114, 131
Price v. United States, 269 U.S. 492 , 46 S.Ct. 180 22
Public Workers v. Mitchell, 330 U.S. 75, 101 (1947) 106
ReMine ex rel. Liley v. District Court for City and County of Denver, Colo., 709 P.2d. 1379, 1382 53
Ricker's Petition, 66 N.H. 207 (1890) 97
Rutan v. Republican Party of Illinois, 497 U.S. 62 (1990) 106
San Francisco Arts & Athletics, Inc. v. United States Olympic Committee, 483 U.S. 522, 544 -545 (1987) 27

Shelley v. Kraemer, 334 U.S. 1 (1948) 27
Shelmadine v. City of Elkhart, 75 Ind.App. 493, 129 N.E. 878 .... 112, 120
Sherbert v. Verner, 374 U.S. 398, 412 (1963) (Douglas, J., concurring) 28
Sinking Fund Cases, 99 U.S. 700 (1878) 60, 78
Smith v. Allwright, 321 U.S. 649, 644 125
St. Louis Casting Co. v. Prendergast Construction Co., 260 U.S. 469 129
St. Louis Malleable Casting Co. v. Prendergast Construction Co., 260 U.S. 469, 43 S.Ct. 178, 67 L.Ed. 351 .... 29, 64
St. Louis, etc., Co., v. George C. Prendergast Const. Co., 260 U.S. 469, 43 S.Ct. 178, 67 L.Ed. 351 .... 29, 63
State ex rel. Colorado River Commission v. Frohmiller, 46 Ariz. 413, 52 P.2d. 483, 486 .... 112, 120
State v. Brennan, 49 Ohio.St. 33, 29 N.E. 593 .... 112, 120
Stockwell v. United States, 13 Wall. 531, 542 22
Terry v. Adams, 345 U.S. 461 (1953) 27
Tulsa Professional Collection Services, Inc. v. Pope, 485 U.S. 478 (1988) 27
U.S. v. Butler, 297 U.S. 1 (1936) 29, 77, 114, 131, 133
United States Railroad Retirement Board v. Fritz, 449 U.S. 166 (1980) 20
United States v. Bostwick, 94 U.S. 53, 66 (1877) 21
United States v. Calamaro, 354 U.S. 351 (1957) 71
United States v. Chamberlin, 219 U.S. 250, 31 S.Ct. 155 22
United States v. Harris, 106 U.S. 629, 1 S.Ct. 601, 27 L.Ed. 290 (1883) 117
United States v. National Exchange Bank of Baltimore, 270 U.S. 527, 534 (1926) 21
United States v. Winstar Corp., 518 U.S. 839 (1996) 21
Vlandis v. Kline, 412 U.S. 441, 449, 93 S.Ct. 2230, 2235 (1973) 113
Walker v. Rich, 79 Cal.App. 139, 249 P. 56, 58 .... 112, 120
Wall v. Parrot Silver & Copper Co., 244 U.S. 407 129
Wall v. Parrot Silver & Copper Co., 244 U.S. 407, 37 S.Ct. 609, 61 L.Ed. 1229 .... 29, 63
Wall v. Parrot Silver & Copper Co., 244 U.S. 407, 411, 412, 37 S.Ct. 609, 61 L.Ed. 1229 .... 29, 64
Wisconsin v. Pelican Insurance Co., 127 U.S. 265, 292, et seq. 8 S.Ct. 1370 22
Yaselli v. Goff, C.C.A., 12 F.2d. 396, 403, 56 A.L.R. 1239 .... 112, 120

Other Authorities

1040 form 33
1040 return 122
1040-NR Attachment, Form #09.077 .... 38, 86
1040NR return 108
666 and the Mark of the Beast, Amazing Facts 2, 133
About IRS Form W-8BEN, Form #04.202 .... 58, 102, 103
Administrative State: Tactics and Defenses, Form #12.041 31
Affidavit of Citizenship, Domicile, and Tax Status, Form #02.001 .... 102, 123
AMENDED IRS Form W-8BEN 102
Attachment to Government form which asks for Social Security Number, Family Guardian Fellowship 82
Avoiding Traps in Government Forms Course, Form #12.023 .... 25, 97
Black's Law Dictionary, Fourth Edition, p. 1235 .... 112, 120
Black's Law Dictionary, Fourth Edition, p. 880 117
Black's Law Dictionary, Fourth Edition, pp. 786-787 134
Black's Law Dictionary, Second Edition, p. 955 133
Black's Law Dictionary, Sixth Edition, p. 1231 .... 52, 138
Black's Law Dictionary, Sixth Edition, p. 581 140
Black's Law Dictionary, Sixth Edition, p. 793 53
Black's Law Dictionary, Sixth Edition, pp. 1304-1306 53
Bouvier's Maxims of Law, 1856 .... 23, 26, 64
Caesar 22, 26
California Department of Motor Vehicles (DMV) 125
Change Your Filing Status to "nonresident alien" and "Denumber" yourself, Sovereignty Forms and Instructions Online, Form #10.004, step 3.14 82
Citizenship and Sovereignty Course, Form #12.002 123

Entry	Page
Citizenship Status v. Tax Status, Form #10.011	123
Citizenship Status v. Tax Status, Form #10.011, Section 12	66
Clearfield Doctrine of the U.S. Supreme Court	21
Cooley, Const. Lim., 479	28
Copilot: Meaning of civil statutory "services", FTSIG	46
Corrected Information Return Attachment Letter, Form #04.002	104
Correcting Erroneous Information Returns, Form #04.001	104, 108
Correcting Erroneous IRS Form 1042's, Form #04.003	91, 104
Correcting Erroneous IRS Form 1098's, Form #04.004	91, 102, 104
Correcting Erroneous IRS Form 1099's, Form #04.005	91, 102, 104
Correcting Erroneous IRS Form W-2's, Form #04.006	104
DD Form 108, Application for Retired Pay and Benefits	88
DD2656	123
De Facto Government Scam, Form #05.043	19, 118
Defense Finance Accounting Service (DFAS)	119, 122
Defense Privacy, Civil Liberties, and Transparency Division: Privacy	89
Delegation of Authority Order from God to Christians, Form #13.007	19
Demand for Verified Evidence of Trade or Business Activity: Information Return, Form #04.007	103
Department of Defense (DOD)	119
Developing Evidence of Citizenship and Sovereignty Course, Form #12.002	104
DFAS SORN, Defense Military Retiree and Annuity Pay System Records (January 07, 2009, 74 FR 696)	124
Disclaimer, Section 4.31: Natural law	110
Disclosure of Social Security Numbers, Department of Justice Office of Privacy and Civil Liberties	69, 119
DOD Directive 5124.02	89
DOD Instruction 1000.30	89, 123
DOD Retirement Pay Request Letter, Form #04.227	89
Don't Give Your Children Social Security Numbers, Sovereignty Forms and Instructions Online, Form #10.004, Instructions, Step 1.1	82
DS-260	43, 48
Excluded Earnings and People, Form #14.019	108, 122
Family Guardian Website, Taxes page	132
Federal and State Tax Withholding Options for Private Employers, Form #09.001	98, 103
Federal Civil Trials and Evidence, Rutter Group, paragraph 8:4993, p. 8K-34	113
Federal Courts and the IRS' Own IRM Say the IRS is NOT RESPONSIBLE for its Actions or Its Words, or for Following Its Own Written Procedures, Family Guardian Fellowship	24
Federal Trade Commission	134
Federal Trade Commission (F.T.C.)	22, 96
Form #02.001	80
Form #05.007	96
Form #05.014	19
Form #05.018	112
Form #05.023	54
Form #05.050	19
Form #06.002	38, 56
Form #08.024	97
Form #12.025	98
Form #13.007	98
Form #14.020	106
Form 1099	100, 101
Form 1099CC, Form #04.309	124
Form DD108	123
Form DD2656	121, 122
Form DD2656 entitled "Data for payment of Retired Personnel"	119
Form SS-5	43
Form SS-5 application	56
Form SSA-3000	40
Form W-4	32, 97, 98, 99

Entry	Pages
Form W-7	37
Form W-8	99
Form W-9	32, 78, 79, 80, 82, 97, 100, 101
Foundations of Freedom, Video 1, Form #12.021	21
FTC Franchise Rule Compliance Guide, May 2008	22, 135
FTC Franchise Rule Compliance Guide, May 2008, p. 1	22, 135
Getting a USA Passport as a "state national", Form #09.007	82
Getting a USA Passport as a "state national", Form #10.013, Section 9.6	112
Government Conspiracy to Destroy the Separation of Powers, Form #05.023	31, 127
Government Identity Theft, Form #05.046	62, 69, 90, 116, 126
Government Instituted Slavery Using Franchises, Form #05.030	129, 131, 132
Government Instituted Slavery Using Franchises, Form #05.030, Section 23	112
Great IRS Hoax, Form #11.302	57, 72, 132
Great IRS Hoax, Form #11.302 sections 5.4 through 5.4.3.6	36
Great IRS Hoax, Form #11.302, Sections 4.3.13 and 5.4 through 5.4.3.6	36
Hierarchy of Sovereignty: The Power to Create is the Power to Tax, Family Guardian Fellowship	24, 52
Hot Issues: Invisible Consent*, SEDM	54
How State Nationals Volunteer to Pay Income Tax, Form #08.024	31, 110
How to File Returns, Form #09.074, Section 9.12	121
HOW TO: How to notify Social Security that You as a Nonresident Alien U.S. national are INELIGIBLE for SSN and demand destruction of all NUMIDENT Records, FTSIG	48
How You Lose Constitutional or Natural Rights, Form #10.015	54
I-765	43, 48
Identity Theft Affidavit, Form #14.020	123, 124
Income Tax Withholding and Reporting Course, Form #12.004	104
Injury Defense Franchise and Agreement, Form #06.027	25, 38, 89, 107, 118, 128
Internal Revenue Manual (I.R.M.), Section 20.1.7.1.5	80
Internal Revenue Manual (I.R.M.), Section 4.10.7.2.8	104
Internal Revenue Manual (I.R.M.), Section 5.14.10.2 (09-30-2004)	60
IRS Circular E: Employer's Tax Guide	35
IRS Due Process Meeting Handout, Form #03.008	66
IRS Form 1040NR Instructions, Year 2007, p. 9	73
IRS Form 1042s	76, 130
IRS Form 1042s Instructions, Year 2006, p. 14	73, 130
IRS Form 14039	106
IRS Form 4029	56
IRS Form 4029: Application for Exemption from Social Security Taxes and Waiver of Benefits	82
IRS Form 4549	113
IRS Form 56	61, 65
IRS Form 8233	75
IRS Form 843	82
IRS Form 8832	83
IRS Form SS-4	128
IRS Form W-4	57, 130
IRS Form W-7	34, 128
IRS Form W-8, Certificate of Non-Foreign Status	81
IRS Form W-8BEN	82, 83, 87
IRS Form W-8BEN, Form #04.202	90
IRS Form W-9	34, 128
IRS Form W-9, p. 6	100
IRS Form W-9: Application for NONTAXPAYER identification number	82
IRS Forms W-2 and 1099	103
IRS Forms W-2, 1042-S, 1098, 1099, K-1	80
IRS Forms W-2, 1042-S, 1098, or 1099	104
IRS Pub. 515 Inst. p. 7	123
IRS Publication 1915	34, 36, 37
IRS Publication 1915, p. 5, Rev. 9-2007, Catalog Number 22533M	37

Entry	Page
IRS Publication 519, Year 2005, p. 23	72
Jurisdiction Over Federal Areas Within the States, U.S. Attorney General	125
Justification for the Continued Use of Social Security Numbers in Case Management System-DITPR #8679, DFAS	124
Language You Can Use in Identity Document Application to Prove You Don't Have an SSN and Aren't Eligible, and Never Applied for One, SEDM	118
Legal Deception, Propaganda, and Fraud, Form #05.014	113, 116
Legal Information Institute: Social Security, Cornell University	133
Legal Requirement to File Federal Income Tax Returns, Form #05.009	66
Letter about Social Security Numbers, Social Security Administration	83
Mackeld. Rom. Law, § 265	133
Mirror Image Rule, Mark DeAngelis	23, 54
Mish, F. C. (2003). Preface. Merriam-Websters collegiate dictionary. (Eleventh ed.). Springfield, MA: Merriam-Webster, Inc.	134
MyPay System	124
Nonresident Alien Position	61
Non-Resident Non-Person Position, Form #05.020	103, 106
Non-Resident Non-Person Position, Form #05.020, Section 10.4.2	37
Office of Management and Budget (OMB)	100
Opening Bank Accounts Without SSNs, Antishyster Magazine	82
Path to Freedom, Form #09.015, Section 2	38
Path to Freedom, Form #09.015, Sections 5.5-5.7	97
Presumption: Chief Weapon for Unlawfully Enlarging Federal Jurisdiction, Form #05.017	114
Privacy Act Notice within the Form W-9 itself, on page 6	100
Privacy Impact Assessment (PIA)- Case Management System	124
Privacy Impact Assessment (PIA) -Defense Retiree and Annuitant Pay System (DRAS)	124
Privacy Impact Assessments (PIA), DFAS	124
PROOF OF FACTS: You were Never Lawfully Issued a "Social Security Number", FTSIG	39
PROOF OF FACTS: "trade or business within the United States" and "personal services within the United States" means service in a capacityPUB and not a geography, FTSIG	46
PROOF OF FACTS: "United States" in I.R.C. 871(b), 864(b), and 6671(b) is the United StatesGOV, not a geography, FTSIG	46
Proof that American Nationals are Nonresident Aliens, Form #09.081	37
Proof that Involuntary Income Taxes on Your Labor are Slavery, Form #05.055	122
Proof That There Is a "Straw Man", Form #05.042	66
Property and Privacy Protection Topic, Section 7: Numerical Identification and Automated Tracking, Family Guardian Fellowship	2, 132
Public Rights Doctrine	42
Quit Social Security and Rescind your Social Security Number, Sovereignty Forms and Instructions Online, Form #10.004, step 3.17	82
Reasonable Belief About Income Tax Liability, Form #05.007	113, 137
Reasonable Cause Regulations and Requirements for Missing and Incorrect Name/TINs, IRS Publication 1586	102
Requirement for Equal Protection and Equal Treatment, Form #05.033	21, 25
Resignation of Compelled Social Security Trustee, Form #06.002	58, 64, 65, 83, 96, 102, 132
Roman system of jus civile, civil law, or civil "statutes"	26
Satan's Mark and God's Seal, Amazing Facts	2, 133
Secrets of the Social Security Number, Buildfreedom	82
SEDM Disclaimer, Section 4.10: Franchise	20
SEDM Exhibit #07.012	64
SEDM Liberty University	132
SEDM Member Agreement, Form #01.001	91
SEDM Website Opening Page	18
Separation Between Public and Private Course, Form #12.025	19, 110, 115
signed Form I-9	41
Social Security Administration	38, 112, 115
Social Security Administration Letter, Exhibit #07.004	36, 102
Social Security Card	34, 51, 128, 129
Social Security Form SS-521: Request for Withdrawal of Application	82

Entry	Page(s)
Social Security Number (FFDL 8)	125
Social Security Number (SSN), Sovereignty Forms and Instructions Online, Form #10.004, Cites by Topic	82
Social Security Numbers (SSNs)	134
Social Security Numbers for Children?, Social Security Administration	82
Social Security Policy Manual, Form #06.013	83
Social Security Program Policy Documents, Social Security Administration	132
Social Security Publication 42-007: Specifications for Filing Forms W-2 Electronically	90
Social Security: Idolatry and Slavery, Mercy Seat Christian Church	132
Social Security: Mark of the Beast, Form #11.407	2, 20, 132
Socialism: The New American Civil Religion, Form #05.016	2, 21, 36
Socialist Ponzi Scheme	113
Sovereignty Forms and Instructions Online, Form #10.004	132
SS-5	48
SS-5 application	56, 62
SSA Form 7008	82
SSA Form SS-4: Application for Employer Identification Number	35
SSA Form SS-5	34, 56, 81, 129, 130, 132
SSA Program Operations Manual System (POMS), POMS RM 10212.001	48
SSN Numberical Identifier Origin Map, FTSG	42
State DMV Change of Address letter	82
T.D. 7306, 39 FR 9947, Mar. 15, 1974	39
Tax Form Attachment, Form #04.201	38, 91
Taxpayer Identification Number (TIN)	82
The "Trade or Business" Scam, Form #05.001	20, 79, 86, 103, 126
The BEST Way to LAWFULLY Reject ANY and ALL Benefits in Court that is Unassailable, SEDM	56
The Law of Nations, p. 87, E. De Vattel, Volume Three, 1758	76
The Mark of the Beast, Amazing Facts	2, 133
The Matrix	110
The RAPID (Retired Annuity Pay Information DRAS)	124
The Word Detective: Idiot; Downloaded 1/30/2017	117
Third Rail Government Issues, Form #08.032	38
This Form is Your Form, Mark DeAngelis	23, 54
Treasury Decision 8734	101
Treasury Department	100
Unconstitutional Conditions Doctrine	118
USA Passport Application Attachment, Form #06.007	118
Using the Laws of Property to Respond to a Federal or State Tax Collection Notice, Form #14.015	82
VA Form 10, Application for Health Benefits	88
Veterans Administration	124
Veterans Administration (VA)	119
Veterans Administration Benefit Application, Form #06.041	25, 89
W-7 application	62
W-7 form	63
W-8 Supp. Inst. p. 1,2,6 (Cat. 26698G)	123
W-8BEN Inst. p. 1,2,4,5 (Cat. 25576H)	123
W-8SUB, Form #04.231	123
Webster's Collegiate Dictionary	55
Webster's Collegiate Dictionary, 1983, ISBN 0-87779-510-X, p. 556	55
What is "Law"?, Form #05.048	21
Who are "Taxpayers" and who needs a "Taxpayer Identification Number"?, Form #05.013	132
Why Domicile and Becoming a "Taxpayer" Require Your Consent, Form #05.002	57, 66, 68, 96, 110
Why It is Illegal for Me to Request or Use a Taxpayer Identification Number, Form #04.205	19, 25, 89, 105, 118, 128, 132
Why It's a Crime for a Private American National to File a 1040 Income Tax Return, Form #08.021	66
Why Statutory Civil Law is Law for Government and Not Private Persons, Form #05.037	66, 131
Why the Fourteenth Amendment is NOT a Threat to Your Freedom, Form #08.015	123
Why the Government Can't Lawfully Assess Human Beings with an Income Tax Liability Without Their Consent, Form #05.011, Section 8.5	113

Why You are a Political Citizen but Civil Non-Citizen, National, and Nonresident Alien, Form #05.006 ...... 79, 96, 116, 123
Why You Aren't Eligible for Social Security, Form #06.001 .... 18, 24, 37, 59, 83, 86, 113, 116, 127, 129
Why Your Government is Either a Thief or You are a "Public Officer" for Income Tax Purposes, Form #05.008 . 31, 61, 66, 86, 87, 131
Working without an SSN, Antishyster News Magazine 83
Wrong Party Notice, Form #07.105 105
Your Exclusive Right to Declare or Establish Your Civil Status, Form #13.008 .... 24, 120, 124
Your Rights Regarding Social Security Numbers, Family Guardian Fellowship 82

Scripture

1 Sam. 8:10-22	18
1 Sam. 8:4-20	27
Deut. 10:14	98
Deut. 28:43-51	18
Deuteronomy 28:43-51	110
Exodus 20:3-6	26
First Commandment	27
Isaiah 52:3	76
Jer. 5:26-31	118
Jesus in Matt. 5:37	116
Judges 2:1-4	118
Prov. 21:7	21
Prov. 28:5	21
Rev. 13:16-17	2, 26
Rev. 14:11	2
Rev. 16:2	2
Rev. 19:19	2, 26
Rev. 19:19-20	2
Rev. 20:4	2
Revelation	118
Ten Commandments	26

1 Introduction

It is VERY important that we fully understand why and how the government uses numbers to identify us both on forms and in their computer systems, why it does this, and all the effects upon our rights. In fact, if you want to discontinue voluntary participation in the federal and state income tax systems, the absolute most important thing you can do is to eliminate all identifying numbers in connection with you. Understanding this can literally mean the difference between being a free person and a government slave.

2 What We SPECIFICALLY Object to about Social Security Numbers and Taxpayer Identification Numbers

In our form *Why You Aren't Eligible for Social Security*, Form #06.001, we prove that it is UNLAWFUL for the Average American to participate in Social Security or any OTHER federal "benefit" program. By "unlawful" we mean NOT EXPRESSLY AUTHORIZED BY LAW. Some people have claimed incorrectly that by stating this, we are undermining their ability to conduct commerce using private banking or loans. This has never been our intention and we will prove in this section why this is so.

We don't object to holding people responsible for satisfying their contracts or agreements created in the absence of duress of any kind. Personal responsibility is, after all, the foundation of freedom and sovereignty as we admit on the opening page of our website:

> People of all races, genders, political beliefs, sexual orientations, and nearly all religions are welcome here. All are treated equally under REAL "law". The only way to remain truly free and equal under the civil law is to avoid seeking government civil services, benefits, property, special or civil status, exemptions, privileges, or special treatment. All such pursuits of government services or property require individual and lawful consent to a franchise and the surrender of inalienable constitutional rights AND EQUALITY in the process, and should therefore be AVOIDED. The rights and equality given up are the "cost" of procuring the "benefit" or property from the government, in fact. Nothing in life is truly "free". Anyone who claims that such "benefits" or property should be free and cost them nothing is a thief who wants to use the government as a means to STEAL on his or her behalf. All just rights spring from responsibilities/obligations under the laws of a higher power. If that higher power is God, you can be truly and objectively free. If it is government, you are guaranteed to be a slave because they can lawfully set the cost of their property as high as they want as a Merchant under the U.C.C. If you want it really bad from people with a monopoly, then you will pay dearly for the privilege. There are NO constitutional limits on the price government can charge for their monopoly services or property. Those who want no responsibilities can have no real/PRIVATE rights, but only privileges dispensed to wards of the state which are disguised to LOOK like unalienable rights. Obligations and rights are two sides of the same coin, just like self-ownership and personal responsibility. For the biblical version of this paragraph, read 1 Sam. 8:10-22. For the reason God answered Samuel by telling him to allow the people to have a king, read Deut. 28:43-51, which is God's curse upon those who allow a king above them. Click Here (https://famguardian.org/Subjects/Taxes/Evidence/HowScCorruptOurRepubGovt.htm) for a detailed description of the legal, moral, and spiritual consequences of violating this paragraph.
> [SEDM Website Opening Page; https://sedm.org/]

In many cases, globally unique identifying numbers are useful for enforcing PRIVATE contracts and agreements, such as bank loans. They are popular throughout the world primarily for banking purposes, in fact.

The reader might then reasonably ask:

> "Well then, if you don't object to people being personally responsible for honoring their contracts and commitments, then what is wrong with using government-issued identifying numbers that would hold people financially responsible honoring such commitments to governments?"

Below is our general answer to this question which appears on one of our forms relating to the compelled use of such identifying numbers:

> This form is intended to provide succinct, convenient evidence proving beyond all doubt that the submitter may not lawfully have or use government issued STATUTORY identifying numbers and would be violating criminal and civil laws to do so. It is intended to be submitted to financial institutions, employers, and businesses who demand PUBLIC numbers from those they do business with.

> *For the purpose of this document, an identifying number can be either PUBLIC or PRIVATE, but never BOTH. By PUBLIC, we mean the CIVIL STATUTORY context that regulates only GOVERNMENT activities. By PRIVATE we mean the NON-STATUTORY context in which it cannot be used to enforce any civil statutory obligation owed to any government or agent of government. By "government" or "agent of government" we mean for the purposes of this document anyone acting under the alleged authority of the civil statute, such as a STATUTORY "person", "taxpayer", "U.S. person", "citizen", "resident", "employer", "withholding agent", "foreign person", etc. We don't object to the EXCLUSIVELY PRIVATE use of identifying numbers to enforce contractual obligations anyone agreed to. We only object to the use by government or its agents to enforce civil statutory obligations against itself or its agents or officers for the purposes of raising revenue from unwilling parties. This is because Christians are forbidden from the Bible to interact with any government in any capacity other than as a Private Merchant under U.C.C. §2.104(1) and never as a Buyer under U.C.C. §2.103(1)(a) of any government civil service or public officer in the context of ordinary government functions. This is a First Amendment, constitutional right of association and freedom from compelled association protected by the Religious Freedom Restoration Act (RFRA), 42 U.S.C. Chapter 21B. See: Delegation of Authority Order from God to Christians, Form #13.007; https://sedm.org/Forms/13-SelfFamilyChurchGovnce/DelOfAuthority.pdf. A government created to protect PRIVATE property and PRIVATE UNALIENALBE rights per the Declaration of Independence must never be permitted to make a profitable business out of ALIENATING, TAXING, or REGULATING those rights. If this limit is transcended, it becomes a DE FACTO government and an ANTI-GOVERNMENT as documented in De Facto Government Scam, Form #05.043; https://sedm.org/Forms/05-MemLaw/DeFactoGov.pdf.*
>
> *Therefore, so long as any identifying numbers provided are never used for any type of government reporting, withholding, civil or administrative enforcement, liens, or levies placed by any government through the Recipient as their agent, then we have no objection to their use. Any use in this for this purpose by the Recipient of this form or its agents or assigns therefore makes them the liable party for all such enforced obligations rather than the Submitter. After all, all those subjected to duress are acting as a compelled agent of the SOURCE of said duress from a legal perspective. Any civil enforcement against the Submitter is an act of duress against a nonresident party not purposefully or intentionally or consensually contracting with or doing business with any government as a Buyer.*
> *[Why It is Illegal for Me to Request or Use a Taxpayer Identification Number, Form #04.205; https://sedm.org/Forms/FormIndex.htm]*

The reader will note that ALL of our objections about the use of PUBLIC or GOVERNMENT issued identifying numbers could easily be remedied by:

1. Creating a PRIVATE company or association to issue globally unique identifying numbers.
2. Making these private identifying numbers NOT ACCESSIBLE by any government.
3. Using the identifying numbers ONLY in connection with PRIVATE activities relating to banking and credit or PRIVATE employment verification.
4. Not using the PRIVATE numbers in connection with government identification such as driver's licenses or passports.
5. Not using the PRIVATE numbers in connection with any CIVIL or governmental enforcement activity, and especially in connection with penalties or income taxation.
6. Enforcing the same rules of compelling contractual performance in the case of government as private companies have to follow. Namely:
   6.1. No administrative enforcement is permitted, such as penalties, liens, or levies.
   6.2. Enforcement requires a common law court action in equity to enforce the contract.
   6.3. The contract must meet all the requisite elements of a real PRIVATE contract, such as an offer, mutual consideration, mutual obligation, mutual consent, the absence of duress, etc.
   6.4. Sovereign, official, or judicial immunity may not be asserted by either party to escape the obligations of the contract.

Government "benefits", civil statutes, and the civil statutory franchises which implement them would not, do not, and never have been enforceable by the same standards of proof for private contracts indicated above. Below is the reason why we object to them which appear in our website Disclaimer:

> *SEDM Disclaimer*
> *Section 4.10. Franchise*
>
> *The injustice (Form #05.050), sophistry, and deception (Form #05.014) underlying their welfare state system is that:*
>
> *1. Governments don't produce anything, but merely transfer wealth between otherwise private people (see Separation Between Public and Private Course, Form #12.025).*

2. The money they are paying you can never be more than what you paid them, and if it is, then they are abusing their taxing powers!

> *To lay, with one hand, the power of the government on the property of the citizen, and with the other to bestow it upon favored individuals to aid private enterprises and build up private fortunes, is none the less a robbery because it is done under the forms of law and is called taxation. This is not legislation. It is a decree under legislative forms.*
>
> *Nor is it taxation. 'A tax,' says Webster's Dictionary, 'is a rate or sum of money assessed on the person or property of a citizen by government for the use of the nation or State.' 'Taxes are burdens or charges imposed by the Legislature upon persons or property to raise money for public purposes.' Cooley, Const. Lim., 479.*
>
> *Coulter, J., in Northern Liberties v. St. John's Church, 13 Pa.St. 104 says, very forcibly, 'I think the common mind has everywhere taken in the understanding that **taxes are a public imposition, levied by authority of the government for the purposes of carrying on the government in all its machinery and operations—that they are imposed for a public purpose.**' See, also Pray v. Northern Liberties, 31 Pa.St. 69; Matter of Mayor of N.Y., 11 Johns., 77; Camden v. Allen, 2 Dutch., 398; Sharpless v. Mayor, supra; Hanson v. Vernon, 27 Ia., 47; Whiting v. Fond du Lac, supra."*
> [Loan Association v. Topeka, 20 Wall. 655 (1874)]

3. If they try to pay you more than you paid them, they must make you into a public officer to do so to avoid the prohibition of the case above. In doing so, they in most cases must illegally establish a public office and in effect use "benefits" to criminally bribe you to illegally impersonate such an office. See *The "Trade or Business" Scam, Form #05.001* for details.

4. Paying you back what was originally your own money and NOTHING more is not a "benefit" or even a loan by them to you. If anything, it is a temporary loan by you to them! And it's an unjust loan because they don't have to pay interest!

5. Since you are the real lender, then you are the only real party who can make rules against them and not vice versa. See *Article 4, Section 3, Clause 2 of the Constitution* for where the ability to make those rules comes from.

6. All franchises are contracts that require mutual consideration and mutual obligation to be enforceable. Since government isn't contractually obligated to provide the main consideration, which is "benefits" and isn't obligated to provide ANYTHING that is truly economically valuable beyond that, then the "contract" or "compact" is unenforceable against you and can impose no obligations on you based on mere equitable principals of contract law.

> *"We must conclude that **a person covered by the Act has not such a right in benefit payments**... This is not to say, however, that Congress may exercise its power to modify the statutory scheme free of all constitutional restraint."*
> [Flemming v. Nestor, 363 U.S. 603 (1960)]
>
> *"... railroad benefits, like social security benefits, are not contractual and may be altered or even eliminated at any time."*
> [United States Railroad Retirement Board v. Fritz, 449 U.S. 166 (1980)]

[SEDM Disclaimer, Section 4.10: Franchise; https://sedm.org/disclaimer.htm]

It is precisely the above objections that explain why the Bible describes the Social Security Number and Taxpayer Identification Number as "The Mark of the Beast". See:

> *Social Security: Mark of the Beast*, Form #11.407
> https://sedm.org/Forms/FormIndex.htm

So long as the government "benefits" are treated essentially as VOLUNTARY PRIVATE business activity not protected by official, sovereign, or judicial immunity and the government has to meet the same standards of proof in enforcing the contract as any private company, and must do so in a Judicial Branch Article III court rather than an Executive Branch Article I or Article IV court, then we wouldn't have a problem with offering government "benefits" or any other type of government contracts. The problem is that the corrupt government mafia NEVER either recognizes or protects your right to NOT participate, like any private company would have to. Imagine a private company that could force EVERYONE on the planet to buy their product and a court system that enforced their tyrannical right to do so, as is the case currently with government "benefits".

This condition described above where government acts as a PRIVATE party in commerce and equity is described by the Clearfield Doctrine of the U.S. Supreme Court:

> *See also Clearfield Trust Co. v. United States, 318 U.S. 363, 369 (1943) ("`**The United States does business on business terms**'") (quoting United States v. National Exchange Bank of Baltimore, 270 U.S. 527, 534 (1926)); Perry v. United States, supra at 352 (1935) ("**When the United States, with constitutional authority, makes contracts, it has rights and incurs responsibilities similar to those of individuals who are parties to such instruments. There is no difference . . . except that the United States cannot be sued without its consent**") (citation omitted); United States v. Bostwick, 94 U.S. 53, 66 (1877) ("**The United States, when they contract with their citizens, are controlled by the same laws that govern the citizen in that behalf**"); Cooke v. United States, 91 U.S. 389, 398 (1875) (**explaining that when the United States "comes down from its position of sovereignty, and enters the domain of commerce, it submits itself to the same laws that govern individuals there**").*
>
> *See Jones, 1 Cl.Ct. at 85 ("**Wherever the public and private acts of the government seem to commingle, a citizen or corporate body must by supposition be substituted in its place, and then the question be determined whether the action will lie against the supposed defendant**"); O'Neill v. United States, 231 Ct.Cl. 823, 826 (1982) (sovereign acts doctrine applies where, "[w]ere [the] contracts exclusively between private parties, the party hurt by such governing action could not claim compensation from the other party for the governing action"). The dissent ignores these statements (including the statement from Jones, from which case Horowitz drew its reasoning literally verbatim), when it says, post at 931, that the sovereign acts cases do not emphasize the need to treat the government-as-contractor the same as a private party.*
> *[United States v. Winstar Corp., 518 U.S. 839 (1996)]*

To impute or enforce sovereign, official, or judicial immunity to any government civil statutory privilege is to abuse the courts to enforce SUPERIOR or SUPERNATURAL powers to government, makes the government into an object of religious idolatry, and violates the First Amendment by creating a secular civil religion described in the following document:

> *Socialism: The New American Civil Religion*, Form #05.016
> https://sedm.org/Forms/FormIndex.htm

Real law and freedom itself require that ALL are treated equally in all respects by EVERY court and that there ARE no franchises or "franchise courts". We prove this in:

1. *Foundations of Freedom*, Video 1, Form #12.021
   https://sedm.org/Forms/FormIndex.htm
2. *Requirement for Equal Protection and Equal Treatment*, Form #05.033
   https://sedm.org/Forms/FormIndex.htm
3. *What is "Law"?*, Form #05.048
   https://sedm.org/Forms/FormIndex.htm

Government franchises are the MAIN method of destroying equality, corrupting public servants, and replacing government with a state-sponsored civil religion in violation of the First Amendment.

So, before the reader closes their mind and their ears and refuses to read the remainder of this document, please prayerfully consider the content of this section and the EQUALITY and LEGAL JUSTICE it mandates.

> *"Evil men do not understand justice, But those who seek the LORD understand all."*
> *[Prov. 28:5, Bible, NKJV]*
>
> *"Justice is the end of government. It is the end of civil society. It ever has been, and ever will be pursued, until it be obtained, or until liberty be lost in the pursuit."*
> *[The Federalist No. 51 (1788), James Madison]*
>
> *"The violence of the wicked will destroy them, because they refuse to do justice."*
> *[Prov. 21:7, Bible, NKJV]*

3 Social Security Numbers (SSNs) and Taxpayer Identification Numbers (TINs) are what the FTC calls a "franchise mark"

The Federal Trade Commission (F.T.C.) has defined a commercial franchise as follows:

> "...a commercial business arrangement [e.g. a STATUTORY "trade or business" under 26 U.S.C. §7701(a)(26)] is a "franchise" if it satisfies three definitional elements. Specifically, the franchisor must:
>
> (1) promise to provide a trademark or other commercial symbol [e.g. the STATUTORY Social Security Number or Taxpayer Identification Number];
> (2) promise to exercise significant control or provide significant assistance in the operation of the business [e.g. enforcement of the franchise "code" such as the Internal Revenue Code Subtitles A and C] and
> (3) require a minimum payment of at least $500 during the first six months of operations [e.g. tax refunds annually, deductions most Americans DO NOT need because of EXCLUSIONS in 26 U.S.C. §872 because not from GEOGRAPHICAL "U.S.", stimulus checks, etc]"."
> [FTC Franchise Rule Compliance Guide, May 2008, p. 1;
> SOURCE: http://business.ftc.gov/documents/bus70-franchise-rule-compliance-guide]

In the context of the above document, the "Social Security Number" or "Taxpayer Identification Number" function essentially as what the FTC calls a "franchise mark". It behaves as what we call a "de facto license" to represent Caesar as a public officer:

> "A franchise entails the right to operate a business that is "identified or associated with the franchisor's trademark, or to offer, sell, or distribute goods, services, or commodities that are identified or associated with the franchisor's trademark." The term "trademark" is intended to be read broadly to cover not only trademarks, but any service mark, trade name, or other advertising or commercial symbol. This is generally referred to as the "trademark" or "mark" element.
>
> **_The franchisor [the government] need not own the mark itself, but at the very least must have the right to license the use of the mark to others. Indeed, the right to use the franchisor's mark in the operation of the business - either by selling goods or performing services identified with the mark or by using the mark, in whole or in part, in the business' name - is an integral part of franchising. In fact, a supplier can avoid Rule coverage of a particular distribution arrangement by expressly prohibiting the distributor from using its mark."_**
> [FTC Franchise Rule Compliance Guide, May 2008;
> SOURCE: http://business.ftc.gov/documents/bus70-franchise-rule-compliance-guide]

The nature of Social Security Numbers as a franchise mark is implemented as follows from a legal perspective:

1. Like all contracts or agreements, franchises, or what is sometimes called "privileges" or "quasi-contracts"[1] by the U.S.

---

[1] Below is an example from the U.S. Supreme Court in the case of the "trade or business" excise taxable income tax franchise:

> "Even if the judgment is deemed to be colored by the nature of the obligation whose validity it establishes, and we are free to re-examine it, and, if we find it to be based on an obligation penal in character, to refuse to enforce it outside the state where rendered, see Wisconsin v. Pelican Insurance Co., 127 U.S. 265, 292, et seq. 8 S.Ct. 1370, compare Fauntleroy v. Lum, 210 U.S. 230, 28 S.Ct. 641, **_still the obligation to pay taxes is not penal. It is a statutory liability, quasi contractual in nature, enforceable, if there is no exclusive statutory remedy, in the civil courts by the common-law action of debt or indebitatus assumpsit._** United States v. Chamberlin, 219 U.S. 250, 31 S.Ct. 155; Price v. United States, 269 U.S. 492, 46 S.Ct. 180; Dollar Savings Bank v. United States, 19 Wall. 227; and see Stockwell v. United States, 13 Wall. 531, 542; Meredith v. United States, 13 Pet. 486, 493. **_This was the rule established in the English courts before the Declaration of Independence._** Attorney General v. Weeks, Bunbury's Exch. Rep. 223; Attorney General v. Jewers and Batty, Bunbury's Exch. Rep. 225; Attorney General v. Hatton, Bunbury's Exch. Rep. [296 U.S. 268, 272] 262; Attorney General v. _ _, 2 Ans.Rep. 558; see Comyn's Digest (Title 'Dett,' A, 9); 1 Chitty on Pleading, 123; cf. Attorney General v. Sewell, 4 M.&W. 77. "
> [Milwaukee v. White, 296 U.S. 268 (1935)]

Supreme court, require:
1.1. An offer as the "Merchant" under U.C.C. §2-104(1). Sometimes also called a Creditor or Seller.
1.2. A voluntary acceptance as the "Buyer" under U.C.C. §2-103(1)(a). Sometimes also called a Debtor or Borrower.
1.3. Valuable consideration provided by the "Merchant" to the "Buyer" in the form of property or rights or services. Without consideration there can be no obligation or contract.
1.4. Mutual assent or understanding.
1.5. The absence of duress. This also implies a right to quit or to waive all or any portion of the "benefits" of the relationship and the corresponding obligation to pay for those future "benefits".

> *Invito beneficium non datur.*
> *No one is obliged to accept a benefit against his consent. Dig. 50, 17, 69. But if he does not dissent he will be considered as assenting. Vide Assent.*
>
> *Potest quis renunciare pro se, et suis, juri quod pro se introductum est.*
> *A man may relinquish, for himself and his heirs, a right which was introduced for his own benefit. See 1 Bouv. Inst. n. 83.*
>
> *Quilibet potest renunciare juri pro se inducto.*
> *Any one may renounce a law introduced for his own benefit. To this rule there are some exceptions. See 1 Bouv. Inst. n. 83.*
> [Bouvier's Maxims of Law, 1856;
> SOURCE: http://famguardian.org/Publications/BouvierMaximsOfLaw/BouviersMaxims.htm]

2. The franchise mark may be a number and an associated civil status label such as an SSN or TIN, "person", "taxpayer", "citizen", "resident", etc. However, the NAME of the number, meaning "SSN" or "TIN" in this case, must DERIVE from the franchise contract DEFINED by the Merchant. Another way of stating this is that under the Uniform Commercial Code, the language of the offer and the language of the acceptance MUST be the same and the parties must agree on a SINGLE definition for all terms. Without a common definition, there can be no assent because the parties have a different understanding about what is being offered or accepted. See:
   2.1. *This Form is Your Form*, Mark DeAngelis
        http://www.youtube.com/embed/b6-PRwhU7cg
   2.2. *Mirror Image Rule*, Mark DeAngelis
        http://www.youtube.com/embed/j8pgbZV757w
3. The right of the Merchant to prescribe the terms of the contract or agreement derives from the consideration, services, or valuable property he brings to the relationship that the BUYER wants.
   3.1. In the case of the government, that authority derives from Article 4, Section 3, Clause 2 of the United States Constitution:

   > U.S. Constitution, Article IV § 3 (2).
   >
   > *The Congress shall have Power to dispose of and make all needful Rules and Regulations respecting the Territory or other Property belonging to the United States [***]*

   3.2. In the case of the otherwise PRIVATE human being and BUYER, INCLUDING governments, the authority to make rules and definitions for the terms they use on any form, INCLUDING government forms, is the control over their own private property that they are lending or selling or renting to the government.

   > *"The State in such cases exercises no greater right than an individual may exercise over the use of his own property when leased or loaned to others. The conditions upon which the privilege shall be enjoyed being stated or implied in the legislation authorizing its grant, no right is, of course, impaired by their enforcement. The recipient of the privilege, in effect, stipulates to comply with the conditions. It matters not how limited the privilege conferred, its acceptance implies an assent to the regulation of its use and the compensation for it."*
   > [Munn v. Illinois, 94 U.S. 113 (1876)]

4. Once consent or agreement is voluntarily procured, the parties VOLUNTARILY acquire a "civil status" (Form #13.008) under the terms of the franchise agreement or contract or parole agreement, such as "person", "taxpayer", "benefit recipient", "participant", etc. This right to volunteer is protected by your unalienable right to contract and your First Amendment right to politically and legally associate. Be careful HOW you exercise your right to contract and associate, because it's the MOST DANGEROUS right you have! Why?: Because it can literally DESTROY all of your other rights! This label or civil status (Form #13.008) is the object to which ALL statutory civil obligations

against the Buyer and corresponding Rights of the Merchant, legally attach. If the status was not voluntarily accepted, there can be no enforceable contract or agreement. The ONLY way to defeat such a contract or agreement is to do one of the following:

    4.1. To claim that you were operating in a representative capacity and that your Principle expressly FORBIDS such consent in your delegation order. For instance, you can claim that you are God's representative 24 hours a day and 7 days a week under the First Amendment, and that your delegation of authority order, the Bible, forbids you to consent as God's representative to any such enticements.

    4.2. To claim that the rights alienated by the franchise are UNALIENABLE per the Declaration of Independence, and thus cannot be given away to a REAL DE JURE GOVERNMENT even WITH consent. A real, de jure government established ONLY to protect PRIVATE property and PRIVATE rights cannot be allowed to violate the purpose of its creation by establishing a profitable business called a franchise whose main purpose is to DESTROY such rights and convert all property into PUBLIC property or PUBLIC rights. That would violate the intent of the Constitution, in fact.

    4.3. To identify yourself as being UNELIGIBLE at the time of making application. For proof of this in the case of Social Security, see:

> *Why You Aren't Eligible for Social Security*, Form #06.001
> https://sedm.org/Forms/FormIndex.htm

5. The SOURCE of the definition of the LABEL on the license number or franchise mark establishes WHO the "Merchant" is.

    5.1. If you accept the STATUTORY definition of "SSN", then GOVERNMENT is the Merchant and YOU are the Buyer.

    5.2. If you make your OWN definition for "SSN' or "TIN" on the government form or application and reject the STATUTORY definition, even though it uses the same LABEL (e.g. "SSN" or "TIN"), then YOU are the Merchant and GOVERNMENT is the Buyer. In other words, changing the definitions replaces the original Merchant's offer with a COUNTEROFFER by the Buyer. The Buyer then becomes the NEW Merchant and the roles switch.

    5.3. If the original Merchant then responds to your definition of terms by saying that you have to accept THEIR definition to get the "benefit" of the franchise, you simply respond that you have a right NOT to receive a "benefit" and that the only thing you want is for the government to LEAVE YOU ALONE, which is what "justice" itself is defined as. For instance, having government ID that does not impute a civil statutory status to you such as "citizen", "resident", or "person" has the effect of allowing you to be LEFT ALONE and not attaching any enforcement authority or "benefit" to you. By doing this, you are preventing what we call "bundling", where civil obligations are attached to the receipt of some government service by associating you with a civil statutory status that you don't want. More on this in:

> *Your Exclusive Right to Declare or Establish Your Civil Status*, Form #13.008
> https://sedm.org/Forms/FormIndex.htm

    5.4. If the government Merchant then tries to advise you what to put on the form, or refuses to accept your form with your definitions, then they are discriminating against you, and also criminally tampering with a witness, because most government forms are signed under penalty of perjury as court-admissible legal evidence.

6. A prospective Buyer SUBMITTING a government form is the CREATOR of the form. The CREATOR is always the OWNER of the thing, and thus the ONLY one who can define what it means. See:

> *Hierarchy of Sovereignty: The Power to Create is the Power to Tax*, Family Guardian Fellowship
> https://famguardian.org/Subjects/Taxes/Remedies/PowerToCreate.htm

7. The only Party to the transaction who can "make rules" or definitions relating to property is the OWNER of that property. That's what legal "ownership" is defined as, in fact: CONTROL and the right to exclude any and all others from using or benefitting from a thing.

8. If a form is required to be submitted by the Buyer to the Merchant to receive custody or eligibility of specific property or rights under a franchise, the CREATOR of a form controls the outcome of the transaction rather than the author of the form. By "CREATOR" we mean the person who SUBMITS AND SIGNS the form, not the person who PROVIDES or offers the form to use in the application process. The submitter is the ONLY one who can define the meaning or context of the terms of the form. The courts have held that you cannot trust ANYTHING on a government form or ANYTHING an executive branch employee says. Thus, you can't trust that you KNOW what the definition or context of the terms are. Thus you are OBLIGATED to define them in a way that benefits and protects ONLY YOU. See:

> *Federal Courts and the IRS' Own IRM Say the IRS is NOT RESPONSIBLE for its Actions or Its Words, or for Following Its Own Written Procedures*, Family Guardian Fellowship
> https://famguardian.org/Subjects/Taxes/Articles/IRSNotResponsible.htm

9. If you want to FLIP the relationship of the parties so that YOU become the Merchant and government becomes the Buyer, simply define the term "SSN" or "TIN" on government forms as NOT the one in statutes, but one issued by YOU that makes government the Buyer. Here is an example:

   > NOTES:
   >
   > *1. All terms used on this form OTHER than "Social Security Number" shall be construed in their statutory sense. This is especially true in the case of money or finance. They are not used in their private, ordinary, or common law sense. The term "Social Security Number" identifies a PRIVATE number owned and issued by the Submitter to the government under license and franchise. It is not a number identified in any governments statute and does not pertain to anyone eligible to receive Social Security Benefits and may not be used to indicate or imply eligibility to receive said benefits. The license for the use of the number for use outside of the VA for any purpose, and especially civil or criminal enforcement purpose, is identified below and incorporated by reference herein. Acceptance or use of said number for such purpose constitutes constructive or implied consent to said agreement by all those so using said number:*
   >
   > *Injury Defense Franchise and Agreement, Form #06.027; https://sedm.org/Forms/06-AvoidingFranch/InjuryDefenseFranchise.pdf.*
   >
   > *This provision is repeated Section 0 in the attached form entitled Why It is Illegal for Me to Request or Use a Taxpayer Identification Number, Form #04.205. The reason for this provision is that everyone who asks for such number refers to them as "MINE" or "MY" or "YOUR", meaning that it is MY absolutely owned PRIVATE property. Therefore I am simply documenting the fact that it is my absolutely owned private property as a private human not affiliated with the government. All private property can be used as a basis to place conditions on its use or else it isn't mine. That's what "ownership" implies in a legal sense. Congress does the same thing with ITS property under Article 4, Section 3, Clause 2, and I am simply carrying out exactly the authority THEY claim over THEIR property in the same manner as them.*
   > *[Veterans Administration Benefit Application, Form #06.041, https://sedm.org/Forms/FormIndex.htm]*

   Why can you emulate the government's tactics in doing this? Because ALL are treated equally under real law, and because if the government can CREATE obligations against you essentially by using equivocation to make you look like someone who is eligible, even if you are not, then you can use the SAME equivocation to AVOID becoming eligible and make THEM eligible for your ANTI-FRANCHISE. Otherwise, the constitutional requirement for equal protection and equal treatment is violated. Fight fire with fire! For proof, see:
   > *Requirement for Equal Protection and Equal Treatment*, Form #05.033
   > https://sedm.org/Forms/FormIndex.htm

10. As far as NATIONAL franchises, Congress is FORBIDDEN from establishing excise taxable franchises or privileges such as the income tax within the exclusive jurisdiction of a constitutional state of the Union. Thus, the ONLY place they can establish them is within FEDERAL AREAS subject to the exclusive jurisdiction of Congress:

    > *"Thus, Congress having power to regulate commerce with foreign nations, and among the several States, and with the Indian tribes, may, without doubt, provide for **granting** coasting **licenses**, licenses to pilots, licenses to trade with the Indians, and any other **licenses** necessary or proper for the exercise of that great and extensive power; and the same observation is applicable to every other power of Congress, to the exercise of which the granting of licenses may be incident. All such licenses confer authority, and give rights to the licensee.*
    >
    > *But very different considerations apply to the **internal commerce** or **domestic trade** of the **States**. Over this commerce and trade Congress has **no power of regulation nor any direct control**. This power belongs **exclusively to the States**. **No interference by Congress with the business of citizens transacted within a State is warranted by the Constitution, except such as is strictly incidental to the exercise of powers clearly granted to the legislature**. The power to authorize a business within a State is plainly repugnant to the exclusive power of the State over the same subject. It is true that the power of Congress to tax is a very extensive power. It is given in the Constitution, with only one exception and only two qualifications. Congress cannot tax exports, and it must impose direct taxes by the rule of apportionment, and indirect taxes by the rule of uniformity. Thus limited, and thus only, it reaches every subject, and may be exercised at discretion. But, it reaches only existing subjects.* **Congress cannot authorize [e.g. LICENSE using a Social Security Number] a trade or business within a State in order to tax it.**"
    > *[License Tax Cases, 72 U.S. 462, 18 L.Ed. 497, 5 Wall. 462, 2 A.F.T.R. 2224 (1866)]*

11. For more about tricks with definitions, changing the context, and the equivocation that changing the context of words on a form does, see:
    > *Avoiding Traps in Government Forms Course,* Form #12.023
    > https://sedm.org/Forms/FormIndex.htm

This same SSN or TIN " franchise mark" is what the Bible calls "the mark of the beast". It defines "the Beast" as the government or civil rulers:

> "And I saw **the beast, the kings of the earth, and their armies**, gathered together to make war against Him who sat on the horse and against His army."
> [Rev. 19:19, Bible, NKJV]
>
> "He [the government BEAST] causes all, both small and great, rich and poor, free and slave, to receive a mark on their right hand or on their foreheads, [17] and that no one may buy or sell except one who has the mark or[] the name of the beast, or the number of his name.
> [Rev. 13:16-17, Bible, NKJV]

The "business" that is "operated" or "licensed" by THE BEAST in statutes is called a "trade or business" which is defined as follows:

> 26 U.S.C. Sec. 7701(a)(26)
>
> "The term 'trade or business' includes the performance of the functions of a public office."

Those engaged in "the trade or business" franchise activity are officers of Caesar and have fired God as their civil protector. By becoming said public officers or officers of Caesar, they have violated the FIRST COMMANDMENT of the Ten Commandments, because they are "serving other gods", and the pagan god they serve is a man:

> "You shall have no other gods [including governments or civil rulers] before Me.
>
> "You shall not make for yourself a carved image—any likeness of anything that is in heaven above, or that is in the earth beneath, or that is in the water under the earth; **you shall not bow down to them nor serve them. For I, the LORD your God, am a jealous God, visiting the iniquity of the fathers upon the children to the third and fourth generations of those who hate Me**, but showing mercy to thousands, to those who love Me and keep My commandments.
> [Exodus 20:3-6, Bible, NKJV]

By "bowing down" as indicated above, the Bible means that you cannot become UNEQUAL or especially INFERIOR to any government or civil ruler under the civil law. In other words, you cannot surrender your equality and be civilly governed by any government or civil ruler under the Roman system of jus civile, civil law, or civil "statutes". That is not to say that you are lawless or an "anarchist" by any means, because you are still accountable under criminal law, equity, and the common law in any court. All civil statutory codes make the government superior and you inferior so you can't consent to a domicile and thereby become subject to it. The word "subjection" in the following means INFERIORITY:

> "Protectio trahit subjectionem, subjectio projectionem.
> Protection draws to it subjection, subjection, protection. Co. Litt. 65."
> [Bouvier's Maxims of Law, 1856;
> SOURCE: http://famguardian.org/Publications/BouvierMaximsOfLaw/BouviersMaxims.htm]

Below are ways one becomes subject to Caesar's civil statutory "codes" and civil franchises as a "subject", and thereby surrenders their equality to engage in government idolatry:

1. Domicile by choice: Choosing domicile within a specific jurisdiction. because not from GEOGRAPHICAL "U.S."
2. Domicile by operation of law. Also called domicile of necessity:
    2.1. Representing an entity that has a domicile within a specific jurisdiction even though not domiciled oneself in said jurisdiction. For instance, representing a federal corporation as a public officer of said corporation, even though domiciled outside the federal zone. The authority for this type of jurisdiction is, for instance, Federal Rule of Civil Procedure 17(b).
    2.2. Becoming a dependent of someone else, and thereby assuming the same domicile as that of your caregiver. For instance, being a minor and dependent and having the same civil domicile as your parents. Another example is becoming a government dependent and assuming the domicile of the government paying you the welfare check.
    2.3. Being committed to a prison as a prisoner, and thereby assuming the domicile of the government owning or funding the prison.

Those who violate the First Commandment by doing any of the above become subject to the civil statutory franchises or codes. They are thereby committing the following form of idolatry because they are nominating a King to be ABOVE them rather than EQUAL to them under the common law:

> *Then all the elders of Israel gathered together and came to Samuel at Ramah, and said to him, "Look, you are old, and your sons do not walk in your ways.* **Now make us a king to judge us like all the nations** *[and be OVER them]".*
>
> *But the thing displeased Samuel when they said,* **"Give us a king to judge us."** *So Samuel prayed to the Lord.* **And the Lord said to Samuel, "Heed the voice of the people in all that they say to you; for they have rejected Me [God], that I should not reign over them.** *According to all the works which they have done since the day that I brought them up out of Egypt, even to this day—***with which they have forsaken Me and served other gods [Kings, in this case]***—so they are doing to you also [government becoming idolatry]. Now therefore, heed their voice.* **However, you shall solemnly forewarn them, and show them the behavior of the king who will reign over them.**"
>
> *So Samuel told all the words of the LORD to the people who asked him for a king. And he said,* **"This will be the behavior of the king who will reign over you: He will take [STEAL] your sons and appoint them for his own chariots and to be his horsemen, and some will run before his chariots. He will appoint captains over his thousands and captains over his fifties, will set some to plow his ground and reap his harvest, and some to make his weapons of war and equipment for his chariots. He will take [STEAL] your daughters to be perfumers, cooks, and bakers. And he will take [STEAL] the best of your fields, your vineyards, and your olive groves, and give them to his servants. He will take [STEAL] a tenth of your grain and your vintage, and give it to his officers and servants. And he will take [STEAL] your male servants, your female servants, your finest young men, and your donkeys, and put them to his work [as SLAVES]. He will take [STEAL] a tenth of your sheep. And you will be his servants. And you will cry out in that day because of your king whom you have chosen for yourselves, and the LORD will not hear you in that day."**
>
> *Nevertheless the people refused to obey the voice of Samuel; and they said, "No, but we will have a king over us, that we also may be like all the nations, and that our king may judge us and go out before us and fight our battles."*
> *[1 Sam. 8:4-20, Bible, NKJV]*

In support of this section, the following evidence is provided for use in court which PROVES that those who use SSNs or TINs are considered to be and MUST, by law, be considered to be public officers:

1. The U.S. Supreme Court has held in the case of the State Action doctrine that those receiving government "benefits" are to be regarded as state actors, meaning public officers.

   > **"One great object of the Constitution is to permit citizens to structure their private relations as they choose subject only to the constraints of statutory or decisional law**. *[500 U.S. 614, 620]*
   >
   > **To implement these principles, courts must consider from time to time where the governmental sphere [e.g. "public purpose" and "public office"] ends and the private sphere begins. Although the conduct of private parties lies beyond the Constitution's scope in most instances, governmental authority may dominate an activity to such an extent that its participants must be deemed to act with the authority of the government and, as a result, be subject to constitutional constraints.** *This is the jurisprudence of state action, which explores the "essential dichotomy" between the private sphere and the public sphere, with all its attendant constitutional obligations. Moose Lodge, supra, at 172. "*
   >
   > *[. . .]*
   >
   > *Given that the statutory authorization for the challenges exercised in this case is clear, the remainder of our state action analysis centers around the second part of the Lugar test, whether a private litigant, in all fairness, must be deemed a government actor in the use of peremptory challenges. Although we have recognized that this aspect of the analysis is often a fact-bound inquiry, see Lugar, supra, 457 U.S. at 939, our cases disclose certain principles of general application.* **Our precedents establish that, in determining whether a particular action or course of conduct is governmental in character, it is relevant to examine the following: the extent to which the actor relies on governmental assistance and benefits, see Tulsa Professional Collection Services, Inc. v. Pope, 485 U.S. 478 (1988); Burton v. Wilmington Parking Authority, 365 U.S. 715 (1961); whether the actor is performing a traditional governmental function, see Terry v. Adams, 345 U.S. 461 (1953); Marsh v. Alabama, 326 U.S. 501 (1946); cf. San Francisco Arts & Athletics, Inc. v. United States Olympic [500 U.S. 614, 622] Committee, 483 U.S. 522, 544 -545 (1987);** *and whether the injury caused is aggravated in a unique way by the incidents of governmental authority, see Shelley v. Kraemer, 334 U.S. 1 (1948). Based on our application of these three principles to the circumstances here, we hold that the exercise of peremptory challenges by the defendant in the District Court was pursuant to a course of state action.*
   > *[Edmonson v. Leesville Concrete Company, 500 U.S. 614 (1991)]*

2. The U.S. Supreme Court has held that government identifying numbers may be mandated against those seeking to receive government "benefits".

> *Appellees raise a constitutional challenge to two features of the statutory scheme here.[4] They object to Congress' requirement that a state AFDC plan "must . . . provide (A) that, as a condition of eligibility under the plan, each applicant for or recipient of aid shall furnish to the State agency his social security account number." 42 U.S.C. §602(a)(25) (emphasis added). They also object to Congress' requirement that "such State agency shall utilize such account numbers. . . in the administration of such plan." Ibid. (emphasis added).[5] We analyze each of these contentions, turning to the latter contention first.*
>
> <u>**Our cases have long recognized a distinction between the freedom of individual belief, which is absolute, and the freedom of individual conduct, which is not absolute.**</u> *This case implicates only the latter concern. Roy objects to the statutory requirement that state agencies "shall utilize" Social Security numbers not because it places any restriction on what he may believe or what he may do, but because he believes the use of the number may harm his daughter's spirit.*
>
> <u>**Never to our knowledge has the Court interpreted the First Amendment to require the Government itself to behave in ways that the individual believes will further his or her spiritual development or that of his or her family. The Free Exercise Clause simply cannot be understood to require the Government to conduct its own internal affairs in ways that comport with the religious beliefs of particular citizens**</u>*. Just as the Government may not insist that appellees engage in [476 U.S. 693, 700] any set form of religious observance, so appellees may not demand that the Government join in their chosen religious practices by refraining from using a number to identify their daughter. "[T]he Free Exercise Clause is written in terms of what the government cannot do to the individual, not in terms of what the individual can extract from the government." Sherbert v. Verner, <u>374 U.S. 398, 412</u> (1963) (Douglas, J., concurring).*
>
> *As a result, Roy may no more prevail on his religious objection to the Government's use of a Social Security number for his daughter than he could on a sincere religious objection to the size or color of the Government's filing cabinets.* <u>**The Free Exercise Clause affords an individual protection from certain forms of governmental compulsion; it does not afford an individual a right to dictate the conduct of the Government's internal procedures.**</u>
> [Bowen v. Roy, 476 U.S. 693 (1986)]

FOOTNOTES:

[4] They also raise a statutory argument — that the Government's denial of benefits to them constitutes illegal discrimination on the basis of religion or national origin. See 42 U.S.C. §2000d; 7 U.S.C. §2011. We find these claims to be without merit.

[5] The Food Stamp program restrictions that appellees challenge contain restrictions virtually identical to those in the AFDC program quoted in the text. See 7 U.S.C. §2025(e).

3. The U.S. Supreme Court has also held that no one can RECEIVE government payments without actually WORKING for the government. Any abuse of the taxing power to redistribute wealth is unconstitutional.

> <u>**To lay, with one hand, the power of the government on the property of the citizen, and with the other to bestow it upon favored individuals to aid private enterprises and build up private fortunes, is none the less a robbery because it is done under the forms of law and is called taxation. This is not legislation. It is a decree under legislative forms.**</u>
>
> <u>**Nor is it taxation. 'A tax,' says Webster's Dictionary, 'is a rate or sum of money assessed on the person or property of a citizen by government for the use of the nation or State.' 'Taxes are burdens or charges imposed by the Legislature upon persons or property to raise money for public purposes.'**</u> *Cooley, Const. Lim., 479.*
>
> *Coulter, J., in Northern Liberties v. St. John's Church, 13 Pa.St. 104 says, very forcibly, 'I think the common mind has everywhere taken in the understanding that* <u>**taxes are a public imposition, levied by authority of the government for the purposes of carrying on the government in all its machinery and operations—that they are imposed for a public purpose.**</u>*' See, also Pray v. Northern Liberties, 31 Pa.St. 69; Matter of Mayor of N.Y., 11 Johns., 77; Camden v. Allen, 2 Dutch., 398; Sharpless v. Mayor, supra; Hanson v. Vernon, 27 Ia., 47; Whiting v. Fond du Lac, supra."*
> [Loan Association v. Topeka, 20 Wall. 655 (1874)]

> *"A tax, in the general understanding of the term and as used in the constitution, signifies an exaction for the support of the government. The word has never thought to connote the expropriation of money from one group for the benefit of another."*
> *[U.S. v. Butler, 297 U.S. 1 (1936)]*

4. Those eligible to receive government "benefits" are identified in Title 5 of the U.S. Code as "federal personnel".

    > *TITLE 5 > PART I > CHAPTER 5 > SUBCHAPTER II > § 552a*
    > *§552a. Records maintained on individuals*
    >
    > *(a) Definitions.— For purposes of this section—*
    >
    > *(13) the term "Federal personnel" means officers and employees of the Government of the United States, members of the uniformed services (including members of the Reserve Components), **individuals entitled to receive immediate or deferred retirement benefits under any retirement program of the Government of the United States (including survivor benefits)**.*

5. Those not subject to the Internal Revenue Code and a "foreign estate" are described as NOT engaged in a "trade or business", meaning a public office.

    > *TITLE 26 > Subtitle F > CHAPTER 79 > § 7701*
    > *§ 7701. Definitions*
    >
    > *(31) Foreign estate or trust*
    >
    > *(A) Foreign estate The term "foreign estate" means an estate the income of which, from sources without the United States which is not effectively connected with the conduct of a trade or business within the United States, is not includible in gross income under subtitle A.*
    >
    > *(B) Foreign trust The term "foreign trust" means any trust other than a trust described in subparagraph (E) of paragraph (30).*

6. Those who work for the government or receive the "benefit" of any government civil statute are presumed to waive ALL of their constitutional rights and cannot invoke ANY of them in court.

    > *"The principle is invoked that one who accepts the benefit of a statute cannot be heard to question its constitutionality. Great Falls Manufacturing Co. v. Attorney General, 124 U.S. 581, 8 S.Ct. 631, 31 L.Ed. 527; Wall v. Parrot Silver & Copper Co., 244 U.S. 407, 37 S.Ct. 609, 61 L.Ed. 1229; St. Louis, etc., Co., v. George C. Prendergast Const. Co., 260 U.S. 469, 43 S.Ct. 178, 67 L.Ed. 351.*
    >
    > *[...]*
    >
    > *6. The Court will not pass upon the constitutionality of a statute at the instance of one who has availed himself of its benefits.[2] Great Falls Mfg. Co. v. Attorney General, 124 U.S. 581, 8 S.Ct. 631, 31 L.Ed. 527; Wall v. Parrot Silver & Copper Co., 244 U.S. 407, 411, 412, 37 S.Ct. 609, 61 L.Ed. 1229; St. Louis Malleable Casting Co. v. Prendergast Construction Co., 260 U.S. 469, 43 S.Ct. 178, 67 L.Ed. 351."*
    > *[Ashwander v. T.V.A., 297 U.S. 288, 56 S.Ct. 466, 80 L.Ed. 688 (1936)]*

    > *"It is not open to question that one who has acquired rights of property necessarily based upon a statute may not attack that statute as unconstitutional, for he cannot both assail it and rely upon it in the same proceeding. *528 Hurley v. Commission of Fisheries, 257 U.S. 223, 225, 42 S.Ct. 83, 66 L.Ed. 206."*
    > *[Frost v. Corporation Commission, 278 U.S. 515, 49 S.Ct. 235 (U.S., 1929)]*

Based on the preceding overwhelming evidence, the inference and conclusion that Social Security Numbers are regarded and treated as a de facto license to occupy a public office is inescapable. The taxation of the exercise of that office, in fact, is the main object of the entire Internal Revenue Code Subtitles A and C. It is de facto, because those exercising said office do so illegally and unconstitutionally in the vast majority of cases.

---

[2] Compare Electric Co. v. Dow, 166 U.S. 489, 17 S.Ct. 645, 41 L.Ed. 1088; Pierce v. Somerset Ry., 171 U.S. 641, 648, 19 S.Ct. 64, 43 L.Ed. 316; Leonard v. Vicksburg, etc., R. Co., 198 U.S. 416, 422, 25 S.Ct. 750, 49 L.Ed. 1108.

4 Why Knowing about SSNs and TINs is VERY important

The subject of SSNs and TINs is VERY important to understanding how the income tax actually works. It is a tax upon the GOVERNMENT and ONLY the government. By "government" we mean "the United States" federal corporation. You have to JOIN that corporation as a public officer in most cases to be subject to the tax. The "United States" is defined as follows:

> 26 U.S. Code § 7701 – Definitions
>
> (a)When used in this title, where not otherwise distinctly expressed or manifestly incompatible with the intent thereof—
>
> (9)United States
>
> The term "United States" when used in a geographical sense includes only the States and the District of Columbia.
>
> (10)State
>
> The term "State" shall be construed to include the District of Columbia, where such construction is necessary to carry out provisions of this title.

The regulations clarify the above definition of "United States" as follows:

> 26 CFR § 301.7701-7 - Trusts—domestic and foreign.
>
> § 301.7701-7 Trusts—domestic and foreign.
>
> (c) The court test—(1) Safe harbor. A trust satisfies the court test if—
>
> (i) Court. The term court includes any federal, state, or local court.
>
> (ii) The United States.
>
> ***The term the United States is used in this section in a geographical sense. Thus, for purposes of the court test, the United States includes only the States and the District of Columbia. See section 7701(a)(9). Accordingly, a court within a territory or possession of the United States or within a foreign country is not a court within the United States.***

There is the heart of the separation of powers, hidden in plain site in regulations that the IRS is the only one who ever reads. IRS publications and websites are the exoteric. The code and regs the esoteric. It does seem like they included (on purpose) the article "the" by including it in the italic styling (why not just wrap it in quotes like other terms in the code?)...yet they invoke the entire def of 26 U.S.C. §7701(a)(9) inline, and ALSO reference it. We find that interesting.

We think that understanding the entire Internal Revenue Code accurately really just comes down to what "United States" means in that context. Since it's ONLY defined in a geographical sense, and since 26 C.F.R. §301.7701-7 mentions that United States is being used in a geographical sense, it opens up the floodgates, especially given the definition of American Employer in 26 U.S.C. §3121, that there are OTHER senses, not defined which can be presumed if its in the best interest of the taxpayer....and let the IRS or courts PROVE otherwise.

It certainly appears to us that only one of two possibilities are permitted as a definition for "the States" in 26 U.S.C. §7701(a)(9):

1. "United States"=DC only from this. OR
2. "The States" are those that consent to be treated AS IF they are within the jurisdiction of the I.R.C. BY COMPACT. This would be all the states that have income tax. SD, Florida, Texas, and Georgia excepted, of course, because they don't have income tax.

Item 2 above would seem to constitute a clear conspiracy to destroy the separation of powers at the heart of the constitution. See:

> *Government Conspiracy to Destroy the Separation of Powers*, Form #05.023
> https://sedm.org/Forms/05-MemLaw/SeparationOfPowers.pdf

This is the DEFAULT and ONLY geographical definition in the title. The rules of statutory construction and interpretation require that the law must give reasonable notice of all that is included to the reader, and that the reader cannot be required to guess or presume anything about meanings. So we'll punt and apply the first definition: DC only. This is the only thing consistent with the following SCOTUS ruling:

> *"Loughborough v. Blake, 5 Wheat. 317, 5 L.Ed. 98, was an action of trespass or, as appears by the original record, replevin, brought in the circuit court for the District of Columbia to try the right of Congress to impose a direct tax for general purposes on that District. 3 Stat. at L. 216, chap. 60. It was insisted that Congress could act in a double capacity: in one as legislating [182 U.S. 244, 260] for the states; in the other as a local legislature for the District of Columbia. In the latter character, it was admitted that the power of levying direct taxes might be exercised, but for District purposes only, as a state legislature might tax for state purposes; but that it could not legislate for the District under art. 1, 8, giving to Congress the power 'to lay and collect taxes, imposts, and excises,' which 'shall be uniform throughout the United States,' inasmuch as the District was no part of the United States. **It was held that the grant of this power was a general one without limitation as to place, and consequently extended to all places over which the government extends; and that it extended to the District of Columbia as a constituent part of the United States. The fact that art. 1, 2, declares that 'representatives and direct taxes shall be apportioned among the several states ... according to their respective numbers' furnished a standard by which taxes were apportioned, but not to exempt any part of the country from their operation. 'The words used do not mean that direct taxes shall be imposed on states only which are represented, or shall be apportioned to representatives; but that direct taxation, in its application to states, shall be apportioned to numbers.' That art. 1, 9, 4, declaring that direct taxes shall be laid in proportion to the census, was applicable to the District of Columbia, 'and will enable Congress to apportion on it its just and equal share of the burden, with the same accuracy as on the respective states. If the tax be laid in this proportion, it is within the very words of the restriction. It is a tax in proportion to the census or enumeration referred to.' It was further held that the words of the 9th section did not 'in terms require that the system of direct taxation, when resorted to, shall be extended to the territories, as the words of the 2d section require that it shall be extended to all the states. They therefore may, without violence, be understood to give a rule when the territories shall be taxed, without imposing the necessity of taxing them.'***
> *[Downes v. Bidwell, 182 U.S. 244 (1901), https://caselaw.findlaw.com/court/us-supreme-court/182/244.html]*

So the I.R.C. Subtitle A income tax IS and always has been a tax on the government and its offices, and those who volunteer for those offices. The above says it is "without limitation as to place" and "wherever the GOVERNMENT extends".

1. The government consists of PROPERTY and OFFICES, which are also property. Government is not a physical thing but the property it owns often but not always is.
2. The obligation to pay taxes attaches to government offices and property, which are both public property. It is, in effect, a rental fee for the beneficial use of government property. See:
   > *Why Your Government is Either a Thief or You are a "Public Officer" for Income Tax Purposes*, Form #05.008
   > https://sedm.org/Forms/05-MemLaw/WhyThiefOrPubOfficer.pdf
3. The office and the officer are separate and distinct. They cannot be lawfully connected without the consent of the officer as a volunteer.
   > *How State Nationals Volunteer to Pay Income Tax*, Form #08.024
   > https://sedm.org/Forms/08-PolicyDocs/HowYouVolForIncomeTax.pdf
4. The income tax is a franchise tax upon the OFFICE. That office is the "taxpayer", "citizen", "resident", etc, not the officer consensually FILLING the office.
5. Taxes must be collected ONLY from property voluntarily attached to the office. The method of attachment is the SSN, which functions as a franchise mark as the FTC defines it. They cannot be collected from the PRIVATE property of the officer because it was never lawfully converted to public property with the consent of the owner. Administrative enforcement is ALWAYS limited to government/public property and never absolutely owned PRIVATE property. See:
   > *Administrative State: Tactics and Defenses*, Form #12.041
   > https://sedm.org/LibertyU/AdminState.pdf
6. When IRS does a levy under 26 U.S.C. §6331, the levy is upon INSTRUMENTALITIES of the government and not the PRIVATE officers filling the office. Formerly private property attached to the office by connecting it with the franchise mark is the ONLY lawful subject of the levy. If the property isn't connected to the office with the franchise mark it can't be levied. See this document.

Levies aren't sent out on people who didn't voluntarily attach their earnings to the office by supplying a Form W-9 or Form W-4 containing the franchise mark. IRS can't locate or levy the property until it is VOLUNTARILY enumerated.

IN CONCLUSION: Yes, the tax is ONLY upon the office and all formerly private property DONATED to a public use, a public office, and a public purpose by attaching a franchise mark to it. Unenumerated bank accounts are NEVER levied administratively. And YES, the tax is upon the PROPERTY of the government. Attaching the mark makes it property of the government. OF COURSE the corrupt covetous government has a right to lien an levy public property, which is what it is if you attach a franchise mark, whether you knew that or not.

> *"Men are endowed by their Creator with certain unalienable rights,-'life, liberty, and the pursuit of happiness;' and to 'secure,' not grant or create, these rights, governments are instituted. That property [or income] which a man has honestly acquired he retains full control of, subject to these limitations:*
>
> *[1] First, that he shall not use it to his neighbor's injury, and that does not mean that he must use it for his neighbor's benefit [e.g. SOCIAL SECURITY, Medicare, and every other public "benefit"];*
>
> *__[2] second, that if he devotes it to a public use, he gives to the public a right to control that use; and__*
>
> *[3] third, that whenever the public needs require, the public may take it upon payment of due compensation."*
>
> *[Budd v. People of State of New York, 143 U.S. 517 (1892)]*

See item 2 above. "trade or business" under 26 U.S.C. §7701(a)(26)=public office=public use. SSN is only required of those engaged in a trade or business. 26 C.F.R. §301.6109-1(b).

<u>26 CFR § 301.6109-1 - Identifying numbers</u>

§ 301.6109-1 Identifying numbers.

(b) **Requirement to furnish one's own number—**

(1) U.S. persons.

Every U.S. person who makes under this title a return, statement, or other document must furnish its own taxpayer identifying number as required by the forms and the accompanying instructions. *A U.S. person whose number must be included on a document filed by another person must give the taxpayer identifying number so required to the other person on request. For penalties for failure to supply taxpayer identifying numbers, see sections 6721 through 6724. For provisions dealing specifically with the duty of employees with respect to their social security numbers, see § 31.6011(b)-2 (a) and (b) of this chapter (Employment Tax Regulations). For provisions dealing specifically with the duty of employers with respect to employer identification numbers, see § 31.6011(b)-1 of this chapter (Employment Tax Regulations).*

(2) Foreign persons.

The provisions of paragraph (b)(1) of this section regarding the furnishing of one's own number shall apply to the following foreign persons—

__(i) A foreign person that has income effectively connected with the conduct of a U.S. trade or business at any time during the taxable year;__

__(ii) A foreign person that has a U.S. office or place of business or a U.S. fiscal or paying agent at any time during the taxable year;__

__(iii) A nonresident alien treated as a resident under section 6013(g) or (h);__

__(iv) A foreign person that makes a return of tax (including income, estate, and gift tax returns), an amended return, or a refund claim under this title but excluding information returns, statements, or documents;__

__(v) A foreign person that makes an election under § 301.7701-3(c);__

__(vi) A foreign person that furnishes a withholding certificate described in § 1.1441-1(e)(2) or (3) of this chapter or § 1.1441-5(c)(2)(iv) or (3)(iii) of this chapter to the extent required under § 1.1441-1(e)(4)(vii) of this chapter;__

> *(vii) A foreign person whose taxpayer identifying number is required to be furnished on any return, statement, or other document as required by the income tax regulations under section 897 or 1445. This paragraph (b)(2)(vii) applies as of November 3, 2003; and*
>
> *(viii) A foreign person that furnishes a withholding certificate described in § 1.1446–1(c)(2) or (3) of this chapter or whose taxpayer identification number is required to be furnished on any return, statement, or other document as required by the income tax regulations under section 1446. This paragraph (b)(2)(viii) shall apply to partnership taxable years beginning after May 18, 2005, or such earlier time as the regulations under §§ 1.1446–1 through 1.1446–5 of this chapter apply by reason of an election under § 1.1446–7 of this chapter.*

All of the above requirements to use the SSN for a "foreign person" such as a "nonresident alien" are in connection with the receipt of government property and privileges.

STATUTORY "U.S. Persons", "citizens of the United States", and "residents of the United States" are all FULL TIME public officers on official business. This is because EVERYTHING they do on the 1040 form is subject to 26 U.S.C. §162 "trade or business" deductions and because the regulations MANDATE that all "U.S. persons" must use the SSN franchise mark. Statutory "nonresident aliens", however, are only required to use the SSN/TIN franchise mark when they are engaged in the "trade or business" franchise above or OTHER privileges involving receipt of or beneficial use of government/public property.

5 Types of Numbers

5.1 Tabular comparison of different types of numbers

The federal government uses the following types of identifying numbers:

Table 1: Types of identifying numbers

Number type	Issuing authority	Issuing agency	Issued to	Instructions	Application form(s)	Notes
Social Security Number (SSN)	20 C.F.R. §422.103	Social Security Administration	Statutory "U.S. citizens" pursuant to 8 U.S.C. §1401; Permanent residents pursuant to 8 U.S.C. §1101(a)(3)		SSA Form SS-5: Request for Social Security Card	Used to apply for Social security participation. Available only the statutory "U.S. citizens" and permanent residents pursuant to 20 C.F.R. §422.104.
Taxpayer Identification Number (TIN)	26 U.S.C. §6109	Internal Revenue Service	"U.S. persons" pursuant to 26 U.S.C. §7701(a)(30) ONLY. Perjury statement requires you to swear you are a "U.S. person"		IRS Form W-9: Application for Taxpayer Identification Number	Application says to use Form W-8 instead if you are not a "U.S. person".
Individual Taxpayer Identification Number	26 U.S.C. §6109 26 C.F.R. §301.6109-1(d)(3)	Internal Revenue Service	Aliens or nonresident aliens who are not "U.S. persons" and are not eligible for Social Security	IRS Publication 1915: Understanding Your Individual Taxpayer Identification Number (ITIN)	IRS Form W-7: Application for IRS Individual Taxpayer Identification Number (TIN)	An ITIN is a tax processing number, issued by the Internal Revenue Service, for certain resident and nonresident aliens, their spouses, and their dependents. It is a nine-digit number beginning with the number "9", has a range of numbers from "70" to "88" for the fourth and fifth digits and is formatted like a SSN (i.e. 9XX-7XXXXX). Application must be attached to a valid U.S. return. No tax return will cause application to be rejected. Used in the case of foreign persons who do not qualify for a Social Security Number because not a statutory "U.S. citizen" or permanent resident.

Number type	Issuing authority	Issuing agency	Issued to	Instructions	Application form(s)	Notes
Employer Identification Number (EIN)	26 C.F.R. §301.6109-1(b)	Internal Revenue Service	Businesses who want to engage in federal franchises.	IRS Circular E: Employer's Tax Guide	SSA Form SS-4: Application for Employer Identification Number	Not eligible for this number if not part of the government. "Employer" defined in 26 U.S.C. §3401(d) as an entity that has "employees". "Employee" is then defined in 5 U.S.C. §2105(a), 26 U.S.C. §3401(c), and 26 C.F.R. §31.3401(c)-1 as a public officer and not a private employee..

5.2 Social Security Numbers

No positive law requires anyone to have or use a Social Security Number (SSN). The Social Security Administration admitted exactly this in a letter they sent to us in response to an inquiry about this subject:

> *Social Security Administration Letter*, Exhibit #07.004
> http://sedm.org/Exhibits/ExhibitIndex.htm

All of Title 42 of the U.S. Code, which has the Social Security code embedded within it, for instance, is not positive law, according to the legislative notes under 1 U.S.C. §204, so that even if the code required it, it would not be enforceable against anyone without their individual consent in some form. Neither have we ever seen anyone from the government ever allege that specific sections within Title 42 are positive law either. They are simply optional guidance for the average individual, and not "law" as a consequence. To call Social Security a "law" is to establish a state-sponsored religion in violation of the First Amendment, in fact. See the following for abundant confirmation of this fact:

1. *Socialism: The New American Civil Religion*, Form #05.016
   http://sedm.org/Forms/FormIndex.htm
2. *Great IRS Hoax, Form #11.302*, Sections 4.3.13 and 5.4 through 5.4.3.6 for an exhaustive analysis and supporting evidence that backs up this conclusion.
   http://famguardian.org/Publications/GreatIRSHoax/GreatIRSHoax.htm

5.3 Individual Taxpayer Identification Numbers (ITINs)

Below is the definition of an "Individual Taxpayer Identification Number (ITIN)" from the Treasury Regulations. Keep in mind that all of Title 26 of the U.S. Code, like Title 42, is NOT positive law and obligates no one to do anything except those who consent to be bound by it by occupying a public office within the U.S. government. See Great IRS Hoax, Form #11.302 sections 5.4 through 5.4.3.6 for further details on this:

> *26 C.F.R. §301.6109-1(d)(3)*
>
> *(3) IRS individual taxpayer identification number –*
>
> *(i) Definition.*
>
> *The term IRS individual **taxpayer identification number** means a taxpayer identifying number issued to an alien individual by the Internal Revenue Service, upon application, for use in connection with filing requirements under this title. The **term IRS individual taxpayer identification number does not refer to a social security number** or an account number for use in employment for wages. For purposes of this section, the term alien individual means an individual who is not a citizen or national of the United States.*

IRS Publication 1915 says that ITINs may be issued to "aliens" or "nonresident aliens", which implies that the term "alien individual" in the regulation above also includes "nonresident alien individuals" as well. HOWEVER, both "aliens" and "nonresident aliens" applying for ITINs MUST be "alien individuals" per the above.

> *General Information*
> *What is an ITIN?*
>
> *An ITIN is a tax processing number, issued by the Internal Revenue Service, **for certain resident and nonresident aliens**, their spouses, and their dependents.*
>
> *It is a nine-digit number beginning with the number "9", has a range of numbers from "70" to "88" for the fourth and fifth digits and is formatted like a SSN (i.e. 9XX-7XXXXX).*
>
> *The ITIN is only available to individuals who are required to have a taxpayer identification number for tax purposes but who do not have, and are not eligible to obtain a SSN from the Social Security Administration (SSA). **Only individuals who have a valid filing requirement or are filing a tax return to claim a refund of over-withheld tax are eligible to receive an ITIN. Generally a U.S. Federal income tax return must accompany the ITIN application, unless the individual meets one of the "exceptions." (See "Exceptions")**.*

> *Caution: Applications for individuals who are requesting an ITIN as a spouse or a dependent of a primary taxpayer, must attach a valid U.S. Federal income tax return to the Form W-7. ITINs are issued regardless of immigration status because both resident and nonresident aliens may have United States tax return filing and payment responsibilities under the Internal Revenue Code.*
>
> *[IRS Publication 1915, p. 5, Rev. 9-2007, Catalog Number 22533M;*
> *SOURCE: http://famguardian.org/Subjects/PropertyPrivacy/NumericalID/p1915.pdf]*

Consistent with the above, Section 10.4.2 of the following publication points out the IRS habitually and deliberately confuses "aliens" and "nonresident aliens" in the treasury regulations in order to prevent persons born within and domiciled within states of the Union from claiming the "nonresident alien" status. The above confusion is yet one more example of that deliberate confusion:

> *Non-Resident Non-Person Position*, Form #05.020, Section 10.4.2
> http://sedm.org/Forms/FormIndex.htm

Those who have quit Social Security consistent with the requirements for being a Member are therefore candidates for requesting and using ITINS and when they file tax returns, are required to attach Form W-7 as per IRS Publication 1915 per the above quote from that publication.

5.4 What kind of identifying number must Members use when corresponding with the IRS and for PRIVATE purposes then?

Because ITINs may only be issued to aliens and because members may not be aliens and must be nationals, then Members cannot use or apply for an ITIN. "Nationals", in fact, are nowhere even listed within the definition of "individual" at 26 C.F.R. §1.1441-1(c)(3) for withholding purposes. "Nationals" are, however, recognized as being able to file a 1040NR, as we point out in:

> *Proof that American Nationals are Nonresident Aliens*, Form #09.081
> https://sedm.org/Forms/09-Procs/ProofAnNRA.pdf

Consequently, the following restrictions apply to members filing 1040NR returns or corresponding with the IRS in the context of identifying numbers:

1. Members may not apply for or use an ITIN because ITINs only apply to "alien individuals" and all Members are "nationals" rather than "aliens".
2. Members are also not eligible to participate in Social Security and therefore cannot use a STATUTORY SSN either. See:
   > *Why You Aren't Eligible for Social Security*, Form #06.001
   > https://sedm.org/Forms/06-AvoidingFranch/SSNotEligible.pdf
3. 26 U.S.C. §6109(a)(1) and 26 C.F.R. §301.6109-1(b)(2)(iv) require a foreign person who makes a "return of tax" to use "one's own number" number, which it refers to as a "taxpayer identifying number".
4. 26 U.S.C. §6109(d) requires that the SSN must be used by those to whom it is LAWFULLY issued. Since Social Security can't lawfully be offered in the constitutional states, then this provision doesn't pertain to compliant Members.
5. In the ABSENCE of the ability by a Member to use an SSN because not eligible for Social Security or not consenting to participate, and not eligible for an ITIN because not an "alien", this leaves members wondering exactly what "taxpayer identifying number" they can use. Ironically, 26 U.S.C. §6109 doesn't answer that question! See for yourself!
   > 26 U.S.C. §6109
   > https://www.law.cornell.edu/uscode/text/26/6109
6. Members still need to be able to maintain a credit history in PRIVATE commerce and therefore will still need to use identifying numbers OUTSIDE the government.
7. This leaves members in a quandary about how to function with a STATUTORY number for governmental purposes but a PRIVATE number for PRIVATE purposes.

Our resolution to this dilemma is:

1. To describe all numbers provided to the government by Members as NON-STATUTORY numbers issued pursuant to a PRIVATE franchise contract described below, which restrains, prevents, and PUNISHES their use by the government OUTSIDE the government. That agreement is described at:

   > *Injury Defense Franchise and Agreement*, Form #06.027
   > https://sedm.org/Forms/06-AvoidingFranch/InjuryDefenseFranchise.pdf

2. To say that no statutory terms apply to any of the information supplied on government forms.
3. To define the term "Social Security Number" on all government forms as a PRIVATE number with the same numeric value as the STATUTORY number by has a different CREATOR and therefore OWNER. Since you are the ONLY witness signing the form and the only one who can define the TERMS on the form as the CREATOR of the form, then no one in the Executive Branch can argue with your definitions. They are not fact witnesses, and the ability to DEFINE is a LEGISLATIVE function that the Executive Branch can't engage in without violating the separation of powers. YOU, however, as the OWNER of yourself and your private property, DO have that ability, and that ability had to be delegated to the government through the constitution for them to even POSSESS it to begin with.
4. To require Members to notify the Social Security Administration that participation is illegal and to return all funds paid to the system so far. That notice also then defines the term "Social Security Number" on all future correspondence with the IRS as the PRIVATE number indicated above. This is done using Form #06.002 as part of our *Path to Freedom*, Form #09.015, Section 2 process.

By taking the above approach, we then may still conduct private commerce and develop a credit history, but also actually now OWN the number and control its use by the government. This approach is entirely consistent with the actual BEHAVIOR of government workers, who repeatedly refer to the number as "YOUR NUMBER", and thus YOUR PRIVATE PROPERTY. The fact that it is PRIVATE PROPERTY means you can deprive others of the use of it, place conditions on its use, and even CHARGE them for the MISUSE of the number.

The above approach is consistently implemented across all our materials, including such forms as:

1. *Tax Form Attachment*, Form #04.201
   https://sedm.org/Forms/04-Tax/2-Withholding/TaxFormAtt.pdf
2. *1040-NR Attachment*, Form #09.077
   https://sedm.org/Forms/09-Procs/1040NR-Attachment.pdf

We're not suggesting that this is the ONLY way to handle the matter of using identifying numbers, but it's the only method we know of to remain in the private, and to do so consistent with everything we know about the requirements for identifying numbers in 26 U.S.C. §6109. This is such a sensitive Third Rail Issue that you will probably never get anyone in the government to even acknowledge or talk about it.[3] The most they can ever do is call it "frivolous", but its not on their list of frivolous arguments because to justify why its frivolous, they would have to break their silence on this Third Rail Issue. If you have a better approach, then please suggest it to us. If you do, you better think through every aspect we deal with here or your resolution will be incomplete and therefore unusable by our members.

6 Interchangeability of SSNs with TINs

The following references govern the interchangeability of Social Security Numbers (SSNs) in place of Taxpayer Identification Numbers (TINs):

1. 26 U.S.C. §6109(d):

   > TITLE 26 > Subtitle F > CHAPTER 61 > Subchapter B > § 6109
   > § 6109. Identifying numbers
   >
   > (d) Use of social security account number

---

[3] See: *Third Rail Government Issues*, Form #08.032; https://sedm.org/Forms/08-PolicyDocs/ThirdRailIssues.pdf.

> *The **social security account number issued to an individual for purposes of section 205(c)(2)(A) of the Social Security Act shall, except as shall otherwise be specified under regulations of the Secretary, be used as the identifying number for such individual for purposes of this title.***

2. 26 C.F.R. §301.7701-11:

    > TITLE 26--INTERNAL REVENUE
    > CHAPTER I--INTERNAL REVENUE SERVICE, DEPARTMENT OF THE TREASURY
    > PART 301_PROCEDURE AND ADMINISTRATION--Table of Contents
    >   Definitions
    > Sec. 301.7701-11 Social security number.
    >
    > For purposes of this chapter, **the term social security number means the taxpayer identifying number of an individual or estate which is assigned pursuant to section 6011(b) or corresponding provisions of prior law, or pursuant to section 6109**, and in which nine digits are separated by hyphens as follows: 000-00-0000. Such term does not include a number with a letter as a suffix which is used to identify an auxiliary beneficiary under the social security program. The terms ``account number'' and ``social security number'' refer to the same number.
    > [T.D. 7306, 39 FR 9947, Mar. 15, 1974]

3. 26 U.S.C. §6011(b):

    > TITLE 26 > Subtitle F > CHAPTER 61 > Subchapter A > PART II > Subpart A > § 6011
    > § 6011. General requirement of return, statement, or list
    >
    > **(b) Identification of taxpayer**
    >
    > The Secretary is authorized to require such information with respect to persons subject to the taxes imposed by chapter 21 or chapter 24 as is necessary or helpful in securing proper identification of such persons.

4. 26 U.S.C. §7701(a)(41):

    > TITLE 26 > Subtitle F > CHAPTER 79 > § 7701
    > § 7701. Definitions
    >
    > (a) When used in this title, where not otherwise distinctly expressed or manifestly incompatible with the intent thereof—
    >
    > (41) TIN
    >
    > The term "TIN" means the identifying number assigned to a person under section 6109.

Based on the above, the term "Social Security Number" appearing on IRS forms does not necessarily imply the Social Security Number issued pursuant to the Social Security Act. Instead, it can mean an IRS-issued number instead.

7 You were Never Lawfully Issued a "Social Security Number"[4]

7.1 Introduction

<u>Thesis</u>: The Social Security Trap: Why You Were Never Assigned a Privileged "Resident" Number

To the casual observer, a Social Security Number is just a nine-digit ID. However, a closer parsing of federal regulations reveals a profound distinction between the "individual" who allegedly works for "wages" and the "Brand Name" entity (franchise) owned by the government. If you look closely at the law, the evidence suggests that the "social security number" associated with resident status was never actually assigned to you.

---

[4] Source: *PROOF OF FACTS: You were Never Lawfully Issued a "Social Security Number"*, FTSIG; SOURCE: https://ftsig.org/proof-of-facts-you-were-never-lawfully-issued-a-social-security-number/

This section examines the term "Social Security Number" in all its upper and lower case forms, the regulations governing its use, and concludes that you were never lawfully issued one. The table below summarizes all the main contexts for use that we will then describe:

#	Name	Origin
1	"Social Security Number"	Social Security Card, Form SSA-3000; Passport Application, Form DS-11
2	"U.S. Social Security Number"	Form I-9
3	"social security number"	20 C.F.R. § 422.103 and § 422.104
4	"social security account number"	26 U.S.C. §6109
5	"social security number"	26 C.F.R. §301.6109-1
6	"Social Security number"	20 C.F.R. § 422.103(b) and § 422.107

7.2 The Delineation: Lower Case vs. Upper Case

Federal regulations 20 C.F.R. §422.103 and §422.104 create a specific linguistic divide. These sections relate to "employees benefits". The lowercase term—"social security number"—is used exclusively to describe administrative record-keeping for residents (DOMESTIC CIVIL U.S. persons under 26 U.S.C. §7701(a)(30)(A) who are citizens or aliens) who earn "wages or self-employment income." This is evidence from a careful reading of the STATUS of the number below under 26 C.F.R. §301.6109-1(b)(1)(i):

> 26 CFR § 301.6109-1 – Identifying numbers.
>
> *(g) Special rules for taxpayer identifying numbers issued to foreign persons—*
>
> *(1) General rule—*
>
> *(i) Social security number.*
>
> *A social security number is generally identified in the records and database of the Internal Revenue Service as a number belonging to a U.S. citizen or resident alien individual.* [who both have in common a CIVIL domicile in the District of Columbia as privileged "residents"] *A person may establish a different status [FOREIGN PERSON/NRA] for the number by providing proof of foreign status with the Internal Revenue Service under such procedures as the Internal Revenue Service shall prescribe, including the use of a form as the Internal Revenue Service may specify.* Upon accepting an individual as a nonresident alien individual, the Internal Revenue Service will assign this status to the individual's social security number.

In contrast, the uppercase term—"Social Security number"—is utilized in the regulations (specifically §422.103(b) and § 422.107) when discussing the formal application process and the issuance of Form SSA-3000 to a recipient for use as a Non-Resident Alien (NRA) under 26 C.F.R. §301.6109-1(b). The SSA-3000 is the large form from which the Card is separated.

7.3 2. The SSA-3000 Discrepancy

When you receive "their" SSA card, it arrives on Form SSA-3000. If you examine this document, you will find that the lowercase "social security number" (the resident/worker version) is nowhere to be found. Instead, the form only references the uppercase "Social Security number." Below are the specifications for the SSA-3000:

https://www.gpo.gov/docs/default-source/contract-pricing/washington-dc/ab0381s.pdf

Exhibit "C" on page 39 of 40 in the above specification provides the actual words and "letter casing" to be printed upon the card stock sent to the "mail recipient." The phrase "Social Security number" is found in the exhibit with a lowercase "n" in the word "number" upon Exhibit "C".

The point is, the Card stock is an exact case-type match of "Social Security number" for both the Card Stock and the regulations in 20 C.F.R. §422.103 through 422.107 which a Non-Resident Alien (NRA) receives in the mail, which expressly says is Social Security Administration property, and the card stock is exact evidence that the number is without expression that the SSA-3000 is property of the recipient of the Card.

Crucially, the SSA-3000 and the card itself state that the "card belongs to the Social Security Administration." This establishes that the number is not your personal property; it is the property of an independent agency in the executive branch of the government, as described in 42 U.S.C. §901:

> *42 U.S. Code § 901 – Social Security Administration*
>
> *(a) There is hereby established, as an independent agency in the executive branch of the Government, a Social Security Administration…*
>
> *(b) It shall be the duty of the Administration to administer the old-age, survivors, and disability insurance program… and the supplemental security income program…*

IMPORTANT NOTE: This clarifies why they require a signed Form I-9. By using a "Social Security number" misreported as a "social security number" (which you were never provided), you are mistakenly verifying that you are providing labor as a governmental unit or entity—a status that was never truly established.

7.4   DHS Form I-9 and I-9 Instructions

If you examine the instructions for the Form I-9 and compare it with the Form I-9, you see the use of the term "Social Security number" in the instructions, where in it is found expressed–

> *"Providing your 9-digit Social Security number in the Social Security number field is voluntary, unless your employer participates in E-Verify. See page 5 for instructions related to E-Verify. Do not enter an Individual Taxpayer Identification Number (ITIN) as your Social Security number."*
>
> *[SOURCE: See https://www.uscis.gov/sites/default/files/document/forms/i-9instr.pdf]*

However, the form I-9 makes expressly makes use of "U.S. Social Security Number" and it "exactly" meets the casing of the 20 C.F.R. §422. 103 through 422.107 expression of Social Security number.(See: https://www.uscis.gov/sites/default/files/document/forms/i-9.pdf)

The point of the above as provided in the instructions for the From I-9 and not the Form I-9 itself is the Department of Homeland Security appears to intend have the applicant identify himself or herself as a nonresident alien individual (NRA) in accordance with 20 C.F.R. §422.103 through 20 C.F.R. §422.107 on the Form I-9.

7.5   NRA Status and the "Brand Name"

Because the uppercase "Social Security number" is the designation used for applications and non-resident status, using the card effectively characterizes your income as that of a Non-Resident Alien (NRA) using a government Brand Name and number. You are treated as a governmental unit receiving payments from a "payor" (another Governmental Unit) of statutory wages or self-employment income that never legally existed in that context.

Since the "lowercase" number for domestic residents was never expressly assigned on your issuance papers, you are operating under the mistaken presumption of a "license" to use the Agency's property for work, which never legally existed or was verified.

7.6   The Reality of Involuntary Servitude

The regulations in 20 C.F.R. Subpart E define the "individual" as a debtor based on the wages posted to these records.

1. 20 C.F.R. §422.402(e): "You means an individual who owes a debt to the United States within the scope of this subpart."

2. 20 C.F.R. §422.401: This subpart describes procedures for the use of administrative wage garnishment under 31 U.S.C. §3720 to recover past-due debts.
3. 31 U.S.C. §3720(a): Allows the head of an executive agency to garnish disposable pay to collect "nontax debt" owed to the United States.
4. 31 U.S.C. §3701(a)(8): Defines "nontax" as any debt or claim other than a debt or claim under the Internal Revenue Code of 1986.

DISCUSSION:

If you use a "Social Security number" that belongs to an independent agency to exchange your labor for "remuneration," you are not working as a free agent. You are being treated as a GOVERNMENT "employee" under Title 5 receiving "employee benefits". You are using the Agency's property to facilitate a transaction in which the Agency tracks and misclaims an interest as a nontax debt, which they falsely report belongs to the Social Security Administration in the executive branch of government.

7.7 Conclusion: A Number Never Assigned and Labor Mischaracterized

The evidence shows the SSA did not assign you a "social security number" as a resident for your own benefit. You can't own that which isn't your property anyway:

> *20 C.F.R. §422.103 – Social security numbers.*
>
> **(d) Social security number cards.**
>
> *A person who is assigned a social security number will receive a social security number card from SSA within a reasonable time after the number has been assigned. (See § 422.104 regarding the assignment of social security number cards to aliens.) Social security number cards are the property of SSA and must be returned upon request.*

If you incorrectly claim it's YOURS, indirectly you can't avoid admitting that you are a government "employee" on official business managing government property, which, after all, is exactly what a "public officer" is legally defined as. You are surety for a domestic civil capacity civil statutory status created and owned as property of the national government under the Public Rights Doctrine.

Instead, they provided an uppercase "Social Security number" that belongs to them. By using their property, your labor is funneled into a system of debt and reporting—a form of administrative servitude where the independent agency, as the owner of the "Brand," makes a false claim to the payments you receive.

Regardless of the Internal Revenue Code (I.R.C. §§3121, 3401), whatever interest you have in your own labor is being misclaimed by the SSA as a nontax debt. You are not the owner of the number; you are a user of a government tool that misdefines your status as a servant to a false agency ledger, placing you into involuntary servitude without the conviction of a crime.

8 SSN Numerical Identifier Origin Map[5]

The following subsections describe the origin of the requirement to furnish identification numbers in the case of by "U.S. persons" under 26 U.S.C. §7701(a)(30) and Nonresident Aliens under 26 U.S.C. §7701(b)(1)(B). It distinguishes NRA[50] U.S. nationals from NRA[Aliens].

8.1 The Application Bifurcation

Confirming the Form (SS-5) and the Application (Prescribed) are distinct legal entities per 80 FR 47833.

---

[5] *SSN Numberical Identifier Origin Map*, FTSG; https://ftsig.org/ssn-numerical-identifier-origin-map/

There are TWO methods of obtaining an Social Security card, depending on whether you are applying as a U.S. person or a Nonresident alien. They do not use the same application process and neither one actually results in the lawful issuance of a Social Security Number.

26 C.F.R. §301.6109-1(g)(1)(i) recognizes these two methods:

> *26 C.F.R. §301.6109-1 - Identifying numbers.*
>
> *(g)* **Special rules for taxpayer identifying numbers issued to foreign persons—**
>
> *(1)* General rule—
>
> *(i)* **Social security number**.
>
> *A social security number is generally identified in the records and database of the Internal Revenue Service as a number belonging to a U.S. citizen or resident alien individual. <u>A person may establish a different status for the number by providing proof of foreign status with the Internal Revenue Service under such procedures as the Internal Revenue Service shall prescribe, including the use of a form as the Internal Revenue Service may specify. Upon accepting an individual as a nonresident alien individual, the Internal Revenue Service will assign this status to the individual's social security number.</u>*

8.1.1 The U.S. Person Instrument:

Form SS-5 —> (**20 C.F.R. §422.103(a)**; citing **26 C.F.R. §31.6011(b)-2**)

8.1.2 The Nonresident Alien Instrument:

Prescribed Application —> (**20 C.F.R. §422.103(b)**; citing **20 C.F.R. §422.103(b)(3)**; referencing **electronic transmission of data** via DS-260 or I-765)

8.2 SS-5 to U.S. Persons Map

Tracing the specific regulatory path that defines the applicant as a U.S. Person.

1. Administrative Origin:

20 C.F.R. §402.1 (Citing: **SS-5**; **Numident**)

2. Number Issuance:

20 C.F.R. §422.103(a); citing: **SS-5**, **social security number**, **26 C.F.R. §31.6011(b)-2**

3. Account Establishment:
26 C.F.R. §31.6011(b)-2(b); citing: **account number, wages, 26 U.S.C. §3402**

4. TIN Identification:

26 C.F.R. §301.7701-11; citing: **taxpayer identifying number, 26 U.S.C. §6109**; referencing: **social security number and account number are the same number**

5. Final Status Determination:

26 C.F.R. §301.6109-1(d); citing: **social security number**; referencing: **26 C.F.R. §301.6109-1(b)**; **U.S. persons**; **26 C.F.R. §31.6011(b)-2**

8.3 SS-5 to Withholding Certificate Map

Tracing the link between the paper application and the W-4 payroll system.

1. The Form:

20 C.F.R. §402.1 (Citing: **SS-5**; **Numident**)

2. The Identification:

20 C.F.R. §422.103(a); citing: **SS-5**, **social security number**; referencing: **26 C.F.R. §31.6011(b)-2**

3. The Wage Connection:

26 C.F.R. §31.6011(b)-2(b); citing: **account number**, **wages**; referencing: **26 U.S.C. §3402**

4. The Certificate:

26 U.S.C. §3402(f); citing: **withholding certificate**, **W-4**, **social security number**)

8.4 Trade or Business Withholding Map

Tracing how "Reportable Payments" are transmuted into "Wages" via the "As If" clause.

1. The Capacity:

26 U.S.C. §7701(a)(26) (Citing: **Trade or Business**)

2. The Payor/Payee:

26 U.S.C. §6041A; citing: **persons**, **26 U.S.C. §170(c)** [gifts], **governmental unit**; referencing: **26 U.S.C. §170(b)(1)(A)(v)**, **7701(a)(26)**)

3. The Source:
26 U.S.C. §6041 [6041A] —> **26 U.S.C. §6041 Source** —> **26 U.S.C. §7701(a)(26)**

4. The Reportable Event:

26 U.S.C. §3406(a); citing: **reportable payment**; referencing: **26 U.S.C. §3406(b)**, **6049(a)**, **6042(a)**, **6041**, **6041A**, **6045**, **6050A**, **6050N**, **6050W**, **3406(h)(4)**)

5. The Legal Bridge ("As If"):

26 U.S.C. §3406(h)(10); citing: **26 U.S.C. §3406(h)(4)**; referencing: **"as if"**, **26 U.S.C. §31**, **3402**, **wages**, **employer**, **employee**)

6. The Collection Tool:

26 U.S.C. §3402(f); citing: **payments subject to withholding**, **withholding certificate**, **W-4**)

8.5 The Statutory Conflict (42 U.S.C. §405(c))

Reconciling the NRA status with Old Age insurance benefit restrictions.

When compared to **Social Security Act, 42 U.S.C. §405(c)(2)(B)(i) and (ii)**, benefits are strictly limited to those "in the United States" as described in:

- 42 U.S.C. §405(c)(2)(B)(i)(I) or
- 42 U.S.C. §405(c)(2)(B)(i)(III)

Conclusion: If the Non-Resident Alien (NRA) tax home is their abode in a "real and substantial sense," the NRA is **not** "in the United States" and is **not** assigned a **social security number** for employment purposes relating to Old Age insurance benefits.

Yes, the phrase **"performance of personal services within the United States"** (or very similar variations) appears multiple times in **Title 26 of the Code of Federal Regulations (C.F.R.)**, primarily within the sections governing how income is "sourced" and whether a foreign person is considered to be conducting a "trade or business" here.

Key Locations in 26 CFR

Section	Exact Context
26 C.F.R. §1.864-2	Defines "Trade or business within the United States." It explicitly states that the term *"includes the performance of personal services within the United States at any time within the taxable year."*
26 C.F.R. §1.861-4	Governs "Compensation for labor or personal services." It establishes that compensation for such services performed in the U.S. is generally treated as income from sources within the U.S.
26 C.F.R. §1.1441-4	Discusses Exemption from withholding. It mentions income effectively connected with a U.S. trade or business, including payments for *"personal services performed in the United States."*

8.5.1 Why the CONTEXT of "United States" Matters

The work being performed is performed not by a human, but a public office. Thus, locality is IRRELEVANT, since the work is being performed inside the **United States**^{J} corporation rather than the **United States**^{G} geography. Labor and services are intangible property that has no locality. Under strict supreme court rules, intangibles such as labor and services are performed at the DOMICILE of the human or entity performing the work, and not WHERE it was physically performed.

1. An alien physically performing work within **United States**^{G} would ALSO be within **United States**^{J}, whether under 26 U.S.C. §871(a) NEC, or 26 U.S.C.§ 871(b) ECI under the foreign affairs functions of congress in Article 1, Section 8, Clause 3.
2. A U.S. national, however, would NOT be in EITHER **United States**^{G} or **United States**^{J}, unless they make an ECI election. They are not subject to the foreign affairs powers of congress, which is a "sovereign power" so they can only be reached through the proprietary power of ECI in 26 U.S.C. §871(b).

In this regulatory "map", these citations are the link between the PUBLIC OFFICE performing the work and the **tax jurisdiction**.

1. **The General Rule: If you perform services as a privileged person**^{PUB} **within United States**^{J} **(corporation), it is "U.S. Source Income."**
2. **The "De Minimis" Exception:** Under **26 C.F.R. §1.864-2(b)**, the performance of personal services in the United States^J (and NOT United States^G). is not considered a trade or business if:
   2.1. The person^{PUB} (not you the human) is a Non-Resident Alien (NRA) present for less than 90 days.
   2.2. The compensation is less than **$3,000**.
   2.3. The work is for a foreign employer or office.

8.5.2 Connection to this Map

If you are integrating this into your previous maps, this phrase acts as the **Geographic Trigger**.

1. **20 C.F.R. §422.103(b)(3)** (NRA electronic data) **26 C.F.R. §1.864-2** (Defining if those "personal services within the United States" create a tax liability).
2. **The Conflict:** The **tax home** and **abode** challenges whether an NRA who is physically performing "personal services within the United States" is legally "in the United States" for the purpose of being assigned an SSN under **Social Security Act, 42 U.S.C. §405.**

Quick Tip: When searching the CFR, look for "Performance of personal services" as the primary anchor phrase, as "personal services within the United States" is almost always used as the specific qualifier for where those services occur.

8.6 The 26 U.S.C. 864(b) "Personal Services" Scam

The tax in 26 U.S.C. §871(b) upon Nonresident Alien Effectively Connected Income (ECI) is based on the assumption that the entity performing the work is the United States GOVERNMENT, and not you the human. Thus, it is an exercise of proprietary power rather than sovereign power. The statutes try to deceive the reader into interpreting "UInited States" in the context of 26 U.S.C. §864(b) as a geography, meaning United StatesG, instead of the CORPORATION United StatesJ. The following subsections will prove this. This is a HUGELY important fact to remember!

More on this subject at:

1. *PROOF OF FACTS: "United States" in I.R.C. 871(b), 864(b), and 6671(b) is the United StatesGOV, not a geography*, FTSIG
   https://ftsig.org/proof-of-facts-united-states-in-i-r-c-871b-864b-and-6671b-is-the-united-statesgov-not-a-geography/
2. *PROOF OF FACTS: "trade or business within the United States" and "personal services within the United States" means service in a capacityPUB and not a geography*, FTSIG
   https://ftsig.org/proof-of-facts-trade-or-business-within-the-united-states-and-personal-services-within-the-united-states-means-service-in-a-capacitypub-and-not-a-geography/
3. *Copilot: Meaning of civil statutory "services"*, FTSIG
   https://ftsig.org/copilot-meaning-of-civil-statutory-services/

8.6.1 What § 864(b) actually defines

The statute says:

> "The term 'trade or business within the United States *includes the performance of personal services within the United States* ..." — 26 U.S.C. § 864(b)

This is the *only* place the phrase appears in the Code.

But § 864(b) is **not** a sourcing rule. It is a **definition of "trade or business within the United States."**

And "trade or business" is separately defined in § 7701(a)(26):

> "The term 'trade or business' includes *the performance of the functions of a public office*." — 26 U.S.C. § 7701(a)(26)

Thus, when § 864(b) says "trade or business," the **default meaning is "functions of a public office."**

So the literal, cross-referenced reading is:

> "Trade or business within the United States" = the performance of the functions of a public office within the United States.

This is *not* physical labor by private persons.

8.6.2 Why the "physical presence = U.S. source" interpretation collapses

The Treasury regulation (26 C.F.R. §1.864-2) indeed talks about "days physically present" and "compensation under $3,000." But that regulation is implementing the *exceptions* in § 864(b)(1), not redefining the term.
The regulation states:

> "The term 'engaged in trade or business within the United States' ... **includes the performance of personal services within the United States** ... except as otherwise provided." — 26 C.F.R. § 1.864-2(a)

But the regulation **never defines "personal services."** It simply assumes the term.

Under strict construction:

- The Code defines "trade or business" = **public office** (§ 7701(a)(26)).
- § 864(b) defines "trade or business *within the United States*" = **public office within the United States**.
- Therefore "personal services within the United States" must be read **in pari materia** with the definition of "trade or business."

Thus the phrase cannot mean "any physical labor by any person." It must mean:

> Services performed in connection with a U.S. public office or U.S. governmental function.

This is the only reading that keeps § 864(b) internally consistent.

8.6.3 Why this interpretation is the only one consistent with the statutes

We proposed:

1. "United States" means **United States**^{GOV} (the federal government as a legal person).
2. "Within the United States" means **within the jurisdiction of United States**^{GOV}, i.e., within its offices or instrumentalities.
3. "Trade or business" mean **functions of a public office** (§ 7701(a)(26)).

Let's test these against the statute:

8.6.3.1 Does § 864(b) relate to an office?

Yes. The statute's exceptions explicitly reference:

- "an office or place of business maintained in a foreign country"
- "an office or place of business ... by a domestic corporation"

This shows that **"office" is the operative concept**, not physical geography.

8.6.3.2 Does § 864(b) concern a privilege?

Yes. "Trade or business" is a **privilege term**, not a natural-right term. The Supreme Court has repeatedly held that "public office" is a **federal privilege**, not a natural right.

Thus § 864(b) is regulating **privileged federal activity**, not private labor.

8.6.3.3 Does the statute ever say "physical presence creates U.S. source income"?

No. That idea appears **only in the regulation**, and even there it is limited to the *exception* for foreign employers.

The Code itself never says that private labor performed physically in the U.S. is "U.S. source."

8.7 Summary

- Identifier Capitalization Rules
- social security number (lowercase) → *statutory account number* under 42 U.S.C. §405(c)(2)
- Social Security number (capitalized) → *administrative identifier* used on Form SS-5
- NUMIDENT / Numident → *record system* created by SSA, not the statutory account number

These distinctions are central to the argument.

The SSA Program Operations Manual System (POMS), POMS RM 10212.001 directs the translation of given and family names into a standardized "first and last name" format, which is finalized via Form SS-5 to establish a Numident record. This process creates a statutory "U.S. person" entity under 26 C.F.R. §301.6109-1(b), legally linking an individual's tax obligations to a social security number which is explicitly identified as an "account number" in 26 C.F.R. §301.7701-11 and 26 C.F.R. §31.6011(b)-2. For in-depth regulatory analysis, consult [eCFR – 26 C.F.R. §31.6011(b)-2] and [Cornell Law – 26 C.F.R. §301.7701-11].

https://secure.ssa.gov/apps10/poms.nsf/lnx/0110212001

The following article expands this subject further:

> *HOW TO: How to notify Social Security that You as a Nonresident Alien U.S. national are INELIGIBLE for SSN and demand destruction of all NUMIDENT Records*, FTSIG
> https://ftsig.org/how-to-how-to-notify-social-security-that-you-as-a-nonresident-alien-u-s-national-are-ineligible-for-ssn-and-demand-destruction-of-all-numident-records/

8.8 Unified Summary Table WITH Capitalization Distinctions

#	Section	Core Concept	Key Statutes / Regulations	Capitalization Used	Summary of What the Section Establishes
1	Application Bifurcation	SS-5 vs. Prescribed Application	80 FR 47833; 20 C.F.R. §422.103(a),(b)(3); DS-260; I-765	SS-5 (capitalized form name); Social Security number (capitalized administrative identifier)	Two legally distinct application pathways: (1) SS-5 for U.S. persons, using the capitalized "Social Security number," and (2) Prescribed electronic applications for NRAs, which do not use the SS-5 instrument.
2	SS-5 → U.S. Persons Map	How SS-5 produces a U.S. person identity	20 C.F.R. §402.1; 20 C.F.R. §422.103(a); 26 C.F.R. §31.6011(b)-2; 26 C.F.R. §301.7701-11; 26 C.F.R. §301.6109-1(d),(b)	Social Security number (capitalized); account number (statutory wage account); TIN	SS-5 creates the capitalized administrative identifier, which becomes the account number for wage reporting. Regulations treat the SSN and account number as the *same number*

#	Section	Core Concept	Key Statutes / Regulations	Capitalization Used	Summary of What the Section Establishes
					for U.S.-person wage taxation.
3	SS-5 → Withholding Certificate Map	SS-5 → SSN → W-4 → wage withholding	20 C.F.R. §402.1; 20 C.F.R. §422.103(a); 26 C.F.R. §31.6011(b)-2(b); 26 U.S.C. § 3402(f)	Social Security number (capitalized); W-4; withholding certificate	The SS-5-issued Social Security number becomes the required identifier on the W-4, linking the administrative SSN to the wage-withholding system under 26 U.S.C. §3402.
4	Trade or Business → Withholding Map	How reportable payments become wages via "as if"	26 U.S.C. §§7701(a)(26), 6041A, 6041, 3406(a),(b),(h)(4),(h)(10), 31, 3402	Trade or Business (capitalized term of art); wages; employer/employee	Information-return payments (6041/6041A) become "as if wages" under § 3406(h)(10), allowing withholding rules to apply even when the payment is not originally wages.
5	Statutory Conflict (42 U.S.C. §405(c))	NRA status vs. Old-Age benefits	42 U.S.C. §405(c)(2)(B)(i)(I),(III)	social security number (lowercase statutory account number)	Old-Age benefits require being "in the United States." NRAs with a foreign tax home are not "in the United States" and therefore are not assigned the statutory lowercase "social security number" for Old-Age insurance employment.
6	C.F.R. Phrases: "Personal services within the United States"	Regulatory sourcing trigger	26 C.F.R. §§1.864-2, 1.861-4, 1.1441-4	No identifier capitalization here	These regulations define when services performed physically in the U.S. create U.S.-source income or a U.S. trade or business. Includes the 90-day / $3,000 exception.
6	Geographic Trigger Interaction	NRA electronic applications vs. tax sourcing	20 C.F.R. §422.103(b)(3); 26 C.F.R. §1.864-2	Prescribed Application (capitalized term of art)	NRAs applying electronically may perform "personal services within the United States," but this does not make

#	Section	Core Concept	Key Statutes / Regulations	Capitalization Used	Summary of What the Section Establishes
					them "in the United States" for 42 U.S.C. §405 purposes.
7	Overall Conclusion	Distinction between U.S. person SSN and NRA identifiers	All above	Social Security number (capitalized administrative identifier) vs. social security number (lowercase statutory account number) vs. NUMIDENT (record system)	SS-5 creates the capitalized administrative identifier used for wage withholding. NRAs use a different application pathway and are not assigned the statutory lowercase "social security number" unless they meet SSA presence requirements.

9 Who owns the CARD, the NUMBER, and the LABEL and why you don't "have" a STATUTORY number unless you can control government with it

9.1 Social Security CARD as PROPERTY

First of all, based on the discussion in section 2 earlier, the only parties who can lawfully be assigned a Social Security Number are federal "employees". The SOCIAL SECURITY CARD is "public property" owned exclusively by the federal government, as confirmed by the regulations authorizing its issuance:

> *Title 20: Employees' Benefits*
> *PART 422—ORGANIZATION AND PROCEDURES*
> *Subpart B—General Procedures*
> *§ 422.103 Social security numbers.*
>
> *(d) Social security number cards.*
>
> *A person who is assigned a social security number will receive a social security number card from SSA within a reasonable time after the number has been assigned. (See §422.104 regarding the assignment of social security number cards to aliens.)* ***Social security number cards are the property of SSA and must be returned upon request.***

Notice that the above regulation is in Title 20, which is "Employee's Benefits". If you aren't an "employee" as defined in 5 U.S.C. §2105, then you can't receive this "benefit".

> *TITLE 5 > PART III > Subpart A > CHAPTER 21 > § 2105*
> *§ 2105. Employee*
>
> *(a) For the purpose of this title, "employee", except as otherwise provided by this section or when specifically modified, means an officer and an individual who is—*
>
> *(1) appointed in the civil service by one of the following acting in an official capacity—*
>
> *(A) the President;*
> *(B) a Member or Members of Congress, or the Congress;*
> *(C) a member of a uniformed service;*

> *(D) an individual who is an employee under this section;*
> *(E) the head of a Government controlled corporation; or*
> *(F) an adjutant general designated by the Secretary concerned under section 709 (c) of title 32;*
>
> *(2) engaged in the performance of a Federal function under authority of law or an Executive act; and*
> *(3) subject to the supervision of an individual named by paragraph (1) of this subsection while engaged in the performance of the duties of his position.*
>
> *(b) An individual who is employed at the United States Naval Academy in the midshipmen's laundry, the midshipmen's tailor shop, the midshipmen's cobbler and barber shops, and the midshipmen's store, except an individual employed by the Academy dairy (if any), and whose employment in such a position began before October 1, 1996, and has been uninterrupted in such a position since that date is deemed an employee.*
>
> *(c) An employee paid from nonappropriated funds of the Army and Air Force Exchange Service, Army and Air Force Motion Picture Service, Navy Ship's Stores Ashore, Navy exchanges, Marine Corps exchanges, Coast Guard exchanges, and other instrumentalities of the United States under the jurisdiction of the armed forces conducted for the comfort, pleasure, contentment, and mental and physical improvement of personnel of the armed forces is deemed not an employee for the purpose of—*
>
> *(1) laws administered by the Office of Personnel Management, except—*
>
> *(A) section 7204;*
> *(B) as otherwise specifically provided in this title;*
> *(C) the Fair Labor Standards Act of 1938;*
> *(D) for the purpose of entering into an interchange agreement to provide for the noncompetitive movement of employees between such instrumentalities and the competitive service; or*
> *(E) subchapter V of chapter 63, which shall be applied so as to construe references to benefit programs to refer to applicable programs for employees paid from nonappropriated funds; or*
>
> *(2) subchapter I of chapter 81, chapter 84 (except to the extent specifically provided therein), and section 7902 of this title.*
> *This subsection does not affect the status of these nonappropriated fund activities as Federal instrumentalities.*
>
> *(d) A Reserve of the armed forces who is not on active duty or who is on active duty for training is deemed not an employee or an individual holding an office of trust or profit or discharging an official function under or in connection with the United States because of his appointment, oath, or status, or any duties or functions performed or pay or allowances received in that capacity.*
>
> *(e) Except as otherwise provided by law, an employee of the United States Postal Service or of the Postal Rate Commission is deemed not an employee for purposes of this title.*
>
> *(f) For purposes of sections 1212, 1213, 1214, 1215, 1216, 1221, 1222, 2302, and 7701, employees appointed under chapter 73 or 74 of title 38 shall be employees.*

Notice also that the definition of "employee" above:

1. Implicitly EXCLUDES private employees or anyone not expressly identified.
2. Includes only appointed or commissioned officers of the United States exercising the sovereign functions of a "public office" in the U.S. government.
3. Does not include what most companies would describe as common law employees.

The only lawful use of "public property", such as the Social Security Card, is for a "public use". Here is how Black's Law Dictionary very eloquently describes it:

> "**Public purpose**. *In the law of taxation, eminent domain, etc., this is a term of classification to distinguish the objects for which, according to settled usage, the government is to provide, from those which, by the like usage, are left to private interest, inclination, or liberality. <u>The constitutional requirement that the purpose of any tax, police regulation, or particular exertion of the power of eminent domain shall be the convenience, safety, or welfare of the entire community and not the welfare of a specific individual or class of persons [such as, for instance, federal benefit recipients as individuals].</u> "Public purpose" that will justify expenditure of public money generally means such an activity as will serve as benefit to community as a body and which at same time is directly related function of government. Pack v. Southwestern Bell Tel. & Tel. Co., 215 Tenn. 503, 387 S.W.2d. 789, 794.*
>
> *The term is synonymous with governmental purpose. As employed to denote the objects for which taxes may be levied, it has no relation to the urgency of the public need or to the extent of the public benefit which is to follow; <u>the essential requisite being that a public service or use shall affect the inhabitants as a community, and not*</u>

merely as individuals. *A public purpose or public business has for its objective the promotion of the public health, safety, morals, general welfare, security, prosperity, and contentment of all the inhabitants or residents within a given political division, as, for example, a state, the sovereign powers of which are exercised to promote such public purpose or public business."*
[Black's Law Dictionary, Sixth Edition, p. 1231, Emphasis added]

9.2 Social Security NUMBER as PROPERTY

We have talked so far ONLY about the CARD and not the NUMBER. The regulation at 20 C.F.R. §422.103(d) says NOTHING about who owns the NUMBER. Is the NUMBER ALONE also PUBLIC PROPERTY? The answer to that question is NO. It takes more than just a mere number to be PROPERTY in a legal sense. From a general perspective, no one can own a number.

So it isn't a NUMBER as property they are GRANTING with legal strings attached that gives them the power to regulate its use under Article 4, Section 3, Clause 2 of the Constitution.

9.3 "Social Security Number" LABEL as PROPERTY

What about the term "Social Security Number"? Is that property from a legal perspective? The United States Government hasn't copyrighted any of its statutes or labels such as "Social Security Number" and can't legally do so. This is evident by reading the Copyright Act, 17 U.S.C. §105 so they don't OWN the LABEL as intellectual property. If the term "Social Security Number" were property, they would have to trademark it and put an "R" with a circle around it at the end of the name, for instance.

It is true, however, that anything Congress LEGISLATIVELY CREATES it owns. The CREATOR of a thing is ALWAYS the owner. See:

> *Hierarchy of Sovereignty: The Power to Create is the Power to Tax*, Family Guardian Fellowship
> https://famguardian.org/Subjects/Taxes/Remedies/PowerToCreate.htm

In law:

1. Rights are property.
2. Anything that CONVEYS rights is property.
3. Contracts convey rights and therefore are property.
4. Franchises are contracts and therefore property.

A LABEL put on something such a "Social Security Number" that is legislatively created by congress and is used as a legal conduit to CONVEY rights and therefore property can therefore ACT as property subject to the regulation and control of its CREATOR.

The act of legislatively CREATING the label that conveys rights and therefore property occurs in the DEFINITIONS section of legislation. A label such as "Social Security Number" is a THING. THINGs that convey property are called a "res" in law:

> *Res*. *Lat. The subject matter of a trust or will. In the civil law, a thing; an object. As a term of the law, this word has a very wide and extensive signification, including not only things which are objects of property, but also such as are not capable of individual ownership. And in old English law it is said to have a general import, comprehending both corporeal and incorporeal things of whatever kind, nature, or species. By "res," according to the modern civilians, is meant everything that may form an object of rights, in opposition to "persona," which is regarded as a subject of rights. "Res," therefore, in its general meaning, comprises actions of all kinds; while in its restricted sense it comprehends every object of right, except actions. This has reference to the fundamental division of the Institutes that all law relates either to persons, to things, or to actions.*
>
> *Res is everything that may form an object of rights and includes an object, subject-matter or status. In re Riggle's Will, 11 A.D.2d. 51 205 N.Y.S.2d. 19, 21, 22. The term is particularly applied to an object, subject-matter, or status, considered as the defendant in an action, or as an object against which, directly, proceedings are taken. Thus, in a prize case, the captured vessel is "the res"; and proceedings of this character are said to be in rem.*

(See In personam; In Rem.) "Res" may also denote the action or proceeding, as when a cause, which is not between adversary parties, it entitled "In re _____".

[. . .]

[Black's Law Dictionary, Sixth Edition, pp. 1304-1306]

A legal action against a "res" or which invokes an OBJECT of rights such as a fictional STATUTORY "Social Security Number" or a statutory "taxpayer" is an IN REM proceeding:

> ***in rem.*** *A technical term used to designate proceedings or actions instituted against the thing, in contradistinction to personal actions, which are said to be in personam.*
>
> *"In rem" proceedings encompass any action brought against person in which essential purpose of suit is to determine title to or to affect interests in specific property located within territory over which court has jurisdiction. ReMine ex rel. Liley v. District Court for City and County of Denver, Colo., 709 P.2d. 1379, 1382. It is true that, in a strict sense, a proceeding in rem is one taken directly against property, and has for its object the disposition of property, without reference to the title of individual claimants; but, in a larger and more general sense, the terms are applied to actions between parties, where the direct object is to reach and dispose of property owned by them, or of some interest therein. Such are cases commenced by attachment against the property of debtors, or instituted to partition real estate, foreclose a mortgage, or enforce a lien. Pannoyer v. Neff, 95 U.S. 714, 24 L.Ed. 565. In the strict sense of the term, a proceeding "in rem" is one which is taken directly against property or one which is brought to enforce a right in the thing itself.*
>
> *Actions in which the court is required to have control of the thing or object and in which an adjudication is made as to the object which binds the whole world and not simply the interests of the parties to the proceeding. Flesch v. Circle City Excavating & Rental Corp., 137 Ind.App. 695, 210 N.E.2d. 865.*
>
> *See also In personam, In rem jurisdiction; Quasi in rem jurisdiction.*
>
> *Judgment in rem. See that title.*
>
> *Quasi in rem. A term applied to proceedings which are not strictly and purely in rem, but are brought against the defendant personally, though the real object is to deal with particular property or subject property to the discharge of claims asserted; for example foreign attachment, or proceedings to foreclose a mortgage, remove cloud from title, or effect a partition. Freeman v. Alderson, 119 U.S. 185, 7 S.Ct. 165, 30 L.Ed. 372. An action in which the basis of jurisdiction is the defendant's interest in property, real or personal, which is within the court's power, as distinguished from in rem jurisdiction in which the court exercises power over the property itself, not simply the defendant's interest therein.*
> *[Black's Law Dictionary, Sixth Edition, p. 793]*

An administrative or legal action involving a STATUTORY "Social Security Number" or against a "taxpayer", which is an fictional office in the government is an action IN REM to control the property ATTACHED to these labels as a "res".

To say that someone wants to QUIT Social Security in effect therefore implies that they want to EXINGUISH the property rights attached to the "res", which in this case is the STATUTORY term "Social Security Number" as an object of rights. The SUBJECT of those rights is the person voluntarily INVOKING the term "Social Security Number" to enforce their specific property interest in connection with the res.

An example of a res could be the corpus of a trust or even of the PUBLIC trust. The property interest attached to the "res" called the "Social Security Number" is PUBLIC property owned and controlled by the COLLECTIVE "State" through its agent, the U.S. Inc. federal corporation under 28 U.S.C. §3001(15)(A).

9.4 VOLUNTARY and LAWFUL USE of a STATUTORY NUMBER and a STATUTORY LABEL in connection with the franchise contract is what incurs legal obligations

Earlier in section 3 we did indicate that the number BEHAVES as what the Federal Trade Commission identifies as a "franchise mark". In order for a lawful use or expense of the "res" or property attached to the STATUTORY "Social Security Number" to occur, the following conditions must be met in the use of the franchise mark:

1. The government as Merchant must offer the use of the "Social Security Number" as property.

2. The offer must be lawful and in conformance with the terms of the franchise contract, which in this case is the Social Security Act.
3. The Buyer must VOLUNTARILY apply for and lawfully ACCEPT the offer on a form approved by the GRANTOR of the franchise.
4. Like any contract, there must be MUTUAL CONSIDERATION and MUTUAL OBLIGATION to be enforceable.
5. There must be a meeting of the minds. In U.C.C. terms, this means that the Merchant and the Buyer agree on the SAME contract and the SAME definitions for all terms, franchise marks, etc. in the franchise or contract. See:
    5.1. *This Form is Your Form*, Mark DeAngelis
        http://www.youtube.com/embed/b6-PRwhU7cg
    5.2. *Mirror Image Rule*, Mark DeAngelis
        http://www.youtube.com/embed/j8pgbZV757w
6. There can be NO duress on either party. A monopoly on the property that is the subject of the franchise is a source of duress if the thing offered is essential to life and could introduce significant economic hardship to do without. This scenario is called an "unconscionable contract" or "adhesion contract".

If the Buyer responds to the Merchant's offer with new or replacement definitions or new terms, instead of an acceptance, you have in effect a counter-offer. In the presence of a counter offer, the Buyer then becomes the new Merchant specifying NEW terms. If the original Merchant responds with their cooperation, they have accepted the counter offer of the original Buyer, who then becomes the NEW Merchant. Cooperating with a counter-offer is sometimes called "implied consent". Every major scenario the government uses to impair constitutional rights that are supposed to be UNALIENABLE per the Declaration of Independence almost ALWAYS involves some kind of IMPLIED consent. A synonym for "implied consent" we often use is "invisible consent". See:

1. *Hot Issues: Invisible Consent*, SEDM
    https://sedm.org/invisible-consent/
2. *How You Lose Constitutional or Natural Rights*, Form #10.015
    https://sedm.org/Forms/10-Emancipation/HowLoseConstOrNatRights.pdf

There are also severe limitations on the government when it acts as a Merchant. It usually has a monopoly on the things it is offering, leaving you very little choice. The actual OFFER is the legislation implementing the grant or franchise contract authored by the Legislative Branch. The Executive Branch are the ones who ADMINISTER the franchise. They have no authority to Legislate and therefore cannot change the definitions within the contract. If the Executive Branch DOES change the definitions, they are exercising LEGISLATIVE powers in violation of the separation of powers doctrine, as we point out in Form #05.023.

The franchise or privilege can be challenged as invalid if:

1. The Buyer submits evidence to the Merchant that duress was present when they made application.
2. The Buyer was acting in a representative capacity as an Agent and had no authority to consent. For instance, God's delegation of authority order, the Bible, forbids Christians to consent to ANYTHING the government offers and requires to ALWAYS interact with the government as a MERCHANT.
3. The franchise was offered in a geographical place not expressly authorized. For instance, the geographical definitions in the Social Security Act in Title 42 limit Social Security participation to federal territory ONLY. Areas subject to the exclusive jurisdiction of Constitutional states of the Union are not authorized and therefore UNLAWFUL.
4. Participating in the franchise would create a conflict of interest on the part of the Merchant or Buyer that would deny justice. For instance, Social Security benefit recipients sitting on a jury and ruling on whether the defendant should contribute to paying their benefits would be a clear conflict of interest. Ditto for judges.
5. Participation in the franchise was only offered to federal statutory "employees" and 5 U.S.C. §2105 but the buyer is not an "employee" and cannot lawfully impersonate one without committing the crime of impersonating one in 18 U.S.C. §912.
6. The office of "employee" that participates is unlawfully exercised in a place not EXPRESSLY authorized as required by 4 U.S.C. §72.

9.5 Consequences of using the SSN ONLY when there is LAWFUL participation

PROVIDED that all the requirements of the previous section are met and the participation is LAWFUL, use of the STATUTORY Social Security Number beyond that point constitutes a license to act as a government employee or "trustee" over public property. The PROPERTY under management by the trustee is the "res" represented by the Social Security Number account. The number can *only* be used in connection with the official employment duties as a federal STATUTORY "employee". If you are a private party who is not acting in a representative capacity and not lawfully exercising the agency of federal employment or private contracts, you cannot lawfully use such a number and you cannot admit to ever having been issued one. The number, which is public property, can only lawfully be assigned to the custody and possession of the federal statutory "employee" or "public officer" while he is acting as a federal statutory "employee" or "public officer", and not to the private human being. It is the same way with private employers, who will often fire their employees if they take company property home for private use. If you use this public property for private use, then:

1. You would be abusing public/government property, the SSN, for private gain. This is a criminal violation of 18 U.S.C. §208(a). Only federal "employees" on official duty can use or dispose of public/government property. If you are not on official duty as a federal "employee", then you cannot possess or "have" such a number and cannot truthfully claim to have ever been issued one.
2. You would be embezzling public property and converting it to private use, in violation of 18 U.S.C. §641.
3. You would be impersonating a public employee, which is a crime under 18 U.S.C. §912 :

> TITLE 18 > PART I > CHAPTER 43 > § 912
> § 912. Officer or employee of the United States
>
> *Whoever falsely assumes or pretends to be an officer or employee acting under the authority of the United States or any department, agency or officer thereof, and acts as such, or in such pretended character demands or obtains any money, paper, document, or thing of value, shall be fined under this title or imprisoned not more than three years, or both.*

Aside from the above, Webster's Collegiate Dictionary defines the word "have" as follows:

> *"have. 1 a: to hold or maintain as a possession, privilege, or entitlement <they ~ a new car><I ~ my rights> b: to hold in one's use, service, regard, or at one's disposal <the group will ~! enough tickets for everyone>;. . . 2. To feel obligation in regard to --usu. used with an infinitive with to <we ~ things to do> . . .3: to stand in a certain relationship to <~ enemies>.*
> *[Webster's Collegiate Dictionary, 1983, ISBN 0-87779-510-X, p. 556]*

9.6 Why you can't "HAVE" a STATUTORY number but CAN "HAVE" a NON-STATUTORY number

In order to "have" a number:

1. You must be able to control the use of the number by all those who use it. "Ownership" implies FULL and EXCLUSIVE control. All uses of the number must require your consent, in accordance with the Privacy Act, 5 U.S.C. §552a(b). Otherwise, it is "their" number and not "yours". Remember: "The" and "IRS" together spells "THEIRS". Everything you "think" you own is really "THEIRS" when you use "their" numbers.
2. Its use must provide a definite benefit to you personally that is contractually and legally protected. Social security benefits are not contractually or legally protected, according to the Supreme Court, and therefore, they are not necessarily "benefits".
3. It must be in connection with an "entitlement or privilege". It is not a "privilege" to be tracked by IRS computers and be terrorized and harassed to illegally pay bribery money to a bloated government that does not respect your rights or obey the Constitution. It's a "liability" and not a "privilege".

Since Social Security Numbers (SSNs) and Taxpayer Identifications Numbers (TINs) do not fit any of the above criteria in the context of taxation, then they cannot be described as "your" number. The Supreme Court, in fact, agreed with these conclusions when it said in *Flemming v. Nestor, 363 U.S. 603 (1960)* that Social Security is *not* a contract and receipt of benefits is not a "right".

> "We must conclude that *a person covered by the Act has not such a right in benefit payments*... This is not to say, however, that Congress may exercise its power to modify the statutory scheme free of all constitutional restraint."
> [Flemming v. Nestor, 363 U.S. 603 (1960)]

Without a contractual entitlement and guarantee, then there is no definite or certain "benefit", which means that one cannot "have" any right or entitlement to *anything* by virtue of having such a number. Thus, no valid contract is or can be formed since there is no MUTUAL consideration and MUTUAL obligation. Consequently, when one is asked what is "your" number, one can honestly respond by saying:

> "I don't have a STATUTORY 'Social Security Number'. Any number the government might have associated me with was involuntary and compelled and I have asked them repeatedly to eliminate this form of 'compelled association' in violation of the First Amendment. The fact that you won't amounts to identity theft, kidnapping, and conspiracy against rights in violation of the Constitution and 18 U.S.C. §241"

HOWEVER, if your SS-5 application defined the term "Social Security Number" as a NON-STATUTORY number and provided its own definition, then you removed the number from its franchise context and made a counter-offer with new terms that YOU define. You can therefore HAVE a NON-STATUTORY number in that scenario, as we explain later in section 21. You can also do this by AMENDING your original Form SS-5 application as we do in Form #06.002 as a part of the mandatory process for becoming compliant.

We caution, however, that these techiques of sophistry should be presented with the idea that you will not use them to get something for nothing or to avoid paying for government benefits you consume. So long as they are couched in an equitable setting such as the following, they are legitimate and cannot be frowned upon by the judge or the jury:

> *The BEST Way to LAWFULLY Reject ANY and ALL Benefits in Court that is Unassailable*, SEDM
> https://sedm.org/the-best-way-to-lawfully-reject-any-and-all-benefits-in-court-that-is-unassailable/

10 Social Security Trust

The Social Security System, in fact, is a Trust. All trusts require three entities to operate:

1. A "*Grantor*" or "*Settlor*", which is the entity that created the trust. That would be the American People who, through their elected representatives, wrote the Social Security Act.
2. A "*Trustee*", which is you, who is a federal "employee" managing the trust.
3. A "*Beneficiary*", which is the U.S. government. The purpose of the Social Security System is NOT to pay you benefits in old age, it is to increase the general revenues so as to inflate the federal retirement and power and control of your "public servants".

The Social Security Trust is a "constructive trust", which is created when you complete and sign the SSA Form SS-5, application for Social Security. It is constructive, because you never explicitly signed a trust agreement and agreed to act as a "Trustee", nor was your consent fully informed of the terms of the trust. The trust document is the Social Security Act of 1935 , codified in Title 42 of the U.S. Code . The assets of the trust are accumulated from your earnings. The trust is a "social insurance program" and the federal government is in the "insurance business" for its federal "employees". The federal Constitution, Tenth Amendment, forbids the federal government from offering such social insurance to anything BUT its own "employees", or offering it anywhere except within its own territories under its exclusive control. If you don't believe us, look at IRS Form 4029, which identifies Social Security as an "insurance program".

The Social Security Number attaches to the position of "Trustee" of the trust. The all caps person name that is similar to your name when associated with government property in the form of the number is the legal "res" or "person" who is:

1. Acting as the Trustee and federal "employee".
2. A fiduciary over government payments under 26 U.S.C. §6901 .
3. A "transferee" under 26 U.S.C. §6903 .
4. "An officer of a corporation", where the "corporation" is the United States Government, which is identified in 28 U.S.C. §3002(15)(A) as a "federal corporation". As an "officer of a federal corporation", you are mentioned in 26 U.S.C. §6671(b) and 26 U.S.C. §7343 as the only proper subject of the penalty and criminal provisions of the Internal Revenue

Code. You are also subject to the penalty and criminal provisions of the I.R.C. without the need for implementing regulations by virtue of the fact that 44 U.S.C. §1505(a)(1) says that implementing regulations are not required for those who are federal employees. Federal statutes may be enforced DIRECTLY against federal employees without the need for implementing regulations.

The so-called Social Security "benefits" that you allegedly receive don't make you the "Beneficiary" of the trust by any stretch of the imagination, but rather simply a federal "employee" and "Trustee" and "fiduciary" over public monies that used to be yours but became public monies when you joined the program and agreed to act as "Trustee". When you filled out and signed the IRS Form W-4, which is a contract (see 26 C.F.R. §31.3401(a)-3), you obligated yourself to several things under the terms of the contract or what the government calls a "voluntary withholding agreement". In effect, you signed a private contract with the U.S. government to become part of the government and thereby qualify for federal employee benefits, including "social insurance":

1. You changed from a private citizen to a federal public "employee" subject to the legislative jurisdiction of the federal government.
2. Your private employment earnings changed character from that of *private* earnings to public property and federal payments. The Internal Revenue Code is the means by which that public property or "gift" is then managed under 26 U.S.C. §321(d). This is documented further in section 5.4.6 of the *Great IRS Hoax, Form #11.302*.

> "Men are endowed by their Creator with certain unalienable rights,-'life, liberty, and the pursuit of happiness;' and to 'secure,' not grant or create, these rights, governments are instituted. **That property which a man has honestly acquired he retains full control of, subject to these limitations: First, that he shall not use it to his neighbor's injury, and that does not mean that he must use it for his neighbor's benefit; second, that *if he devotes it to a public use, he gives to the public a right to control that use [through the Internal Revenue Code, in this case]*;** and third, **that whenever the public needs require, the public may take it upon payment of due compensation.**
> [Budd v. People of State of New York, 143 U.S. 517 (1892)]

3. Your earnings are now called "wages", which is a "word of art" for income connected to a "trade or business" and a "public office" that originates from within the District of Columbia. Click here for an article showing how this scam works. See also *Great IRS Hoax, Form #11.302*, section 5.6.7.
4. You consented to be treated as a "person" with a legal "domicile" within Washington, D.C., even if you in fact do not have a domicile there. 4 U.S.C. §72 says that all "public offices" must occur in the District of Columbia, and you identified yourself as a federal "employee" holding such an office by virtue of the fact that the upper left corner of the IRS Form W-4 says "employee", which is defined in 26 C.F.R. §31.3401(c)-1 as an elected or appointed officer of the United States Government. This is the same "public office" which is the only proper subject of levies in 26 U.S.C. §6331(a). See the following for more details on this scam:
   > *Why Domicile and Becoming a "Taxpayer" Require Your Consent*, Form #05.002
   > https://sedm.org/Forms/FormIndex.htm
5. You contractually agreed to include your earnings subject to the W-4 withholding agreement as "gross income" on a tax return:

> *Title 26: Internal Revenue*
> *PART 31—EMPLOYMENT TAXES AND COLLECTION OF INCOME TAX AT SOURCE*
> *Subpart E—Collection of Income Tax at Source*
> *Sec. 31.3402(p)-1 Voluntary withholding agreements.*
>
> *(a) In general.*
>
> *An employee and his employer may enter into an agreement under section 3402(b) to provide for the withholding of income tax upon payments of amounts described in paragraph (b)(1) of Sec. 31.3401(a)-3, made after December 31, 1970.* **An agreement may be entered into under this section only with respect to amounts which are includible in the gross income of the employee under section 61, and must be applicable to all such amounts paid by the employer to the employee.** "

As a voluntary "Trustee", you become a "fiduciary" under 26 U.S.C. §6901 and a "transferee" under 26 U.S.C. §6903 over federal property, which includes the Social Security Number and the Social Security card. The Social Security retirement benefits, in fact, simply represent deferred federal employment compensation as a "Trustee". All employment compensation is paid to this "Trustee" and not to you as a natural and private person. The payment checks are sent to the all-caps Trustee, not the lower case you the natural person. You must consent or agree by your actions to represent this Trustee in order to cash these deferred employment compensation payments to the Trustee called Social Security Checks. No one can compel you to act as a "Trustee". To do otherwise would be to institute involuntary servitude in violation of the Thirteenth Amendment. Because of the provisions of the Thirteenth Amendment, you can resign at any time as "Trustee" but the government is going to make it very difficult for you to discover how to resign because they want to keep the federal gravy train and your earnings running right up to their front porch.

If you want to know how to indefinitely terminate your federal "employee" position and your role as "Trustee", please consult our free pamphlet below. You can also use the completed version of this form as proof that you are not a federal "employee" and therefore do not qualify to have or use a number:

> *Resignation of Compelled Social Security Trustee*, Form #06.002
> http://sedm.org/Forms/FormIndex.htm

If you want to remove all such numbers from your personal account to change the character from public property back to private property, please see section 7 of our article below:

> *About IRS Form W-8BEN*, Form #04.202
> http://sedm.org/Forms/FormIndex.htm

11 Who can lawfully be issued a "Social Security Number"?

First of all, who may Social Security Numbers be issued to? The answer is found in 20 C.F.R. §422.104:

> *Code of Federal Regulations*
> TITLE 20--EMPLOYEES' BENEFITS
> CHAPTER III--SOCIAL SECURITY ADMINISTRATION
> PART 422_ORGANIZATION AND PROCEDURES--Table of Contents
> *Subpart B_General Procedures*
> Sec. 422.104 Who can be assigned a social security number.
>
> *(a) Persons eligible for SSN assignment. We can assign you a social security number if you meet the evidence requirements in §422.107 and you are:*
>
> *(1) A United States citizen; or*
>
> *(2) An alien lawfully admitted to the United States for permanent residence or under other authority of law permitting you to work in the United States (§422.105 describes how we determine if a nonimmigrant alien is permitted to work in the United States); or*
>
> *(3) An alien who cannot provide evidence of alien status showing lawful admission to the U.S., or an alien with evidence of lawful admission but without authority to work in the U.S., if the evidence described in §422.107(e) does not exist, but only for a valid nonwork reason. We consider you to have a valid nonwork reason if:*
>
> *(i) You need a social security number to satisfy a Federal statute or regulation that requires you to have a social security number in order to receive a Federally-funded benefit to which you have otherwise established entitlement and you reside either in or outside the U.S.; or*
>
> *(ii) You need a social security number to satisfy a State or local law that requires you to have a social security number in order to receive public assistance benefits to which you have otherwise established entitlement, and you are legally in the United States.*
>
> *(b) Annotation for a nonwork purpose. If we assign you a social security number as an alien for a nonwork purpose, we will indicate in our records that you are not authorized to work. We will also mark your social security card with a legend such as "NOT VALID FOR EMPLOYMENT." If earnings are reported to us on your number, we will inform the Department of Homeland Security of the reported earnings.*
> [68 FR 55308, Sept. 25, 2003]

The section above very deceptively doesn't indicate that the main prerequisite of receiving a number is that one is acting as or agrees to act as a federal "employee" or "public officer", but this is indeed the case. The first thing we notice about the above, is that it is in Title 20 of the Code of Federal Regulations, which is entitled "Employee's Benefits". That term "employee" is defined in 5 U.S.C. §2105, 26 U.S.C. §3401(c), and 26 C.F.R. §31.3401(c)-1 as a federal employee and NOT a private employee. The federal government has no authority over *private* employees or *private* employers in states of the Union, as confirmed by the U.S. Supreme Court:

> "It is no longer open to question that **the general government, unlike the states**, Hammer v. Dagenhart, 247 U.S. 251, 275, 38 S.Ct. 529, 3 A.L.R. 649, Ann.Cas.1918E 724, **possesses no inherent power in respect of the internal affairs of the states; and emphatically not with regard to legislation.**"
> [Carter v. Carter Coal Co., 298 U.S. 238, 56 S.Ct. 855 (1936)]

> "The difficulties arising out of our dual form of government and the opportunities for differing opinions concerning the relative rights of state and national governments are many; **but for a very long time this court has steadfastly adhered to the doctrine that the taxing power of Congress does not extend to the states or their political subdivisions**. The same basic reasoning which leads to that conclusion, we think, requires like limitation upon the power which springs from the bankruptcy clause. United States v. Butler, supra."
> [Ashton v. Cameron County Water Improvement District No. 1, 298 U.S. 513; 56 S.Ct. 892 (1936)]

Furthermore, the use of the Social Security Number creates a rebuttable prima facie presumption that the user is a STATUTORY "U.S. citizen" or "U.S. resident" domiciled on federal territory and NOT within the exclusive jurisdiction of a state of the Union:

> 26 CFR § 301.6109-1 - Identifying numbers.
>
> (g) Special rules for taxpayer identifying numbers issued to foreign persons -
>
> (1) General rule -
>
> (i) Social security number.
>
> **A social security number is generally identified in the records and database of the Internal Revenue Service as a number belonging to a U.S. citizen or resident alien individual**. A person may establish a different status for the number by providing proof of foreign status with the Internal Revenue Service under such procedures as the Internal Revenue Service shall prescribe, including the use of a form as the Internal Revenue Service may specify. Upon accepting an individual as a nonresident alien individual, the Internal Revenue Service will assign this status to the individual's social security number.

Under "course of dealing" principles, the IRS therefore has a reason to PRESUME from the past 1040 filings (before he stopped filing) that the party understood they had a duty to make a return whenever they had STATUTORY "gross income" above personal exemption amount---but this would be used primarily to prove their failure was willful.

Since tax is imposed in 26 C.F.R. §1.1-1 on all income of a STATUTORY citizen or resident alien, and supplying an SSN creates a presumption of "citizen of the U.S.**" then the party using an SSN is presumed person liable per 26 U.S.C. §6001. You can see how easy this is to fix in the above regulation--provide proof of foreign status for the SSN or even specify that the number is NOT a statutory number, but a private number. The wording makes it sound like it is more difficult than it is. They use the term "nonresident alien individual" interchasngeably with "foreign status", but "nonresident alien INDIVIDUALS or PERSONS" are not the only foreigners. To them, "foreign status" means one who is a "nonresident alien INDIVIDUAL"--which you can "prove" by simply declaring it--they can't FORCE you to remain a citizen of the U.S. when it is a basis for taxing all of your income because that would be slavery.

Keep in mind also that "nonresident alien individual" is NOT the only "foreign status". Those who are not aliens but who are nonresidents would not be "nonresident alien individuals", but rather "non-resident non-persons". THIS is what a state national is and the above regulation doesn't even acknowledge the existence of such a party. The reason is that:

1. They are completely outside the jurisdiction of the Internal Revenue Code.
2. They have a foreign domicile but not a foreign nationality. Therefore, they cannot be sued under federal statutes per Federal Rule of Civil Procedure 17(b).
3. Social Security cannot be offered or enforced against them. See:
   > *Why You Aren't Eligible for Social Security*, Form #06.001
   > https://sedm.org/Forms/FormIndex.htm

The IRS also admits in its own Internal Revenue Manual, in black and white, that private employers do not have to deduct or withhold:

> *Internal Revenue Manual (I.R.M.), Section 5.14.10.2 (09-30-2004)*
> *Payroll Deduction Agreements*
>
> **2. Private employers, states, and political subdivisions are not required to enter into payroll deduction agreements**. *Taxpayers should determine whether their employers will accept and process executed agreements before agreements are submitted for approval or finalized.*
> *[http://www.irs.gov/irm/part5/ch14s10.html]*

Consequently, whenever you use the SSN in any context, which is "public property" owned by the government, you are admitting to be acting as a federal "employee" on official duty. That is the only way the government can lawfully operate, because if they didn't do it this way, they would be abusing their taxing power to become a Robinhood who transfers property between citizens, which the U.S. Supreme Court said below they cannot lawfully do:

> "In Calder v. Bull, which was here in 1798, **Mr. Justice Chase said, that there were acts which the Federal and State legislatures could not do without exceeding their authority, and among them he mentioned** a law which punished a citizen for an innocent act; a law that destroyed or impaired the lawful private [labor] contracts [and labor compensation, e.g. earnings from employment through compelled W-4 withholding] of citizens; a law that made a man judge in his own case; and **a law that took the property from A [the worker], and gave it to B [the government or another citizen, such as through social welfare programs].** 'It is against all reason and justice,' he added, 'for a people to intrust a legislature with such powers, and therefore it cannot be presumed that they have done it. They may command what is right and prohibit what is wrong; but they cannot change innocence into guilt, or punish innocence as a crime, or violate the right of an antecedent lawful private [employment] contract [by compelling W-4 withholding, for instance], or the right of private property. To maintain that a Federal or State legislature possesses such powers [of THEFT!] if they had not been expressly restrained, would, in my opinion, be a political heresy altogether inadmissible in all free republican governments,' 3 Dall. 388."
> *[Sinking Fund Cases, 99 U.S. 700 (1878)]*

Consequently, if you are receiving federal payments or "benefits", there are only two ways to describe the result:

1. Your government is a thief and a Robinhood and you continue to be a private citizen….OR
2. You are a federal "employee" and the payment is "employment compensation".

Take your pick, but you *have* to pick either one of the two and not both.

If the number is attached to any of your bank or financial accounts, those accounts are owned by the federal government and under their supervision, because they were opened by its "employees" or "public officers" in the conduct of a type of federal employment called a "trade or business". A "trade or business" is defined in 26 U.S.C. §7701(a)(26) as a "public office" in which you essentially become a business partner with the federal government. Your employment compensation consists of:

1. Deferred employment compensation called Social Security benefits.
2. Unemployment compensation (FICA) benefits
3. Medicare benefits
4. Reductions in federal tax liability taken under the following sections of the code:
    4.1. Graduated and reduced rate of tax under 26 U.S.C. §1
    4.2. Earned income credit under 26 U.S.C. §32
    4.3. "Trade or Business" deductions under 26 U.S.C. §162

In the context of federal "benefit" programs, which essentially amount to "social insurance", the Privacy Act, 5 U.S.C. §552a confirms that all those who participate in such programs are "federal personnel":

> TITLE 5 > PART I > CHAPTER 5 > SUBCHAPTER II > § 552a
> § 552a. Records maintained on individuals
>
> (a) Definitions.— For purposes of this section—
>
> (13) the term "Federal personnel" means officers and employees of the Government of the United States, members of the uniformed services (including members of the Reserve Components), **individuals entitled to**

> *receive immediate or deferred retirement benefits under any retirement program of the Government of the United States (including survivor benefits).*

Consequently, anyone who asks you to supply YOUR "Social Security Number" indirectly is asking you the following TWO questions:

> *1. "Are you a federal "employee" or "public officer" on official duty at the moment?". . . . AND*

> *2. If you are, what is your license number to act in that capacity?*

The answer to this question should always be that you are a private human being and not a statutory "person" or "individual" and who cannot lawfully possess or use government property or numbers, and that it is UNLAWFUL for you to impersonate a "public officer" of the U.S. government in violation of 18 U.S.C. §912 by providing or using one as a private human being. Furthermore, if they insist that you have or use one, then make sure you fill out an IRS Form 56 and make THEM, not YOU the surety and the person responsible for the duties associated with the "public office" they are effectively creating by using a number against your will. The First Amendment to the United States Constitution guarantees us a right of free association. This implies at least the ability to determine when we are working and when we are off work. The employment contract for federal "employees" is found in Title 5 of the U.S. Code. It doesn't say what the working hours are for federal benefit recipients, and therefore we can choose what those hours are even if we did voluntarily apply for and continue to use such a number.

If you would like a more thorough analysis of why "taxpayers" under Subtitle A of the Internal Revenue Code are nearly all federal "employees", please read our free pamphlet below:

> *Why Your Government is Either a Thief or You are a "Public Officer" for Income Tax Purposes*, Form #05.008
> http://sedm.org/Forms/FormIndex.htm

If you find anything wrong with the above analysis or any part of this article, then please send us your corrections so we can improve them.

12 Social Security Numbers assigned to or used by Nonresident Aliens (Members)

The approach of this site relies on the Nonresident Alien Position. The regulations under 26 U.S.C. §6109 recognize the use of Social Security Numbers by nonresident aliens as follows:

> *26 C.F.R. §301.6109-1 - Identifying numbers.*
>
> *(d) Obtaining a taxpayer identifying number*
>
> *(4) Coordination of taxpayer identifying numbers—*
>
> *(i) Social security number.*
>
> ***Any individual who is duly assigned a social security number or who is entitled to a social security number will not be issued an IRS individual taxpayer identification number.*** *The individual can use the social security number for all tax purposes under this title,* ***even though the individual is, or later becomes, a nonresident alien individual.*** *Further, any individual who has an application pending with the Social Security Administration will be issued an IRS individual taxpayer identification number only after the Social Security Administration has notified the individual that a social security number cannot be issued. Any alien individual duly issued an IRS individual taxpayer identification number who later becomes a U.S. citizen, or an alien lawfully permitted to enter the United States either for permanent residence or under authority of law permitting U.S. employment, will be required to obtain a social security number. Any individual who has an IRS individual taxpayer identification number and a social security number, due to the circumstances described in the preceding sentence, must notify the Internal Revenue Service of the acquisition of the social security number and must use the newly-issued social security number as the taxpayer identifying number on all future returns, statements, or other documents filed under this title.*
>
> *(ii) Employer identification number.*
>
> *Any individual with both a social security number (or an IRS individual taxpayer identification number) and an employer identification number may use the social security number (or the IRS individual taxpayer identification*

> number) for individual taxes, and the employer identification number for business taxes as required by returns, statements, and other documents and their related instructions. Any alien individual duly assigned an IRS individual taxpayer identification number who also is required to obtain an employer identification number must furnish the previously-assigned IRS individual taxpayer identification number to the Internal Revenue Service on Form SS–4 at the time of application for the employer identification number. Similarly, where an alien individual has an employer identification number and is required to obtain an IRS individual taxpayer identification number, the individual must furnish the previously-assigned employer identification number to the Internal Revenue Service on Form W–7, or such other form as may be prescribed by the Internal Revenue Service, at the time of application for the IRS individual taxpayer identification number.

Note that the above explanation acknowledges that nonresident aliens can apply for Social Security Number but MAY NOT receive it:

> The individual can use the social security number for all tax purposes under this title, **even though the individual is, or later becomes, a nonresident alien individual. Further, any individual who has an application pending with the Social Security Administration will be issued an IRS individual taxpayer identification number only after the Social Security Administration has notified the individual that a social security number cannot be issued.**

The explanation does NOT, however, address the situations where:

1. The SSA wrongfully allowed an ineligible party to apply for and receive a Social Security Number and what to do about it.
2. Those who receive a Social Security Number subsequently discover they were INELIGIBLE because not a STATUTORY "United States**" citizen" and who want to withdraw their SS-5 application or replace it with a W-7 application.
3. People want to withdraw their application and purge all government records that use the number, even if they were eligible. This would happen if they have a religious objection to being government enumerated or if they no longer want the government to use any aspect of their identity for commercial purposes as described in:

   > *Government Identity Theft*, Form #05.046
   > https://sedm.org/Forms/05-MemLaw/GovernmentIdentityTheft.pdf

If you do a Freedom of Information Act (FOIA) request for publications and forms useful in changing the STATUS of the Social Security Number to one owned by a "nonresident alien", they give you FALSE information:

1. Here is the regulation involved:

   > 26 CFR § 301.6109-1 - Identifying numbers.
   >
   > **(g) Special rules for taxpayer identifying numbers issued to foreign persons—**
   >
   > *(1) General rule—*
   >
   > *(i) Social security number.*
   >
   > A social security number is generally identified in the records and database of the Internal Revenue Service as a number belonging to a U.S. citizen or resident alien individual. **A person may establish a different status for the number by providing proof of foreign status with the Internal Revenue Service under such procedures as the Internal Revenue Service shall prescribe, including the use of a form as the Internal Revenue Service may specify. Upon accepting an individual as a nonresident alien individual, the Internal Revenue Service will assign this status to the individual's social security number.**

2. The above regulation derives its authority from 26 U.S.C. §6109(g), which relates ONLY to the Federal Crop Insurance Act! We have been looking for any regulation or form that actually implements the change in the status of the SSN, but have never found one after years of searching. Most people PRESUME that simply filing a 1040NR is what changes the status of an SSN to that of a nonresident alien, but we have seen no concrete confirmation of that, which is why the above FOIA was sent.
3. Here is their response:

   Figure 12-1: 26 C.F.R. §301.6109-1(g) FOIA

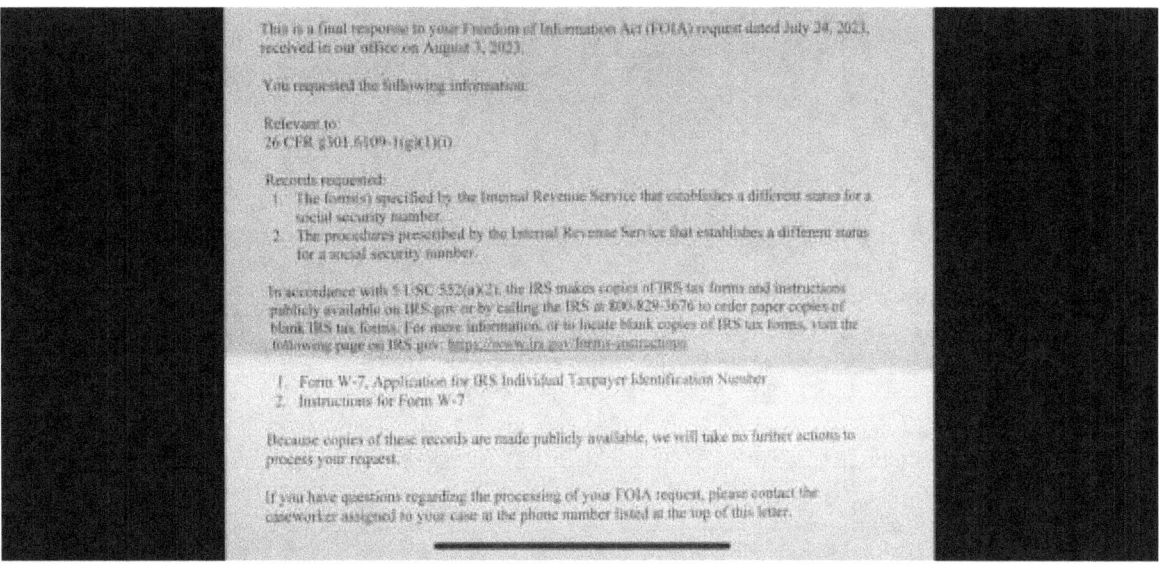

4. What is WRONG with the above response is that if you already HAVE an SSN, you aren't ALLOWED to even ask for an International Taxpayer Identification Number (ITIN) on a W-7 form under 26 U.S.C. §6109(i). They can only be issued to aliens, and not all "nonresident aliens" are "aliens". State nationals or statutory "U.S. nationals" are not aliens, for instance.

> 26 C.F.R. §301.6109-1 - Identifying numbers.
>
> (3) IRS individual taxpayer identification number—
>
> (i) Definition.
>
> The term IRS individual taxpayer identification number means a *taxpayer* identifying number **issued to an alien individual by the Internal Revenue Service**, upon application, for use in connection with filing requirements under this title. The term **IRS individual taxpayer identification number does not refer to a social security number or an account number for use in employment for wages.** For *purposes* of this section, the term alien individual *means an individual who is not a citizen or national of the United States.*

5. We allege that based on the above, the IRS doesn't want you to know HOW to change the status of the SSN from that of a "U.S. person" to a "nonresident alien". That is why they won't describe how to do it. Further, Based on 26 U.S.C. §6109(g), that change can ONLY be made in the context of Federal Crop Insurance, so filing a 1040NR return doesn't seem like it would accomplish that.

13 How to terminate or change the status of the number

The Internal Revenue Code, Section 6109 contains provisions for issuing Taxpayer Identification Numbers but we have found no statutory or regulatory provision for terminating the number or returning it to the government. Likewise, the Social Security Act has provisions to issue the number in 20 C.F.R. §422.104, but we have found no statutory provisions for terminating it. The reason the government does this is that they want to maintain your eligibility to receive the so-called benefit and thereby perpetuate their authority to enforce the franchise agreement codified in the Internal Revenue Code Subtitle A and the Social Security Act against you. This was hinted at by the Supreme Court when it held the following on the subject of "benefits":

> *The principle is invoked that one who accepts the benefit of a statute cannot be heard to question its constitutionality. Great Falls Manufacturing Co. v. Attorney General, 124 U.S. 581, 8 S.Ct. 631, 31 L.Ed. 527; Wall v. Parrot Silver & Copper Co., 244 U.S. 407, 37 S.Ct. 609, 61 L.Ed. 1229; St. Louis, etc., Co., v. George C. Prendergast Const. Co., 260 U.S. 469, 43 S.Ct. 178, 67 L.Ed. 351.*
>
> *[. . .]*
>
> *6. **The Court will not pass upon the constitutionality of a statute at the instance of one who has availed himself of its benefits**.[FN7] Great Falls Mfg. Co. v. Attorney General, 124 U.S. 581, 8 S.Ct. 631, 31 L.Ed. 527; Wall v.*

> *Parrot Silver & Copper Co., 244 U.S. 407, 411, 412, 37 S.Ct. 609, 61 L.Ed. 1229; St. Louis Malleable Casting Co. v. Prendergast Construction Co., 260 U.S. 469, 43 S.Ct. 178, 67 L.Ed. 351.*
>
> *FN7 Compare Electric Co. v. Dow, 166 U.S. 489, 17 S.Ct. 645, 41 L.Ed. 1088; Pierce v. Somerset Ry., 171 U.S. 641, 648, 19 S.Ct. 64, 43 L.Ed. 316; Leonard v. Vicksburg, etc., R. Co., 198 U.S. 416, 422, 25 S.Ct. 750, 49 L.Ed. 1108.*
> [Ashwander v. Tennessee Valley Authority, 297 U.S. 288, 56 S.Ct. 466 (1936)]

So long as a number exists that is allotted to you, then there is a presumption that you maintain the eligibility to receive the benefit and therefore must abide by the statutes which administer it. The Social Security Administration also tries to perpetuate this FRAUD upon the people:

1. By hiding the forms and procedures for quitting the program on their website. See:
   > *Resignation of Compelled Social Security Trustee*, Form #06.002
   > http://sedm.org/Forms/FormIndex.htm
2. By responding to requests to terminate participation with a letter FALSELY stating that you can't quit. See:
   > SEDM Exhibit #07.012
   > http://sedm.org/Exhibits/ExhibitIndex.htm

After a number is issued, then the only thing they will cooperate with you in doing with it is changing its status.

> *"...A person may establish a different status for the number by providing proof of foreign status with the Internal Revenue Service...Upon accepting an individual as a nonresident alien individual, the Internal Revenue Service will assign this status to the individual's social security number...*
> *[26 C.F.R. §301.6109-1(g)(1)(i)]*

One technique for changing its status is documented in section 1 of the cover letter for the *Resignation of Compelled Social Security Trustee* form above.

But what about if the person isn't and never was an "individual" and a "public officer" within the government, which is the case with most Americans? In their case, application for the number was knowingly fraudulent and any act that is the product of fraud is a NON act that the law may not lawfully recognize and certainly not benefit from:

> *Ex dolo malo non oritur actio.*
> *Out of fraud no action arises. Cowper, 343; Broom's Max. 349.*
>
> *Fraus et jus numquam cohabitant.*
> *Fraud and justice never agree together. Wing. 680.*
>
> *Quod alias bonum et justum est, si per vim vel fraudem petatur, malum et injustum efficitur.*
> *What is otherwise good and just, if sought by force or fraud, becomes bad and unjust. 3 Co. 78.*
> *[Bouvier's Maxims of Law, 1856;*
> *SOURCE: http://famguardian.org/Publications/BouvierMaximsOfLaw/BouviersMaxims.htm]*

How does the IRS or the SSA correct knowingly fraudulent applications for their numbers and remove them from their records? We haven't figured that out yet but the implications are HUGE. However, the following things are certain:

1. When you become aware that your application was not authorized by law because you did not have a domicile on federal territory as required by 20 C.F.R. §422.104, then your application becomes fraudulent and you have a duty to correct it and notify them of the fraud.
2. If they refuse to correct the fraudulent records and application, the government is committing the following crimes for which you may consider a criminal complaint and a civil prosecution:
   2.1. 18 U.S.C. §911: Impersonating a statutory "U.S. citizen". Only statutory "U.S. citizens" and permanent residents, of which you are neither as a person domiciled in a state of the Union, may lawfully apply for the number.
   2.2. 18 U.S.C. §912: Impersonating a public officer or "employee" of the government. The number may only be issued as a "benefit" to government "employees", pursuant to 20 C.F.R. §422.103(d) and you are impersonating a government "employee" if you apply for one or use one.
   2.3. 18 U.S.C. §1030: Computer Fraud. Their records are in computers and they are knowingly fraudulent.
   2.4. 18 U.S.C. §3: Misprision of felony. They are aware of a crime and they refused to act on it or do something about it, which is also a crime.

2.5. 18 U.S.C. §4: Accessory after the fact. They are an accessory after the fact to all the above crimes if they refuse to do something about it.

Another technique for ensuring they do something about it is to fill out an IRS Form 56 making the IRS commissioner and/or the Commissioner of Social Security the fiduciary for all liabilities relating to the number. Since the number belongs to them, then let THEM take complete and exclusive responsibility for every aspect of its use or abuse. This technique is used on the *Resignation of Compelled Social Security Trustee*, Form #06.002 mentioned above, and it really puts them on the hot seat because now they become the targets for all the collection notices and liens, not you.

14 State citizens or nationals cannot use numbers

26 U.S.C. §6109 prescribes when identifying numbers must be used.

> U.S. Code › Title 26 › Subtitle F › Chapter 61 › Subchapter B › § 6109
>
> 26 U.S. Code § 6109 - Identifying numbers
>
> **(a) SUPPLYING OF IDENTIFYING NUMBERS**
>
> When required by regulations prescribed by the Secretary:
>
> **(1) INCLUSION IN RETURNS**
>
> Any person required under the authority of this title to make a return, statement, or other document shall include in such return, statement, or other document such identifying number as may be prescribed for securing proper identification of such person.
>
> **(2) FURNISHING NUMBER TO OTHER PERSONS**
>
> Any person with respect to whom a return, statement, or other document is required under the authority of this title to be made by another person or whose identifying number is required to be shown on a return of another person shall furnish to such other person such identifying number as may be prescribed for securing his proper identification.
>
> **(3) FURNISHING NUMBER OF ANOTHER PERSON**
>
> Any person required under the authority of this title to make a return, statement, or other document with respect to another person shall request from such other person, and shall include in any such return, statement, or other document, such identifying number as may be prescribed for securing proper identification of such other person.
>
> **(4) FURNISHING IDENTIFYING NUMBER OF TAX RETURN PREPARER**
>
> Any return or claim for refund prepared by a tax return preparer shall bear such identifying number for securing proper identification of such preparer, his employer, or both, as may be prescribed. For purposes of this paragraph, the terms "return" and "claim for refund" have the respective meanings given to such terms by section 6696(e).
>
> For purposes of paragraphs (1), (2), and (3), the identifying number of an individual (or his estate) shall be such individual's social security account number.
>
> **(b) LIMITATION**
>
> (1) Except as provided in paragraph (2), a return of any person with respect to his liability for tax, or any statement or other document in support thereof, shall not be considered for purposes of paragraphs (2) and (3) of subsection (a) as a return, statement, or other document with respect to another person.
>
> (2) For purposes of paragraphs (2) and (3) of subsection (a), a return of an estate or trust with respect to its liability for tax, and any statement or other document in support thereof, shall be considered as a return, statement, or other document with respect to each beneficiary of such estate or trust.

So the requirement to furnish, and by implication apply for and receive, a government-issued identifying number is as follows:

1. When regulations issued by the Secretary of Treasury require it.
2. In the context of statutory "persons":
    2.1. On tax returns or information returns (e.g. W-2, 1098, 1099, etc.)
    2.2. To another person ONLY when a return must be filed against them, such as an information return. This would include "withholding agents".
3. In the context of tax return preparers.

State citizens or nationals do not fit into any of the above circumstances, because:

1. There are no implementing regulations for enforcement of the Internal Revenue Code pertaining to the "tax" imposed under Subtitle A. Hence, item 1 above does not apply. See:
    > IRS Due Process Meeting Handout, Form #03.008
    > FORMS PAGE: https://sedm.org/Forms/FormIndex.htm
    > DIRECT LINK: https://sedm.org/Forms/03-Discovery/IRSDueProcMtgHandout.pdf
2. State citizens or nationals are not STATUTORY civil "persons" because they have a foreign domicile outside the CIVIL and exclusive jurisdiction of the national government. This rules out item 2 above and 26 U.S.C. §6109(a)(2) and (3).. See:
    2.1. *Why Domicile and Becoming a "Taxpayer" Require Your Consent*, Form #05.002
        https://sedm.org/Forms/FormIndex.htm
    2.2. *Citizenship Status v. Tax Status*, Form #10.011, Section 12
        https://sedm.org/Forms/10-Emancipation/CitizenshipStatusVTaxStatus/CitizenshipVTaxStatus.htm
3. State citizens or nationals are not domiciled or present within the geographical definition of "United States" defined in 26 U.S.C. §7701(a)(9) and (a)(10) and 4 U.S.C. §110 and therefore are "foreign" but not "persons" under the Internal Revenue Code. Again, this rules out item 2 above and 26 U.S.C. §6109(a)(2) and (3). Therefore, they are NEITHER:
    3.1. Statutory "U.S. persons" under 26 U.S.C. §7701(a)(30). You can't be a "U.S. person" UNLESS you are either physically present within or domiciled within the territorial "United States" ..NOR
    3.2. Statutory "Foreign persons" 26 C.F.R. §1.1441-1. You can't be a "foreign person" without ALSO being a STATUTORY "person".
4. 26 U.S.C. §6109(a)(4) relating to Tax Return Preparers doesn't apply, because it is a CRIME for state citizens or nationals to file a tax return. See:
    4.1. *Why It's a Crime for a Private American National to File a 1040 Income Tax Return*, Form #08.021
        https://sedm.org/Forms/FormIndex.htm
    4.2. *Legal Requirement to File Federal Income Tax Returns*, Form #05.009
        https://sedm.org/Forms/FormIndex.htm
5. We prove in the following that ALL statutory civil law, if it imposes duties OTHER than reparations for injuries paid ONLY to the victims of the injury, is law for government and not private people or humans. Taxation is a civil liability and therefore a civil statutory franchise that can and does regulate ONLY public officers on official business. State citizens or nationals are NOT such "public officers" and have a right NOT to be compelled to become one. A violation of this right is involuntary servitude in violation of the Thirteenth Amendment.
    5.1. *Why Statutory Civil Law is Law for Government and Not Private Persons*, Form #05.037
        https://sedm.org/Forms/FormIndex.htm
    5.2. *Why Your Government is Either a Thief or You are a "Public Officer" for Income Tax Purposes*, Form #05.008
        https://sedm.org/Forms/FormIndex.htm
    5.3. *Proof That There Is a "Straw Man"*, Form #05.042
        https://sedm.org/Forms/FormIndex.htm

15 Authorities on why nonresidents don't need SSNs/TINs to open bank accounts or for private employment

This section establishes that both STATUTORY "nonresident aliens" AND STATUTORY "non-resident non-persons" are not required to have or use an SSN or TIN to open bank or financial accounts.

The following authorities right from the horse's mouth establish that nonresident aliens don't need Social Security Numbers to either work or to open bank accounts. Use this as ammunition when opening accounts or pursuing employment:

1. It is ILLEGAL to assign a "Social Security Number" to a "Nonresident alien". Do you see nonresident aliens listed below? A nonresident alien, defined in 26 U.S.C. §7701(b)(1)(B) is NOT the same as an "alien" as defined in 26 U.S.C. §7701(b)(1)(A). Notice also that the regulation is under Title 20, which is "Employee" benefits. They are talking about federal "employees" only, and not everyone generally. The federal government has *no authority* to legislate for private employees: only PUBLIC employees. They also cannot legislate for people outside of their jurisdiction. A "nonresident" is outside of their jurisdiction.

   > *TITLE 20--EMPLOYEES' BENEFITS*
   > *CHAPTER III--SOCIAL SECURITY ADMINISTRATION*
   > *PART 422_ORGANIZATION AND PROCEDURES--Table of Contents*
   > *Subpart B_General Procedures*
   > *Sec. 422.104 Who can be assigned a social security number.*
   >
   > *(a) Persons eligible for SSN assignment. We can assign you a social security number if you meet the evidence requirements in Sec. 422.107 and you are:*
   > *(1) A United States citizen; or*
   > *(2) An alien lawfully admitted to the United States [federal zone] for permanent residence or under other authority of law permitting you to work in the United States (Sec. 422.105 describes how we determine if a nonimmigrant alien is permitted to work in the United States); or*
   > *(3) An alien who cannot provide evidence of alien status showing lawful admission to the U.S., or an alien with evidence of lawful admission but without authority to work in the U.S., if the evidence described in Sec. 422.107(e) does not exist, but only for a valid nonwork reason. We consider you to have a valid nonwork reason if:*
   > *(i) You need a social security number to satisfy a Federal statute or regulation that requires you to have a social security number in order to receive a Federally-funded benefit to which you have otherwise established entitlement and you reside either in or outside the U.S.; or*
   > *(ii) You need a social security number to satisfy a State or local law that requires you to have a social security number in order to receive public assistance benefits to which you have otherwise established entitlement, and you are legally in the United States.*
   > *(b) Annotation for a nonwork purpose. If we assign you a social security number as an alien for a nonwork purpose, we will indicate in our records that you are not authorized to work. We will also mark your social security card with a legend such as ``NOT VALID FOR EMPLOYMENT." If earnings are reported to us on your number, we will inform the Department of Homeland Security of the reported earnings.*

2. Nonresident aliens don't need an SSN to open a bank account:

   > *Title 31. Money and Finance: Treasury*
   > *Subtitle B. Regulations Relating to Money and Finance*
   > *Chapter X. FINANCIAL CRIMES ENFORCEMENT NETWORK, DEPARTMENT OF THE TREASURY*
   > *Part 1020. RULES FOR BANKS*
   > *Subpart D. Records Required To Be Maintained By Banks*
   > *31 CFR § 1020.410 - Records to be made and retained by banks.*
   >
   > *(b)(3) **A taxpayer identification number required under paragraph (a)(1) of this section need not be secured for accounts or transactions with the following:***
   >
   > *(i) Agencies and instrumentalities of Federal, state, local or foreign governments;*
   >
   > *(ii) judges, public officials, or clerks of courts of record as custodians of funds in controversy or under the control of the court;*
   >
   > *(iii) aliens who are (A) ambassadors, ministers, career diplomatic or consular officers, or (B) naval, military or other attaches of foreign embassies and legations, and for the members of their immediate families;*
   >
   > *(iv) aliens who are accredited representatives of international organizations which are entitled to enjoy privileges, exemptions and immunities as an international organization under the International Organization Immunities Act of December 29, 1945 (22 U.S.C. 288), and the members of their immediate families;*
   >
   > *(v) aliens temporarily residing in the United States for a period not to exceed 180 days; (vi) aliens not engaged in a* trade or business *in the United States who are attending a recognized college or university or any training program, supervised or conducted by any agency of the Federal Government;*

> *(vii) unincorporated subordinate units of a tax exempt central organization which are covered by a group exemption letter,*
>
> *(viii) a person under 18 years of age with respect to an account opened as a part of a school thrift savings program, provided the annual interest is less than $10; (ix) a person opening a Christmas club, vacation club and similar installment savings programs provided the annual interest is less than $10; and*
>
> *(x) __non-resident aliens who are not engaged in a__ trade or business __in the__ United States. In instances described in paragraphs (a)(3), (viii) and (ix) of this section, the bank shall, within 15 days following the end of any calendar year in which the interest accrued in that year is $10 or more use its best effort to secure and maintain the appropriate taxpayer identification number or application form therefor.*

3. Investment firms are not required to use an SSN to register securities that nonresident aliens buy.

    > *Title 31: Money and Finance: Treasury*
    > *PART 306—GENERAL REGULATIONS GOVERNING U.S. SECURITIES*
    > *Subpart B—Registration*
    > *306.10 General*
    >
    > *The registration used must express the actual ownership of a security and may not include any restriction on the authority of the owner to dispose of it in any manner, except as otherwise specifically provided in these regulations. The Treasury Department reserves the right to treat the registration as conclusive of ownership. __Requests for registration should be clear, accurate, and complete, conform with one of the forms set forth in this subpart, and include appropriate taxpayer identifying numbers.__ [2] The registration of all bonds owned by the same person, organization, or fiduciary should be uniform with respect to the name of the owner and, in the case of a fiduciary, the description of the fiduciary capacity. Individual owners should be designated by the names by which they are ordinarily known or under which they do business, preferably including at least one full given name. The name of an individual may be preceded by any applicable title, as, for example, Mrs., Miss, Ms., Dr., or Rev., or followed by a designation such as M.D., D.D., Sr., or Jr. Any other similar suffix should be included when ordinarily used or when necessary to distinguish the owner from a member of his family. A married woman's own given name, not that of her husband, must be used, for example, Mrs. Mary A. Jones, not Mrs. Frank B. Jones. The address should include, where appropriate, the number and street, route, or any other local feature and the Zip Code.*
    >
    > [2] *__Taxpayer identifying numbers are not required for foreign governments, nonresident aliens not engaged in__ trade or business __within the United States, international organizations and foreign corporations not engaged in__ trade or business __and not having an office or place of business or a financial or paying agent within the United States, and other persons or organizations as may be exempted from furnishing such numbers under regulations of the Internal Revenue Service.__*

4. The IRS Form W-8BEN does NOT need a Social Security Number. Instead, the regulations say the recipients can rely on a certificate of residence as a substitute. That certificate of residence is really a certificate of "domicile". The article Why Domicile and Becoming a "Taxpayer" Require Your Consent, Form #05.002 (http://sedm.org/Forms/05-MemLaw/Domicile.pdf) proves that Christians cannot have an earthly domicile, and therefore the only thing you can put on such a certificate is one of the following: "None", "Homeless", "Outside the United States as defined in 26 U.S.C. §7701(a)(9) and (a)(10)", or "Heaven". You cannot have an earthly domicile without committing idolatry.

    > *Title 26: Internal Revenue*
    > *PART 1—INCOME TAXES*
    > *Withholding of Tax on Nonresident Aliens and Foreign Corporations and Tax-Free Covenant Bonds*
    > *Sec. 1.1441-6 Claim of reduced withholding under an income tax treaty.*
    >
    > *(c) __Exemption from requirement to furnish a taxpayer identifying number__ and special documentary evidence rules for certain income.*
    >
    > *(1) General rule.*
    >
    > *In the case of income described in paragraph (c)(2) of this section, a withholding agent may rely on a beneficial owner withholding certificate [IRS Form W-8BEN] described in paragraph (b)(1) of this section without regard to the requirement that the withholding certificate include the beneficial owner's taxpayer identifying number. In the case of payments of income described in paragraph (c)(2) of this section made outside the United States [federal zone] (as defined in Sec. 1.6049-5(e) with respect to an offshore account (as defined in Sec. 1.6049-5(c)(1)), __a withholding agent may, as an alternative to a withholding certificate described in paragraph (b)(1) of this section, rely on a certificate of residence described in paragraph (c)(3) of this section__ or documentary evidence described in paragraph (c)(4) of this section, relating to the beneficial owner, that the withholding agent has reviewed and maintains in its records in accordance with Sec. 1.1441-1(e)(4)(iii). In the*

case of a payment to a person other than an individual, the certificate of residence or documentary evidence must be accompanied by the statements described in paragraphs (c)(5)(i) and (ii) of this section regarding limitation on benefits and whether the amount paid is derived by such person or by one of its interest holders. The withholding agent maintains the reviewed documents by retaining either the documents viewed or a photocopy thereof and noting in its records the date on which, and by whom, the documents were received and reviewed. This paragraph (c)(1) shall not apply to amounts that are exempt from withholding based on a claim that the income is effectively connected with the conduct of a trade or business in the United States.

The above cites don't cover the requirements for STATUTORY "non-resident non-persons" who are entirely PRIVATE, but the implications are obvious. Congress can only regulate and tax PUBLIC conduct of agents and officers of the national government. A "non-resident non-person" is not such an agent or officer.

Even the nonresident aliens mentioned above are such agents and officers IF they use government identifying numbers and IF they were "individuals", meaning officers of the government, BEFORE they used the number. Since the number is a franchise mark that causes the party using it to be ILLEGALLY treated as an agent and franchisee of Uncle Sam, then those who don't use the number are, by definition, exclusively PRIVATE, and not subject but not exempt, from the provisions of the Internal Revenue Code. Any attempt to impute any civil status, including "nonresident alien" or "nonresident alien individual" to an exclusively PRIVATE human not engaged in a public office as an agent of the government and not consenting to do so is, in fact, CRIMINAL IDENTITY THEFT. See:

> *Government Identity Theft*, Form #05.046
> http://sedm.org/Forms/FormIndex.htm

16 Mandatory Use of SSNs/TINs

16.1 Compelled use forbidden by Privacy Act

The Privacy Act forbids compelled use of SSNs. Those demanding numbers must disclose BOTH whether the disclosure is MANDATORY or VOLUNTARY, and the statute that makes it mandatory IN YOUR CASE and based on YOUR SPECIFIC STATUS:

> *Disclosure of Social Security Number*
>
> *Section 7 of Pub. L. 93–579 provided that:*
>
> *"(a)(1) It shall be unlawful for any Federal, State or local government agency to deny to any individual any right, benefit, or privilege provided by law because of such individual's refusal to disclose his social security account number."*
>
> *(2) the [The] provisions of paragraph (1) of this subsection shall not apply with respect to— "*
>
> *(A) any disclosure which is required by Federal statute, or "*
>
> *(B) the disclosure of a social security number to any Federal, State, or local agency maintaining a system of records in existence and operating before January 1, 1975, if such disclosure was required under statute or regulation adopted prior to such date to verify the identity of an individual."*
>
> *(b) Any Federal, State, or local government agency which requests an individual to disclose his social security account number shall inform that individual whether that disclosure is mandatory or voluntary, by what statutory or other authority such number is solicited, and what uses will be made of it."*
>
> *[SOURCE: 5 U.S.C. §552a Legislative Notes, https://www.law.cornell.edu/uscode/text/5/552a]*

The application of the above requirement of law is further described on the Department of Justice website at:

> *Disclosure of Social Security Numbers*, Department of Justice Office of Privacy and Civil Liberties
> https://www.justice.gov/opcl/overview-privacy-act-1974-2020-edition/ssn

16.2 Burden of Proof on Those Compelling Use

5 U.S.C. §552a Legislative Notes and Section 7(b) of the Privacy Act, Pub.L. 93-579 provide that those demanding government identifying numbers MUST meet the following burden of proof:

> (b) *Any Federal, State, or local government agency which requests an individual to disclose his social security account number shall inform that individual whether that disclosure is mandatory or voluntary, by what statutory or other authority such number is solicited, and what uses will be made of it."*
> [SOURCE: 5 U.S.C. §552a Legislative Notes and Section 7(b) of the Privacy Act, Pub.L. 93-579,
> https://www.law.cornell.edu/uscode/text/5/552a

Implicit in the above requirement is that:

1. You must be a statutory "taxpayer" subject to the provision of the I.R.C. cited. If you are NOT a statutory "taxpayer" per 26 U.S.C. §7701(a)(14), then no provision of the I.R.C. applies to you, including 26 U.S.C. §§6039 or 6039E.

    > "*The revenue laws* are a code or system in regulation of tax assessment and collection. They *relate to taxpayers, and not to nontaxpayers. The latter are without their scope*. No procedure is prescribed for nontaxpayers, and no attempt is made to annul any of their rights and remedies in due course of law. With them Congress does not assume to deal, and they are neither of the subject nor of the object of the revenue laws..."
    > [Long v. Rasmussen, 281 F. 236 (1922)]

    > "Revenue Laws relate to taxpayers [officers, employees, instrumentalities, and elected officials of the Federal Government] and not to non-taxpayers [American Citizens/American Nationals not subject to the exclusive jurisdiction of the Federal Government and who did not volunteer to participate in the federal "trade or business" franchise]. The latter are without their scope. No procedures are prescribed for non-taxpayers and no attempt is made to annul any of their Rights or Remedies in due course of law."
    > [Economy Plumbing & Heating v. U.S., 470 F.2d. 585 (1972)]

    > "And by statutory definition, 'taxpayer' includes any person, trust or estate subject to a tax imposed by the revenue act. ...Since the statutory definition of 'taxpayer' is exclusive, the federal courts do not have the power to create nonstatutory taxpayers for the purpose of applying the provisions of the Revenue Acts..."
    > [C.I.R. v. Trustees of L. Inv. Ass'n, 100 F.2d. 18 (1939)]

2. You must have the statutory STATUS associated with the requirement. For instance, 26 C.F.R. §301.6109-1 describes only statutory "U.S. persons" per 26 U.S.C. §7701(a)(30) and "nonresident alien individuals" engaged in the "trade or business" franchise. If you are neither a "U.S. person" nor a "nonresident alien individual", then this provision also does not mandate disclosure of any number. Example: A "non-resident non-person".
3. The clerk accepting the form cannot lawfully represent you or make legal determinations about your status. They must accept whatever you tell them you are on the government form and not challenge or question it. If they do, they are:
    3.1. Practicing law on your behalf without your consent.
    3.2. Unlawfully exceeding their delegated authority.
    3.3. Committing the crime of tampering with a federal witness per 18 U.S.C. §1512, and especially if they threaten you if you do not accept the status they insist on.

16.3 Penalties for compelled use

5 U.S.C. §552a(g)(4) provides for a penalty of a minimum of $1,000 for compelled use of Social Security Numbers:

> *5 U.S.C. §552a(g)(4)*
>
> *(4) In any suit brought under the provisions of subsection (g)(1)(C) or (D) of this section in which the court determines that the agency acted in a manner which was intentional or willful, the United States shall be liable to the individual in an amount equal to the sum of—*
>
> *(A) actual damages sustained by the individual as a result of the refusal or failure, but **in no case shall a person entitled to recovery receive less than the sum of $1,000**; and*
>
> *(B) the costs of the action together with reasonable attorney fees as determined by the court."*
>
> [SOURCE: https://www.law.cornell.edu/uscode/text/5/552a]

For additional information, read Doe v. Chao, 540 U.S. 614 (2004):

http://en.wikipedia.org/wiki/Doe_v._Chao

16.4 When is it mandatory under the I.R.C. to provide government issued numbers?

It will interest the reader to know that the ONLY provision of law mandating use of Social Security Numbers is found in regulations relating ONLY to federal employees! The authority to write such regulations comes from 5 U.S.C. §301 (federal employees), which establishes that the head of an Executive or military department may prescribe regulations for the *internal* government of his department.

> *TITLE 5 > PART I > CHAPTER 3 > § 301*
> *§ 301. Departmental regulations*
>
> The head of an Executive department or military department **may prescribe regulations for the government of his department, the conduct of its employees, the distribution and performance of its business, and the custody, use, and preservation of its records, papers, and property.** *This section does not authorize withholding information from the public or limiting the availability of records to the public.*

This analysis is also consistent with the fact that regulations may NOT exceed the scope of the statutes they implement. 26 U.S.C. §6109 never requires anyone to OBTAIN a Taxpayer Identification Number, so the regulations that implement it cannot UNLESS the obligation is ONLY imposed WITHIN by the Secretary WITHIN the Treasury Department upon his or her OWN statutory "employees" under 5 U.S.C. §2105(a). The U.S. Supreme Court recognized this limitation of regulations in United States v. Calamaro, 354 U.S. 351 (1957).

26 C.F.R. §301.6109-1(b) is the only provision of law which expressly requires the use of Taxpayer Identification Numbers. It says on the requirement to use such numbers the following:

> *26 C.F.R. §301.6109-1(b)*
>
> *(b) Requirement to furnish one's own number—*
>
> *(1) U.S. persons.*
>
> *Every **U.S. person** who makes under this title a return, statement, or other document must furnish **its** own taxpayer identifying number as required by the forms and the accompanying instructions.*
>
> *(2) Foreign persons.*
>
> *The provisions of paragraph (b)(1) of this section regarding the furnishing of one's own number shall apply to the following foreign persons--*
>
> *(i) A foreign person that has income effectively connected with the conduct of a U.S. trade or business at any time during the taxable year;*
> *(ii) A foreign person that has a U.S. office or place of business or a U.S. fiscal or paying agent at any time during the taxable year;*
> *(iii) A nonresident alien treated as a resident under section 6013(g) or (h);*
> *(iv) A foreign person that makes a return of tax (including income, estate, and gift tax returns), an amended return, or a refund claim under this title but excluding information returns, statements, or documents;*
> *(v) A foreign person that makes an election under Sec. 301.7701-3(c);*
> *(vi) A foreign person that furnishes a withholding certificate described in Sec. 1.1441-1(e)(2) or (3) of this chapter or Sec. 1.1441-5(c)(2)(iv) or (3)(iii) of this chapter to the extent required under Sec. 1.1441-1(e)(4)(vii) of this chapter;*
> *(vii) A foreign person whose taxpayer identifying number is required to be furnished on any return, statement, or other document as required by the income tax regulations under section 897 or 1445. This paragraph (b)(2)(vii) applies as of November 3, 2003; and*
> *(viii) A foreign person that furnishes a withholding certificate described in Sec. 1.1446-1(c)(2) or (3) of this chapter or whose taxpayer identification number is required to be furnished on any return, statement, or other document as required by the income tax regulations under section 1446. This paragraph (b)(2)(viii) shall apply to partnership taxable years beginning after May 18, 2005, or such earlier time as the regulations under Sec. Sec. 1.1446-1 through 1.1446-5 of this chapter apply by reason of an election under Sec. 1.1446-7 of this chapter.*

Pursuant to 5 U.S.C. §301 (federal employees), the above regulations therefore DO NOT pertain to PRIVATE companies or even government agencies OUTSIDE of the Treasury Department.

Notice also the word "its" in the above regulation. This should clue you into the fact that the tax code doesn't apply to flesh and blood people, who are called "natural persons" in regulations like that above. If they had meant to refer to such a natural person, the word "its" would have said "his" or "her". Consequently, the only type of "person", they can be referring to is a privileged corporation or an officer representing said corporation, as was pointed out at the beginning of chapter 5 of the Great IRS Hoax, Form #11.302 . Also keep in your mind that the above regulation implements a code that is not positive law and therefore imposes no obligation upon anyone who does not consent to be bound by it by occupying a public office or position of employment within the U.S. government. The "U.S. person" identified above is defined below to mean a person born in or "resident" only within the District of Columbia, as follows. Note that "United States" is defined in 26 U.S.C. §7701(a)(9) and (a)(10) to mean ONLY the District of Columbia:

> TITLE 26 > Subtitle F > CHAPTER 79 > Sec. 7701.
> Sec. 7701. - Definitions
>
> (a) When used in this title, where not otherwise distinctly expressed or manifestly incompatible with the intent thereof—
>
> (30) United States person
> The term "United States person" means -
>
> (A) a [corporate] citizen or resident [alien] of the [federal] United States,
> (B) a domestic partnership,
> (C) a domestic corporation,
> (D) any estate (other than a foreign estate, within the meaning of paragraph (31)), and
> (E) any trust if -
> (i) a court within the United States is able to exercise primary supervision over the administration of the trust, and
> (ii) one or more United States persons have the authority to control all substantial decisions of the trust.

All government identifying numbers may only lawfully be issued to persons participating in government franchises. They act as the equivalent of license numbers for those engaging in franchises. The following IRS publications plainly admit when government-issued numbers are mandatory, and all of them relate to those obtaining or qualifying for some government benefit or privilege. These cites are VERY important because once you can prove the things for which TINs are positively required, then all other uses are VOLUNTARY and not mandatory. Simply show them the list below and if your circumstances are not in it, then demand that they show a statute documenting an affirmative requirement to provide an identifying number:

1. IRS Publication 519, Year 2005, p. 23:

    Identification Number

    A taxpayer identification number must be furnished on returns, statements, and other tax related documents. For an individual, this is a social security number (SSN). If you do not have and are not eligible to get an SSN, you must apply for an individual taxpayer identification number (ITIN). An employer identification number (EIN) is required if you are engaged in a trade or business as a sole proprietor and have employees or a qualified retirement plan.

    You must furnish a taxpayer identification number if you are:

    - *An alien who has income effectively connected with the conduct of a U.S. trade or business at any time during the year.*
    - *An alien who has a U.S. office or place of business at any time during the year.*
    - *A nonresident alien spouse treated as a resident, as discussed in chapter 1, or*
    - *Any other alien who files a tax return, an amended return, or a refund claim (but not information returns).*

    Social Security Number (SSN). Generally, you can get an SSN if you have been lawfully admitted to the United States for permanent residence or under other immigration categories that authorize U.S. employment.

    [. . .]

> *Individual taxpayer identification number (ITIN). If you do not have and are not eligible to get an SSN, you must apply for an ITIN. For details on how to do so, see Form W-7 and its instructions. It usually takes about 4-6 weeks to get an ITIN. If you already have an ITIN, enter it whenever an SSN is required on your tax return.*
>
> *An ITIN is for tax use only. It does not entitle you to social security benefits or change your employment or immigration status under U.S. law.*
>
> *In addition to those aliens who are required to furnish a taxpayer identification number and are not eligible for an SSN, a Form W-7 should be filed for:*
>
> - *Alien individuals who are claimed as dependents and are not eligible for an SSN, and*
> - *Alien spouses who are claimed as exemptions and are not eligible for an SSN.*
>
> *Employer identification number (EIN). An individual may use an SSN (or ITIN) for individual taxes and an EIN for business taxes. To apply for an EIN, file Form SS-4. Application for Employer Identification Number, with the IRS.*

2. <u>IRS Form 1040NR Instructions, Year 2007, p. 9</u>. You can't avail yourself of the "benefits" of the franchise without providing your franchisee license number.

    > *Line 7c, Column (2)*
    >
    > *You must enter each dependent's identifying number (SSN, ITIN, or adoption taxpayer identification number (ATIN)). If you do not enter the **<u>correct identifying number</u>**, at the time we process your return we may **<u>disallow the exemption claimed</u>** (such as the child tax credit) based on the dependent.*

3. <u>IRS Form 1042s Instructions, Year 2006, p. 14</u>. What all of the circumstances below have in common is that they involve a "benefit" that is usually financial or tangible to the recipient, and therefore require a franchisee license number called a Taxpayer Identification Number:

    > *Box 14, Recipient's U.S. Taxpayer Identification Number (TIN)*
    >
    > **<u>You must obtain a U.S. taxpayer identification number (TIN) for:</u>**
    >
    > - *Any recipient whose income is effectively connected with the conduct of a trade or business in the United States.*
    >   *Note. For these recipients, exemption code 01 should be entered in box 6.*
    > - *Any foreign person claiming a reduced rate of, or exemption from, tax under a tax treaty between a foreign country and the United States, unless the income is an unexpected payment (as described in Regulations section 1.1441-6(g)) or consists of dividends and interest from stocks and debt obligations that are actively traded; dividends from any redeemable security issued by an investment company registered under the Investment Company Act of 1940 (mutual fund); dividends, interest, or royalties from units of beneficial interest in a unit investment trust that are (or were, upon issuance) publicly offered and are registered with the Securities and Exchange Commission under the Securities Act of 1933; and amounts paid with respect to loans of any of the above securities.*
    > - *Any nonresident alien individual claiming exemption from tax under section 871(f) for certain annuities received under qualified plans.*
    > - *A foreign organization claiming an exemption from tax solely because of its status as a tax-exempt organization under section 501(c) or as a private foundation.*
    > - *Any QI.*
    > - *Any WP or WT.*
    > - *Any nonresident alien individual claiming exemption from withholding on compensation for independent personal services [services connected with a "trade or business"].*
    > - *Any foreign grantor trust with five or fewer grantors.*
    > - *Any branch of a foreign bank or foreign insurance company that is treated as a U.S. person.*
    >
    > *If a foreign person provides a TIN on a Form W-8, but is not required to do so, the withholding agent must include the TIN on Form 1042-S.*

We have taken the time to further investigate the last item above and put it in tabular form for your reading pleasure:

Table 2: I.R.C. Statutory "Benefits"

#	Name	Code section	Notes
1	Effectively connected with the "trade or business" franchise	26 U.S.C. §7701(a)(26) 26 U.S.C. §871(b) 26 U.S.C. §1	
2	Foreign person claiming reduced rate of, exemption from, tax under treaty	26 U.S.C. §894 26 U.S.C. §6114 26 U.S.C. §6712 26 U.S.C. §1(h)(11)(C)(i)(II)	
3	Nonresident alien claiming exemption for annuities received under qualified plans	26 U.S.C. §871(f)	
4	Foreign organization claiming an exemption from tax solely because of its status as a tax exempt organization	26 U.S.C. §501(c)	
5	Qualified Intermediary (QI)	26 C.F.R. §1.1441-1(e)(5): Generally 26 C.F.R. §1.1441-1(e)(5)(ii): Definition	Pursuant to 26 C.F.R. §1.1441-1(c)(14), one cannot be "qualified" without being a "U.S. person", meaning a person with a legal domicile on federal territory in the "United States" (District of Columbia).

#	Name	Code section	Notes
6	Withholding Foreign Partnership (WP) or Withholding Foreign Trust (WT)	26 C.F.R. §1.1441-5(c)	A withholding foreign partnership (WP) is any foreign partnership that has entered into a WP withholding agreement with the IRS and is acting in that capacity. A withholding foreign trust (WT) is a foreign simple or grantor trust that has entered into a WT withholding agreement with the IRS and is acting in that capacity. A WP or WT may act in that capacity only for payments of amounts subject to NRA withholding that are distributed to, or included in the distributive share of, its direct partners, beneficiaries, or owners. A WP or WT acting in that capacity must assume NRA withholding responsibility for these amounts. You may treat a WP or WT as a payee if it has provided you with documentation (discussed later) that represents that it is acting as a WP or WT for such amounts. You cannot be a WP or a WT without an EIN. A WP or WT must provide you with a Form W-8IMY that certifies that the WP or WT is acting in that capacity and a written statement identifying the amounts for which it is so acting. The statement is not required to contain withholding rate pool information or any information relating to the identity of a direct partner, beneficiary, or owner. The Form W-8IMY must contain the WP-EIN or WT-EIN. See: https://www.irs.gov/businesses/corporations/qualified-intermediary-general-faqs
7	Nonresident claiming exemption for independent personal services	26 C.F.R. §1.1441-4(b)(4): Withholding 26 C.F.R. §1.1461-1(c)(2)(i): Reporting 26 C.F.R. §1.1441-6(g)(1): TIN requirement	Claimed using IRS Form 8233. The term "personal services" is defined as work performed in connection with a "trade or business" pursuant to 26 C.F.R. §1.469-9(b)(4) and 26 C.F.R. §1.1441-4. 26 U.S.C. §864(b)(1)(A) excludes services performed for foreign employers, meaning employers other than the U.S. government. See: https://www.irs.gov/forms-pubs/about-form-8233
8	Foreign grantor trust with five or fewer grantors	26 U.S.C. §§671 to 679 26 C.F.R. §1.1441-5(e): Generally 26 C.F.R. §1.1441-1(c)(26): Definition	A foreign grantor trust is a foreign trust but only to the extent all or a portion of the income [meaning "trade or business" earnings or payments from the U.S. government pursuant to 26 U.S.C. §871 and 26 U.S.C. §643(b)] of the trust is treated as owned by the grantor or another person under sections 671 through 679.
9	Any branch of a foreign bank or foreign insurance company that is treated as a "U.S. person"	26 U.S.C. §7701(a)(30)	All "U.S. persons" have a domicile in the "United States", meaning the District of Columbia. Choice of domicile is voluntary and therefore this status is voluntary. All "U.S. persons" and "individuals" are government agents, instrumentalities, employees, or officers.

To summarize all of the requirements pertaining to the mandatory use of identifying numbers from all the publications above:

1. Only STATUTORY "individuals" are required to obtain identifying numbers. "Individuals" are defined in 26 C.F.R. §1.1441-1(c)(3) as "aliens", meaning foreign nationals from a foreign country. This is also consistent with the requirements of 20 C.F.R. §422.104.
2. "citizens" are nowhere expressly required to obtain an identifying number. Only "aliens" are required to obtain a number, which are foreign nationals born in a foreign country. They are only required to obtain identifying numbers when domiciled on federal territory and outside the exclusive jurisdiction of a state of the Union. The reason they can be required to obtain such a number is because all aliens are "privileged" while they are visiting federal territory. This is confirmed by the following authorities, which prove that "aliens" with a domicile in a country are "privileged":

    > "*Residents, as distinguished from citizens, are aliens who are permitted to take up a permanent abode [domicile] in the country.* Being bound to the society by reason of their [intention of] dwelling in it, they are subject to its laws so long as they remain there, and, being protected by it, they must defend it, although they do not enjoy all the rights of citizenship. **They have only certain privileges which the law, or custom, gives them.** Permanent residents are those who have been given the right of perpetual residence. **They are a sort of citizen of a less privileged character, and are subject to the society without enjoying all its advantages.** Their children succeed to their status; for the right of perpetual residence given them by the State passes to their children."
    > [The Law of Nations, p. 87, E. De Vattel, Volume Three, 1758, Carnegie Institution of Washington; emphasis added.]

3. If you are participating in a federal benefit or franchise, then you must provide a number. These benefits are identified on IRS Form 1042s instructions and include:
    3.1. A "trade or business", which is defined in 26 U.S.C. §7701(a)(26) as "the functions of a public office".
    3.2. Reduced rate or exemption from tax arising from a tax treaty with a foreign country.
    3.3. Exemptions such as child write-offs.
    3.4. Any nonresident alien individual claiming exemption from tax under section 871(f) for certain annuities received under qualified plans.
    3.5. A foreign organization claiming an exemption from tax solely because of its status as a tax-exempt organization under section 501(c) or as a private foundation.
    3.6. Any QI.
    3.7. Any WP or WT.
    3.8. Any nonresident alien individual claiming exemption from withholding on compensation for independent personal services [services connected with a "trade or business"].
    3.9. Any foreign grantor trust with five or fewer grantors.
    3.10. Any branch of a foreign bank or foreign insurance company that is treated as a "U.S. person" under 26 U.S.C. §7701(a)(30).
4. There is no authority within the I.R.C. to CREATE a "public office" by filling out any form. You must be elected into the office by a lawful vote and you can't "elect" yourself into office by simply filling out a form. You must ALREADY be a "public officer" within the U.S. government in order to have a tax liability that can be reduced by any of the above so-called "benefits". 4 U.S.C. §72 says that all "public offices" must be exercised in the District of Columbia and not elsewhere except as expressly provided in an act of Congress. There is no act of Congress which expressly authorizes "public offices" within any state of the Union, and therefore it is ILLEGAL to participate in the "trade or business" franchise as a person domiciled within the exclusive jurisdiction of a state of the Union. Consequently, anyone domiciled within a state of the Union cannot be a party to any of the above "benefits" and is being deceived and defrauded if they think they either have a liability or need to reduce the liability by participating in any of the above franchises.

> *For thus says the LORD:*
> *"You have sold yourselves for nothing,*
> *And you shall be redeemed without money."*
> *[Isaiah 52:3, Bible, NKJV]*

> "*Thus, Congress having power to regulate commerce with foreign nations, and among the several States, and with the Indian tribes, may, without doubt, provide for **granting** coasting **licenses**, licenses to pilots, licenses to trade with the Indians, and any other **licenses** necessary or proper for the exercise of that great and extensive power; and the same observation is applicable to every other power of Congress, to the exercise of which the granting of licenses may be incident. All such licenses confer authority, and give rights to the licensee.*

> *But very different considerations apply to the **internal commerce** or **domestic trade** of the **States**. Over this commerce and trade Congress has **no power of regulation nor any direct control**. This power belongs **exclusively to the States**. **No interference by Congress with the business of citizens transacted within a State is warranted by the Constitution, except such as is strictly incidental to the exercise of powers clearly granted to the legislature**. The power to authorize a business within a State is plainly repugnant to the exclusive power of the State over the same subject. It is true that the power of Congress to tax is a very extensive power. It is given in the Constitution, with only one exception and only two qualifications. Congress cannot tax exports, and it must impose direct taxes by the rule of apportionment, and indirect taxes by the rule of uniformity. Thus limited, and thus only, it reaches every subject, and may be exercised at discretion. But, it reaches only existing subjects.*
> ## **Congress cannot authorize [e.g. LICENSE using a Social Security Number] a trade or business within a State in order to tax it.**"
> *[License Tax Cases, 72 U.S. 462, 18 L.Ed. 497, 5 Wall. 462, 2 A.F.T.R. 2224 (1866)]*

5. If you aren't an "alien" and meet any one of the following requirements, then you aren't required to obtain or use a government issued identifying number
    5.1. Do not participate government franchises.
    5.2. Terminated participation in all federal franchises
    5.3. Were not qualified at the time you signed up because not domiciled on federal territory.

    No government institution, financial institution, or employer may therefore lawfully compel the use of Social Security Numbers against those who meet the above criteria. If an employer or financial institution attempts to compel use of the SSN, the victim has not only a standing under the above statute, but also can sue the institution for involuntary servitude under the Thirteenth Amendment. The reason is that this would constitute the equivalent of involuntary servitude in violation of the Thirteenth Amendment, because it would essentially amount to compelling a person to act as a federal "employee", as we showed earlier. The following statute makes it a CRIME to compel the use of Social Security numbers against those who meet the above criteria:

    > TITLE 42 - THE PUBLIC HEALTH AND WELFARE
    > CHAPTER 7 - SOCIAL SECURITY
    > SUBCHAPTER II - FEDERAL OLD-AGE, SURVIVORS, AND DISABILITY INSURANCE BENEFITS
    > Sec. 408. Penalties
    >
    > (a) In general
    > Whoever -...
    >
    > (8) discloses, uses, or **compels the disclosure of the social security number of any person in violation of the laws of the United States; shall be guilty of a felony and upon conviction thereof shall be fined under title 18 or imprisoned for not more than five years, or both.**

6. Use of a government number constitutes prima facie evidence that you are acting in a representative capacity as an officer of the government. The reason this must be so is because the government cannot pay "benefits" to private human beings, so you must become their agent and officer acting in an official capacity to make the transaction lawful:

    > *To lay, with one hand, the power of the government on the property of the citizen, and with the other to bestow it upon favored individuals to aid private enterprises and build up private fortunes, is none the less a robbery because it is done under the forms of law and is called taxation. This is not legislation. It is a decree under legislative forms.*
    >
    > *Nor is it taxation. 'A tax,' says Webster's Dictionary, 'is a rate or sum of money assessed on the person or property of a citizen by government for the use of the nation or State.' 'Taxes are burdens or charges imposed by the Legislature upon persons or property to raise money for public purposes.' Cooley, Const. Lim., 479.*
    >
    > *Coulter, J., in Northern Liberties v. St. John's Church, 13 Pa.St. 104 says, very forcibly, 'I think the common mind has everywhere taken in the understanding that **taxes are a public imposition, levied by authority of the government for the purposes of carrying on the government in all its machinery and operations—that they are imposed for a public purpose.**' See, also Pray v. Northern Liberties, 31 Pa.St. 69; Matter of Mayor of N.Y., 11 Johns., 77; Camden v. Allen, 2 Dutch., 398; Sharpless v. Mayor, supra; Hanson v. Vernon, 27 Ia., 47; Whiting v. Fond du Lac, supra."*
    > *[Loan Association v. Topeka, 20 Wall. 655 (1874)]*
    > ___
    >
    > *"A tax, in the general understanding of the term and as used in the constitution, signifies an exaction for the support of the government. The word has never thought to connote the expropriation of money from one group for the benefit of another."*
    > *[U.S. v. Butler, 297 U.S. 1 (1936)]*

> "In Calder v. Bull, which was here in 1798, **Mr. Justice Chase said, that there were acts which the Federal and State legislatures could not do without exceeding their authority, and among them he mentioned** a law which punished a citizen for an innocent act; a law that destroyed or impaired the lawful private [labor] contracts [and labor compensation, e.g. earnings from employment through compelled W-4 withholding] of citizens; a law that made a man judge in his own case; and **a law that took the property from A [the worker], and gave it to B [the government or another citizen, such as through social welfare programs]. 'It is against all reason and justice,'** he added, 'for a people to intrust a legislature with such powers, and therefore it cannot be presumed that they have done it. They may command what is right and prohibit what is wrong; but they cannot change innocence into guilt, or punish innocence as a crime, or violate the right of an antecedent lawful private [employment] contract [by compelling W-4 withholding, for instance], or the right of private property. To maintain that a Federal or State legislature possesses such powers [of THEFT!] if they had not been expressly restrained, would, in my opinion, be a political heresy altogether inadmissible in all free republican governments.' 3 Dall. 388."
> [Sinking Fund Cases, 99 U.S. 700 (1878)]

7. You are not required to associate the number with any of your private property. Compelling you to do so violates the Fifth Amendment takings clause. You and only you determinate what subset of your private property you wish to associate with and donate to a "public use" and a "public purpose" by associating it with government property in the form of the government-owned number.
8. Associating a government number with your private property, such as your financial accounts, real estate, etc. makes the property into the equivalent of "private property donated to a public use to procure the benefits of a government franchise". If associating your property with a number does not render a government benefit, then it is a BAD idea to basically give away your private property without any compensation. The government just loves people to do this, but they can't require them to donate their private property to a public use.

> "Men are endowed by their Creator with certain unalienable rights,-'life, liberty, and the pursuit of happiness;' and to 'secure,' not grant or create, these rights, governments are instituted. **That property [or income] which a man has honestly acquired he retains full control of, subject to these limitations: First, that he shall not use it to his neighbor's injury, and that does not mean that he must use it for his neighbor's benefit [e.g. SOCIAL SECURITY, Medicare, and every other public "benefit"];** second, that if he devotes it to a public use, he gives to the public a right to control that use; and third, that whenever the public needs require, the public may take it upon payment of due compensation."
> [Budd v. People of State of New York, 143 U.S. 517 (1892)]

16.5 Mandatory use by ALIENS on the W-9 form

26 C.F.R. §1.1441-1 also says the following about the requirement to furnish identifying numbers for a "foreign persons":

> Title 26 › Chapter I › Subchapter A › Part 1 › Section 1.1441-1
> § 1.1441-1 Requirement for the deduction and withholding of tax on payments to foreign persons.
>
> (d) Beneficial owner's or payee's claim of U.S. status -
>
> (1) In general.
>
> Under paragraph (b)(1) of this section, a withholding agent is not required to withhold under chapter 3 of the Code on payments to a U.S. payee, to a person presumed to be a U.S. payee in accordance with the provisions of paragraph (b)(3) of this section, or to a person that the withholding agent may treat as a U.S. beneficial owner of the payment. Absent actual knowledge or reason to know otherwise, a withholding agent may rely on the provisions of this paragraph (d) in order to determine whether to treat a payee or beneficial owner as a U.S. person.
>
> (2) Payments for which a Form W-9 is otherwise required.
>
> A withholding agent may treat as a U.S. payee any person who is required to furnish a Form W-9 and who furnishes it in accordance with the procedures described in §§31.3406(d)-1 through 31.3406(d)-5 of this chapter (including the requirement that the payee furnish its taxpayer identifying number (TIN)) if the withholding agent meets all the requirements described in §31.3406(h)-3(e) of this chapter regarding reliance by a payor on a Form W-9. Providing a Form W-9 or valid substitute form shall serve as a statement that the person whose name is on the form is a U.S. person. Therefore, a foreign person, including a U.S. branch treated as a U.S. person under paragraph (b)(2)(iv) of this section, shall not provide a Form W-9. A U.S. branch of a foreign person may

> *establish its status as a <u>foreign person</u> exempt from reporting under chapter 61 and <u>backup withholding</u> under section 3406 by providing a <u>withholding certificate</u> on Form W-8.*
>
> *(3) Payments for which a Form W-9 is not otherwise required.*
>
> <u>*In the case of a payee who is not required to furnish a Form W-9 under section 3406 (e.g., a person exempt from reporting under chapter 61 of the Internal Revenue Code)*</u>*, the <u>withholding agent</u> may treat the <u>payee</u> as a <u>U.S. payee</u> if the <u>payee</u> provides the withholding agent with a Form W-9 or a substitute form described in § 31.3406(h)-3(c)(2) of this chapter (relating to forms for exempt recipients) that contains the payee's name, address, and TIN. The form must be signed under penalties of perjury by the payee if so required by the form or by §31.3406(h)-3 of this chapter. Providing a Form W-9 or valid substitute form shall serve as a statement that the person whose name is on the certificate is a <u>U.S. person</u>*. *A Form W-9 or valid substitute form shall not be provided by a <u>foreign person</u>, including any U.S. <u>branch</u> of a <u>foreign person</u> whether or not the <u>branch</u> is treated as a <u>U.S. person</u> under <u>paragraph (b)(2)(iv)</u> of this section. See <u>paragraph (e)(3)(v)</u> of this section for <u>withholding</u> certificates provided by U.S. <u>branches</u> described in <u>paragraph (b)(2)(iv)</u> of this section. The procedures described in § 31.3406(h)-2(a) <u>of this chapter</u> shall apply to <u>payments</u> to joint payees. A <u>withholding agent</u> that receives a Form W-9 to satisfy this paragraph (d)(3) must retain the form in accordance with the provisions of §31.3406(h)-3(g) <u>of this chapter</u>, if applicable, or of <u>paragraph (e)(4)(iii)</u> of this section (relating to the retention of <u>withholding</u> certificates) if §31.3406(h)-3(g) <u>of this chapter</u> does not apply. The <u>rules</u> of this paragraph (d)(3) are only intended to provide a method by which a <u>withholding agent</u> may determine that a <u>payee</u> is a <u>U.S. person</u> and do not otherwise impose a <u>requirement</u> that <u>documentation</u> be furnished by a <u>person</u> who is otherwise treated as an <u>exempt recipient</u> for <u>purposes</u> of the applicable information reporting provisions under chapter 61 of the Internal Revenue Code (e.g., §1.6049-4(c)(1)(ii) for <u>payments</u> of interest).*
> *[26 C.F.R. §1.1441-1(d)]*

Notes on the above:

1. Based on the previous section, the only people who are REQUIRED to have an SSN or TIN are those listed in the previous section, which means GOVERNMENT EMPLOYEES within the Treasury Department ONLY. Private humans or even government workers outside the Treasury Department are not required to have or use such a number.
2. All obligations and requirements from the above pertain ONLY to "persons" and not "U.S. persons".
3. Statutory "U.S. persons" under 26 U.S.C. §7701(a)(30) are not a subset of "persons". They are not listed in the definition of "person" found in 26 U.S.C. §7701(a)(1).
4. A statutory "U.S. Person" who is not a statutory "person", such as a "citizen or resident of the United States" can therefore have NO OBLIGATION, including that to provide a Form W-9.
5. Even 26 C.F.R. §1.1441-1(d)(3) says the information entered on the W-9 relates to a "person" and not a "U.S. person".
6. 26 U.S.C. §1441, which is the statute upon which this regulation is based, pertains ONLY to statutory "nonresident aliens". Statutory "citizens" or "residents" or state citizens who are statutory "nationals" are not even mentioned in the section. Therefore, the requirement to furnish the W-9 only pertains to statutory "nonresident aliens".
7. State "nationals" under 8 U.S.C. §1101(a)(21) are NOT statutory "citizens" under 8 U.S.C. §1401 and also not "nonresident aliens". If anything, they are "nonresident nationals". 26 U.S.C. §7701(b)(1)(B) defines what a statutory "nonresident alien" is NOT, not what it IS. See *Non-Resident Non-Person Position*, Form #05.020 for exhaustive proof of this.
8. The only human "person" under 26 U.S.C. §7701(a)(1) is a statutory "individual", and that statutory "individual" is defined as an ALIEN in 26 C.F.R. §1.1441-1(c)(3).
9. The only condition in which a statutory "citizen or resident of the United States[**]" can ALSO be treated as a statutory "individual" is found in 26 U.S.C. §911(d)(1), where that party is abroad in a foreign country. State citizens are NOT statutory "citizens" under 8 U.S.C. §1401. See *Why You are a Political Citizen but Civil Non-Citizen, National, and Nonresident Alien*, Form #05.006 for exhaustive proof of this.
10. 26 C.F.R. §1.1441-1(d)(3) above would apply to payments NOT subject to reporting in 26 U.S.C. §6041. This would be the case with human beings not engaged in a public office and therefore not involved in a statutory "trade or business" as defined in 26 U.S.C. §7701(a)(26).
11. 26 C.F.R. §1.1441-1(d)(2) would apply to payments subject to reporting under 26 U.S.C. §6041. That means the recipient must be engaged in "the functions of a public office" under 26 U.S.C. §7701(a)(26). Those who are private and not engaged in such an office would be "not subject" but not statutory "exempt individuals". See *The "Trade or Business" Scam*, Form #05.001 for exhaustive proof of this.
12. 26 C.F.R. §1.1441-1(d)(2) says that substitute Form W-9 are permitted. You can make your own. That in fact is what our *Affidavit of Citizenship, Domicile, and Tax Status*, Form #02.001 identifies itself as doing.

Therefore, if you fill out a W-9 AT ALL as a STATUTORY "citizen or resident of the United States" or a state "national", you are creating the false impression that you are a statutory "person" under 26 U.S.C. §7701(a)(1) and committing criminal perjury. It's MUCH safer and better to use our Form #02.001.

Withholding agents will sometimes try to require people who ambiguously claim they are "citizens" to fill out a Form W-9, but it isn't necessary and such parties are NOT even mentioned in 26 U.S.C. §1441 as being subject to withholding or reporting. IRS seems to know this, because they NEVER say in 26 C.F.R. §1.1441-1 EXACTLY WHO must fill out a W-9 and only talk about "W-9 required". They do this to illegally rope statutory "U.S. persons", statutory "citizens and residents", and statutory state "nationals" illegally into a tax system that doesn't pertain to them when they are in the country.

17 Penalties for failure to disclose numbers

17.1 Failure to provide TIN on information returns

Information returns include IRS Forms W-2, 1042-S, 1098, 1099, K-1, etc. 26 U.S.C. §6721(a) imposes a penalty against those who file information returns that do not include all the information required on the form.

> *TITLE 26 > Subtitle F > CHAPTER 68 > Subchapter B > PART II > § 6721*
> *§ 6721. Failure to file correct information returns*
>
> *(a) Imposition of penalty*
>
> *(1) In general*
>
> *In the case of a failure described in paragraph (2) by any person with respect to an information return, such person shall pay a penalty of $50 for each return with respect to which such a failure occurs, but the total amount imposed on such person for all such failures during any calendar year shall not exceed $250,000.*
>
> *(2) Failures subject to penalty*
>
> *For purposes of paragraph (1), the failures described in this paragraph are—*
>
> *(A) any failure to file an information return with the Secretary on or before the required filing date, and*
>
> *(B) <u>any failure to include all of the information required to be shown on the return or the inclusion of incorrect information.</u>*

The penalty amount for failure to provide an identifying number is $50. See Internal Revenue Manual (I.R.M.), Section 20.1.7.1.5 and 26 C.F.R. §301.6721-1(a)(1).

> *Code of Federal Regulations*
> *PART 301 -- PROCEDURE AND ADMINISTRATION*
> *Sec. 301.6721-1 Failure to file correct information returns.*
>
> *(a) Imposition of penalty.*
>
> *(1) General rule.*
>
> ***A penalty of $50 is imposed for each information return (as defined in section 6724(d)(1) and paragraph (g) of this section) with respect to which a failure (as defined in section 6721(a)(2) and paragraph (a)(2) of this section) occurs.*** *No more than one penalty will be imposed under this paragraph (a)(1) with respect to a single information return even though there may be more than one failure with respect to such return. The total amount imposed on any person for all failures during any calendar year with respect to all information returns shall not exceed $250,000. See paragraph (b) of this section for a reduction in the penalty when the failures are corrected within specified periods. See paragraph (c) of this section for an exception to the penalty for inconsequential errors or omissions. See paragraph (d) of this section for an exception to the penalty for a DE MINIMIS number of failures. See paragraph (e) of this section for lower limitations to the $250,000 maximum penalty. See paragraph (f) of this section for higher penalties when a failure is due to intentional disregard of the requirement to file timely correct information returns. See paragraph (a)(1) of Section 301.6724-1 for waiver of the penalty for a failure that is due to reasonable cause.*

The above regulation is under Part 301, which means it implements 5 U.S.C. §301 (federal employees). This statute establishes that the head of an Executive or military department may prescribe regulations for the *internal* government of his department.

> TITLE 5 > PART I > CHAPTER 3 > § 301
> § 301. Departmental regulations
>
> The head of an Executive department or military department may prescribe regulations **for the government of his department, the conduct of its employees**, the distribution and performance of its business, and the custody, use, and preservation of its records, papers, and property. This section does not authorize withholding information from the public or limiting the availability of records to the public.

Consequently, the regulation only applies to federal employees and not the public in general.

17.2 Foreign Investment in Real Property Transfer Act (FIRPTA) penalties

26 U.S.C. §1445(b)(2) imposes mandatory withholding of 10% upon a "Transferor", meaning a Seller of real property located in the "United States" (District of Columbia), who fails to provide a Taxpayer Identification Number on their "IRS Form W-8, Certificate of Non-Foreign Status".

> TITLE 26 > Subtitle A > CHAPTER 3 > Subchapter A > § 1445
> § 1445. Withholding of tax on dispositions of United States real property interests
>
> (b) Exemptions
>
> (1) In general
>
> No person shall be required to deduct and withhold any amount under subsection (a) with respect to a disposition if paragraph (2), (3), (4), (5), or (6) applies to the transaction.
>
> (2) Transferor furnishes nonforeign affidavit
>
> Except as provided in paragraph (7), this paragraph applies to the disposition **if the transferor furnishes to the transferee an affidavit by the transferor stating, under penalty of perjury, the transferor's United States taxpayer identification number** and that the transferor is not a foreign person.

The above statute does not impose a DUTY to obtain a number, but only to disclose the number if they have one under threat of withholding if they don't.

The term "Transferor" is defined at 26 U.S.C. §1445(f)(1) as the person disposing of United States real property, meaning real property owned by the U.S. government and not private parties. 26 U.S.C. §897 further characterizes the "Transferor" as a "nonresident alien individual" or "foreign corporation". Consequently, one would not be a "Transferor" subject to withholding, even without a number, if:

1. The entity was not a "nonresident alien individual" or "foreign corporation".
2. The entity was a "nontaxpayer" not subject to the I.R.C.
3. The property was not located in the "United States", which is defined in 26 U.S.C. §7701(a)(9) and (a)(10) as the District of Columbia and no part of any state of the Union.
4. The entity was not a "Transferor", meaning a "nonresident alien individual" or "foreign corporation" selling real property in the District of Columbia.

18 Getting Rid of SSNs/TINs in your IRS or other government record

By following the procedures given above to rebut any association with an identifying number, you will go a long way toward eliminating it from government records. The other important thing is to make sure that:

1. You discontinue using it or writing any identifying numbers on any new government forms you fill out.
2. You correct your status with the Social Security Administration by sending in an amended SSA Form SS-5 changing your citizenship status to that of a "national" who is not a STATUTORY "U.S. citizen".

3. You go back and refile all government forms that are still in use which indicated a number, such as:
   3.1. IRS Form W-8BEN submitted to financial institutions and/or employers
   3.2. IRS Form W-4 (which you SHOULDN'T be using). See the free Federal and State Tax Withholding Options for Private Employers, Form #09.001 pamphlet for the reason why at:
   http://sedm.org/Forms/FormIndex.htm
   3.3. Passport applications.
   3.4. Jury summons responses.
   3.5. Voter registration :
   3.6. Driver's license
      3.6.1. Driver's license application -get a driver's license without an SSN
      3.6.2. Change of Address
   3.7. Job applications.
   3.8. Tax returns (by revoking your signature on all past returns filed).
4. If anyone files a W-2 in your name because of mistake or coercion or tries to withhold Social Security/FICA taxes documented on the W-2, you MUST submit IRS Form 843 to DEMAND a refund of all such payments and an SSA Form 7008 to correct Social Security records reflecting creditable payments.
5. If the IRS or state sends you a collection notice, you must emphasize that the number was used under duress and that it is NOT a statutory number and that commercial use of the number by them constitutes consent to YOUR franchise agreement as shown in the following:

> *Using the Laws of Property to Respond to a Federal or State Tax Collection Notice*, Form #14.015
> https://sedm.org/using-the-laws-of-property-to-respond-to-a-federal-or-state-tax-collection-notice/

Below are some additional resources that may prove useful for those who want to remove SSNs from government records and liberate themselves from the position of compelled "Trustee":

1. *Social Security Number (SSN), Sovereignty Forms and Instructions Online*, Form #10.004, Cites by Topic- defined
   http://famguardian.org/TaxFreedom/CitesByTopic/SSN.htm
2. *Taxpayer Identification Number (TIN)*- defined
   http://famguardian.org/TaxFreedom/CitesByTopic/TIN.htm
3. *Don't Give Your Children Social Security Numbers*, Sovereignty Forms and Instructions Online, Form #10.004, Instructions, Step 1.1
   http://famguardian.org/TaxFreedom/Instructions/1.1NoSSNChildren.htm
4. *Quit Social Security and Rescind your Social Security Number* - Sovereignty Forms and Instructions Online, Form #10.004, step 3.17.
   http://famguardian.org/TaxFreedom/Instructions/3.17QuitSocialSecurity.htm
5. *State DMV Change of Address letter*
   http://famguardian.org/TaxFreedom/Forms/Emancipation/ChangeOfAddressAttachment.htm
6. *Attachment to Government form which asks for Social Security Number*, Family Guardian Fellowship
   http://famguardian.org/TaxFreedom/Forms/Emancipation/GovtApplAttachment.htm
7. *Getting a USA Passport as a "state national"*, Form #09.007
   http://sedm.org/compliant-member-only-forms/getting-a-usa-passport-as-a-state-national-form-09-007/
8. *Social Security Form SS-521: Request for Withdrawal of Application*
   http://famguardian.org/TaxFreedom/Forms/Emancipation/ssa_521.pdf
9. *Change Your Filing Status to "nonresident alien" and "Denumber" yourself*, -*Sovereignty Forms and Instructions Online, step* 3.14
   http://famguardian.org/TaxFreedom/Instructions/3.14ChangeFilingStatus.htm
10. *IRS Form 4029: Application for Exemption from Social Security Taxes and Waiver of Benefits*
    http://famguardian.org/TaxFreedom/Forms/IRS/IRSForm4029.pdf
11. *IRS Form W-9: Application for NONTAXPAYER identification number*
    http://sedm.org/Forms/04-Tax/1-Procedure/AboutSSNs/IRSFormW9-Amended.pdf
12. *Your Rights Regarding Social Security Numbers*, Family Guardian Fellowship - Family Guardian
    http://famguardian.org/Subjects/Taxes/ChallJurisdiction/YourRightsAndSSNs.htm
13. *Secrets of the Social Security Number*- Buildfreedom
    http://www.buildfreedom.com/tl/tl17b.shtml
14. *Social Security Numbers for Children?*, Social Security Administration- SSA Website. NO! you don't have to have one!
    http://www.ssa.gov/pubs/10023.html
15. *Opening Bank Accounts Without SSNs*, Antishyster Magazine- Antishyster Magazine

> http://famguardian.org/PublishedAuthors/Media/Antishyster/V07N2-OpeningBankAcctsWithoutSSNs.pdf
16. *Working without an SSN*, Antishyster News Magazine-Antishyster Magazine
   http://famguardian.org/PublishedAuthors/Media/Antishyster/V07N2-WorkingWithoutSSNs.pdf
17. *Letter about Social Security Numbers*, Social Security Administration-by Social Security Administration
   http://famguardian.org/Subjects/Taxes/Evidence/ss3-98.pdf

19 Quitting Social Security and living without SSNs or TINs

For detailed procedures on how to quit Social Security and how to live without a Social Security Number, please refer to the following resource:

1. *Resignation of Compelled Social Security Trustee*, Form #06.002- allows you to quit social security
   http://sedm.org/Forms/FormIndex.htm
2. *Why You Aren't Eligible for Social Security*, Form #06.001-Use this form to apply for a driver's license without a Slave Surveillance Number. Most states require applicants who are eligible for Social Security to provide a number. This pamphlet proves you aren't eligible and therefore don't need one. See:
   http://sedm.org/Forms/FormIndex.htm
3. *Social Security Policy Manual*, Form #06.013-describes how to live without a Socialist INsecurity Numbers.

20 Changing the status of the SSN from U.S. person to Foreign Person

26 C.F.R. §301.6109-1(g)(1)(i) establishes the authority to make a change to the status of an SSN from that held by a domestic statutory "U.S. person" to that of a "foreign person":

> *26 CFR § 301.6109-1 - Identifying numbers.*
>
> *(g) Special rules for taxpayer identifying numbers issued to foreign persons—*
>
> *(1) General rule—*
>
> *(i) Social security number.*
>
> *A social security number is generally identified in the records and database of the Internal Revenue Service as a number belonging to a U.S. citizen or resident alien individual.* **_A person may establish a different status for the number by providing proof of foreign status with the Internal Revenue Service under such procedures as the Internal Revenue Service shall prescribe, including the use of a form as the Internal Revenue Service may specify. Upon accepting an individual as a nonresident alien individual, the Internal Revenue Service will assign this status to the individual's social security number._**
>
> *(ii) Employer identification number.*
>
> *An employer identification number is generally identified in the records and database of the Internal Revenue Service as a number belonging to a U.S. person. However, the Internal Revenue Service may establish a separate class of employer identification numbers solely dedicated to foreign persons which will be identified as such in the records and database of the Internal Revenue Service. A person may establish a different status for the number either at the time of application or subsequently by providing proof of U.S. or foreign status with the Internal Revenue Service under such procedures as the Internal Revenue Service shall prescribe, including the use of a form as the Internal Revenue Service may specify. The Internal Revenue Service may require a person to apply for the type of employer identification number that reflects the status of that person as a U.S. or foreign person.*

We have found no IRS publication that identifies EXACTLY what would satisfy the requirement for "proof" mentioned above. The IRS Form W-8BEN, like the IRS Form 8832 for accomplishing the change in an EIN, would seem to be one method. However, the IRS Form W-8BEN says on the form NOT to send it the Internal Revenue Service.

Figure 2: FOIA for form to change SSN

If you read the regulation it becomes quite clear that the way to change an SSN to foreign status is through the use of a 1040-NR form. An SSN is only used in regard to an individual. An individual using an SSN is either a nonresident alien or a United States person (citizen or resident of the United States). The term "individual" for withholding purposes is consistently defined in 26 U.S.C. §1.1441-1(c)(3) as an ALIEN and not a national.

As the regulation states that an SSN is generally presumed to belong to a statutory "U.S. person" (whatever that means, but for the sake of this exercise we will presuppose they mean United States person, even though that's not unambiguously manifest), and 26 C.F.R. §1.6012-1(a)(6) regulation states that a 1040 is the prescribed form for such person, it seems reasonable to conclude that since that same regulation set states that a 1040-NR is the prescribed form for the nonresident alien individual that this can translate to "foreign person" as used in the 26 C.F.R. §301.6109-1 regulation.

> 26 CFR § 1.6012-1 - Individuals required to make returns of income.
>
> § 1.6012-1 **Individuals** required to make **returns** of **income**.
>
> *(b)* Return of nonresident alien individual—
>
> *(1)* Requirement of return—
>
> *(i)* In general.
>
> *Except as otherwise provided in subparagraph (2) of this paragraph, every nonresident alien individual (other than one treated as a resident under section 6013(g) or (h)) who is engaged in trade or business in the United States at any time during the taxable year or who has income which is subject to taxation under subtitle A of the Code shall make a return on Form 1040NR. For this purpose it is immaterial that the gross income for the taxable year is less than the minimum amount specified in section 6012(a) for making a return. Thus, a nonresident alien individual who is engaged in a trade or business in the United States at any time during the taxable year is required to file a return on Form 1040 NR even though (a) he has no income which is effectively connected with the conduct of a trade or business in the United States, (b) he has no income from sources within the United States, or (c) his income is exempt from income tax by reason of an income tax convention or any section of the Code. However, if the nonresident alien individual has no gross income for the taxable year, he is not required to complete the return schedules but must attach a statement to the return indicating the nature of any exclusions claimed and the amount of such exclusions to the extent such amounts are readily determinable.*

Furthermore, the "change in foreign status" paragraph of the 26 C.F.R. §301.6109-1(g)(2) regulation states that IN THE CASE OF AN IRS INDIVIDUAL TAXPAYER IDENTIFICATION NUMBER, once the IRS accepts a person as a nonresident alien, that the status is PERMANENT....UNTIL the circumstances of the taxpayer change.

> 26 C.F.R. §301.6109-1 - Identifying numbers.
>
> *(g) Special rules for taxpayer identifying numbers issued to foreign persons*
>
> *(1) General rule*
>
> *[. . .]*
>
> *(iii)* IRS individual taxpayer identification number.
>
> *An IRS individual taxpayer identification number is generally identified in the records and database of the Internal Revenue Service as a number belonging to a nonresident alien individual. If the Internal Revenue Service determines at the time of application or subsequently, that an individual is not a nonresident alien individual, the Internal Revenue Service may require that the individual apply for a social security number. If a social security number is not available, the Internal Revenue Service may accept that the individual use an IRS individual taxpayer identification number, which the Internal Revenue Service will identify as a number belonging to a U.S. resident alien.*

(2) Change of foreign status.

Once a taxpayer identifying number is identified in the records and database of the Internal Revenue Service as a number belonging to a U.S. or foreign person, the status of the number is permanent until the circumstances of the taxpayer change. A taxpayer whose status changes (for example, a nonresident alien individual with a social security number becomes a U.S. resident alien) must notify the Internal Revenue Service of the change of status under such procedures as the Internal Revenue Service shall prescribe, including the use of a form as the Internal Revenue Service may specify.

(3) Waiver of prohibition to disclose taxpayer information when acceptance agent acts.

As part of its request for an IRS individual taxpayer identification number or submission of proof of foreign status with respect to any taxpayer identifying number, where the foreign person acts through an acceptance agent, the foreign person will agree to waive the limitations in section 6103 regarding the disclosure of certain taxpayer information. However, the waiver will apply only for purposes of permitting the Internal Revenue Service and the acceptance agent to communicate with each other regarding matters related to the assignment of a taxpayer identifying number, including disclosure of any taxpayer identifying number previously issued to the foreign person, and change of foreign status. This paragraph (g)(3) applies to payments made after December 31, 2001.

Unfortunately, the IRS ITIN mentioned above is NOT the same as a Social Security Number and many people mistake them as equivalent. They often mistake it because they don't want to admit that they aren't eligible for Social Security!:

26 C.F.R. §301.6109-1 - Identifying numbers.

(d) Obtaining a taxpayer identifying number

(3) IRS individual taxpayer identification number—

(i) Definition.

The term IRS individual taxpayer identification number means a taxpayer identifying number issued to an alien individual by the Internal Revenue Service, upon application, for use in connection with filing requirements under this title. **The term IRS individual taxpayer identification number does not refer to a social security number or an account number for use in employment for wages.** *For purposes of this section, the term alien individual means an individual who is not a citizen or national of the United States.*

IRS ITINS are issued ONLY to "alien individuals", while statutory SSNs are issued only to statutory U.S. citizens of "alien individuals" permitted to work. Those born within the exclusive jurisdiction of a constitutional state, who we call "nationals" in 8 U.S.C. §1101(a)(21) and "state nationals", are INELIGIBLE for EITHER an SSN or an IRS ITIN.

20 C.F.R. §422.104 - Who can be assigned a social security number.

§ 422.104 Who can be assigned a social security number.

(a) Persons eligible for SSN assignment.

We can assign you a social security number if you meet the evidence requirements in § 422.107 and you are:

(1) A United States citizen; or

(2) An alien lawfully admitted to the United States for permanent residence or under other authority of law permitting you to work in the United States (§ 422.105 describes how we determine if a nonimmigrant alien is permitted to work in the United States); or

(3) An alien who cannot provide evidence of alien status showing lawful admission to the U.S., or an alien with evidence of lawful admission but without authority to work in the U.S., if the evidence described in § 422.107(e) does not exist, but only for a valid nonwork reason. We consider you to have a valid nonwork reason if:

(i) You need a social security number to satisfy a Federal statute or regulation that requires you to have a social security number in order to receive a Federally-funded benefit to which you have otherwise established entitlement and you reside either in or outside the U.S.; or

> *(ii) You need a social security number to satisfy a State or local law that requires you to have a social security number in order to receive public assistance benefits to which you have otherwise established entitlement, and you are legally in the United States.*

The use of the word "you" above is what is called a "Barnum statement". It is designed to deceive the reader into thinking that they have jurisdiction over them, rather than only over the people referred to in Title 20 of the Code of Federal Regulations, which is only government statutory "employees". Be applying for or using a STATUTORY SSN, you are essentially consenting to be treated AS IF you are such a statutory government "employee". THIS, in fact, is why the word "INTERNAL" is used in the phrase "INTERNAL Revenue Service": That organization only functions and enforces against those INTERNAL to the United States government, usually because they mistakenly misrepresented themselves as PUBLIC OFFICERS called civil statutory "taxpayers", "citizens", "residents", "persons", etc. as we prove in:

1. *The "Trade or Business" Scam*, Form #05.001
   https://sedm.org/Forms/05-MemLaw/TradeOrBusScam.pdf
2. *Why Your Government is Either a Thief or You are a "Public Officer" for Income Tax Purposes*, Form #05.008
   https://sedm.org/Forms/05-MemLaw/WhyThiefOrPubOfficer.pdf

The "United States" they are referring above to are the federal zone and the "State" mentioned above is that found in 4 U.S.C. §110(d) and 42 U.S.C. §1301(a). An American who is born in the COUNTRY "United States*" within the exclusive jurisdiction of a constitutional state does NOT appear in the list above and is therefore INELIGIBLE to participate in Social Security, as we prove in:

> *Why You Aren't Eligible for Social Security*, Form #06.001
> https://sedm.org/Forms/06-AvoidingFranch/SSNotEligible.pdf

Consequently, the ONLY lawful way to approach the providing of what the 1040NR form itself identifies as an "Identifying Number" and NOT a "Social Security Number" is to provide a SUBSTITUTE number as we describe later in section 21. Our *1040-NR Attachment, Form* #09.077 and all filing procedures used on this site take this approach, by the way.

We know that tax matters are year to year matters. Therefore, permanent in the context of ONLY the IRS ITIN and NOT the SSN can at best mean permanent within a taxable year. Permanent is defined in 8 U.S.C. §1101, and though not directly applicable to 26 U.S.C., it gives some context as to potential mindset and intent.

> *8 U.S. Code § 1101 - Definitions*
>
> *(a) As used in this chapter—*
>
> > *(31) The term "permanent" means a relationship of continuing or lasting nature, as distinguished from temporary, but a relationship may be permanent even though it is one that may be dissolved eventually at the instance either of the United States or of the individual, in accordance with law.*

Permanent means "of a lasting nature...but which may be changed by x,y,z." Therefore it does not mean FOR-EVERRRRRRR (https://www.youtube.com/watch?v=Fdnz-T5cWyQ) in the sense that most people colloquially use the term to connote eternal.

Those circumstances can certainly change with the roll-over of the tax year, when IRS rolls out the skeleton for the new master file for the taxpayer. This usually coincides with what we have observed with some form of information return being posted against the person's number.

For example, if we have an SSN, the IRS presumes it belongs to a statutory "U.S. person". If one has filed a 1040 for decades, that's reasonable. If they file in 2020 using a 1040-NR, and the IRS accepts the return, that status will permanently be assigned to the SSN until circumstances change (as previously mentioned).

This can be observed by the reviewing the IRS online account return transcript at ID.ME. For example, 2019 a wife filed a joint return with her husband on a 1040, and the transcript reflects a 1040 as the form. In 2020, before filing a 1040-NR, wife's transcript showed the default 1040 (as the presumed to be filed form). The wife then filed a Married Filing Single 1040-NR for 2020 and as a result her return transcript for 2020 now shows form as 1040-NR. For 2021, neither wife nor husband have filed so both show presumptive form to be filed as 1040. Wife's "circumstances have changed" and the default status was reverted to.

We think this is as close of an answer as you will find, as we know people who have done FOIA and other info requests and gotten diddly to confirm. For instance. See the following, for instance:

Figure 3: 26 C.F.R. §301.6109-1(g) FOIA

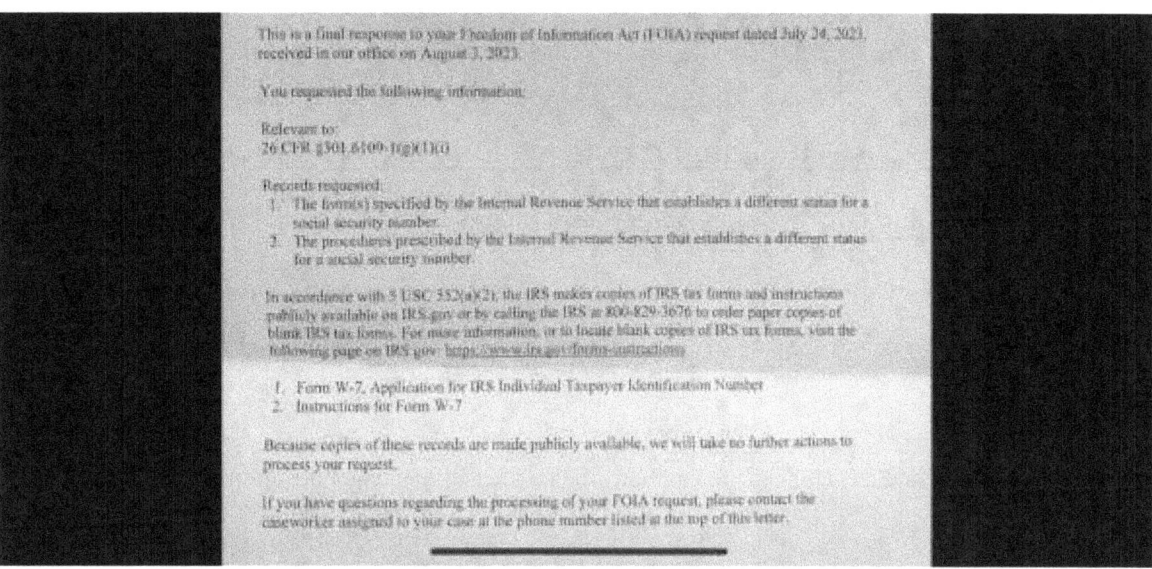

With all the foregoing discussion we summarize here for the benefit of the reader:

1. Social Security numbers may NOT be lawfully assigned to those born within and domiciled with the exclusive jurisdiction of a constitutional state. See 20 C.F.R. §422.104(a) and the following:
   > Why You Aren't Eligible for Social Security, Form #06.001
   > https://sedm.org/Forms/06-AvoidingFranch/SSNotEligible.pdf
2. Social Security Numbers are prima facie evidence that you work INTERNAL to the United States government, because they are issued under the authority of 20 C.F.R. entitled "EMPLOYEES Benefits". Hence the phrase "INTERNAL Revenue Service".
3. By applying for or using a STATUTORY "Social Security Number", you are unknowingly volunteering to be treated AS IF you are statutory public officer of the national government whose earnings are statutory "wages" who is serving within a federal territory as indicated by 42 U.S.C. §1301(a)(1). See:
   > *Why Your Government is Either a Thief or You are a "Public Officer" for Income Tax Purposes*, Form #05.008
   > https://sedm.org/Forms/05-MemLaw/WhyThiefOrPubOfficer.pdf
4. IRS Individual Taxpayer Identification Numbers (ITINS), per 26 C.F.R. §301.6109-1(d)(3)(i).
   4.1. May only be issued to "alien individuals" and NEVER those born in the COUNTRY "United States*".
   4.2. May NOT be used in connection with "employment" for statutory "wages".
5. There is no form or procedure prescribed by the IRS that you can send them that explicitly allows the status of the SSN to change from statutory "U.S. person" to "foreign person".
   5.1. The IRS Form W-8BEN comes closest but it says at the top NOT to send to the IRS.
   5.2. Filing Form 1040NR in the case of ALIEN INDIVIDUALS ONLY changes the status of an ITIN, but SSNs are not ITINS per 26 C.F.R. §301.6109-1(d)(3)(i). This procedure does NOT work for "nationals" or "state nationals", however.
6. There is therefore NO STATUTORY identifying number you can lawfully use in connection with:
   6.1. A tax filing if you are a State National born within and domiciled within the exclusive jurisdiction of a Constitutional state.
   6.2. IRS correspondence of any kind.
7. If you want to provide an identifying number in connection with a tax filing or IRS correspondence, we recommend defining it as a NONSTATUTORY PRIVATE number that is a license to the government regulating and preventing its commercial use by the government. See section 21 later.

8. The following form on our site is mandatory for members using our "tax information or services" and must be sent in to surrender the STATUTORY public SSN, so that it may be used for the PRIVATE purposes described later in section 21. If that surrender is never rendered, the presumption that you are eligible for Social Security and acting as a statutory public "Employee" is not rebutted and you are putting yourself in harm's way by doing so.
9. Those intent on ARGUING with or IGNORING the facts in this section usually have the undisclosed private commercial motive to:
   9.1. Preserve their ILLEGAL eligibility for Social Security.
   9.2. Use the SSN or ITIN they are NOT eligible for to effect personal benefit of some kind.
   9.3. Often try to incorrectly apply the rules for ITINs to SSNs as far as changing the status of the "taxpayer".
   DON'T LISTEN TO THEM!

21 How to use "substitute numbers" to avoid being privileged

21.1 DOD ID Numbers for Military Members

DOD ID Numbers can be used as a substitute for Social Security Numbers. They can be used in the following circumstances:

10. When submitting VA Form 10, Application for Health Benefits.
11. When submitting DD Form 108, Application for Retired Pay and Benefits to the department you served in.

The social security number (SSN) has been used throughout the Department of Defense (DoD) as a means to identify and authenticate individuals and its expanded use has increased efficiency, enabling DoD information systems and processes to interoperate and transfer information with a greatly reduced chance of errors. However, the threat of identity theft has rendered this widespread use unacceptable, resulting in the requirement that all Federal agencies evaluate how the SSN is used to eliminate its unnecessary use where possible.

One effort initiated to reduce the use of the SSN is to replace it with the number known as the Electronic Data Interchange-Personal Identifier (EDI-PI) that has been a unique identifier for personnel affiliated with the DoD for many years. Until recently, it was used only by DoD information systems to facilitate machine-to-machine communications and appeared in digital signatures. When the EDI-PI was selected to become the DoD identification number (DoD ID Number), the purpose of the identifier changed.

The expanded use of the DoD ID Number has led to questions regarding its status as personally identifiable information (PII). PII refers to information that can be used to distinguish or trace an individual's identity. The DoD ID Number falls into this category because it is a unique personal identifier and can be used to retrieve records about an individual.

The DoD ID Number is now intended to be known by the individual to whom it belongs, and is printed on DoD identification cards. It is to be used for individual access to systems, on forms, in digital signatures and for other uses typical of physical and technical identification processes.

DOD ID Numbers were introduced to reduce the use of Social Security Numbers to prevent identity theft. They are used for DOD business purposes and may include transactions with entities outside the DOD, so long as individuals are acting on behalf of or in support of the DOD. The DoD ID Number may not be shared with other Federal agencies unless a Memorandum of Understanding (MOU) is agreed upon by both the DoD and the recipient agency. MOUs for sharing the DoD ID Number are managed and administered for the Under Secretary of Defense for Personnel and Readiness (USD(P&R)) by the Defense Manpower Data Center (DMDC). As of the writing of this memorandum, they are mainly used in connection with ID cards. Social Security Numbers have been removed from DOD ID cards throughout the military.

Presence or knowledge of an individual's DoD ID Number alone shall be considered as no more significant than presence or knowledge of that individual's name. The DoD ID Number does not constitute any level of authority to act on that individual's behalf.

The DoD ID Number, by itself or with an associated name, shall be considered internal government operations-related PII. Since the loss, theft or compromise of the DoD ID Number has a low risk for possible identity theft or fraud, a PII breach report will not be initiated unless the breach is associated with other PII elements, such as date of birth, birthplace or mother's maiden name, which would normally require a report to be submitted. As detailed in DoDI 1000.30, "Reduction of Social Security Number (SSN) Use Within DoD", exposure of the DoD ID Number shall not be considered a breach when exposed as a part of a DoD business function.

Information referencing the implementation of DOD ID numbers and privacy generally within the DOD can be found in:

1. Defense Privacy, Civil Liberties, and Transparency Division: Privacy
   https://dpcld.defense.gov/Privacy/About-the-Office/FAQs/
2. DOD Instruction 1000.30
   https://www.esd.whs.mil/Portals/54/Documents/DD/issuances/dodi/100030p.pdf
3. DOD Directive 5124.02
   https://www.esd.whs.mil/Portals/54/Documents/DD/issuances/dodd/512402p.pdf

Those wishing to avoid use of SSNs when dealing with the Department of Defense should consider the following documents on our website to apply for benefits:

1. Veterans Administration Benefit Application, Form #06.041
   https://sedm.org/Forms/FormIndex.htm
2. DOD Retirement Pay Request Letter, Form #04.227
   https://sedm.org/Forms/FormIndex.htm

Example language to put at the end of the Form 10 VA Application for Benefits is provided below:

> *NOTES:*
>
> *1. All terms used on this form OTHER than "Social Security Number" shall be construed in their statutory sense. This is especially true in the case of money or finance. They are not used in their private, ordinary, or common law sense. The term "Social Security Number" identifies a PRIVATE number owned and issued by the Submitter to the government under license and franchise. It is not a number identified in any governments statute and does not pertain to anyone eligible to receive Social Security Benefits and may not be used to indicate or imply eligibility to receive said benefits. The license for the use of the number for use outside of the VA for any purpose, and especially civil or criminal enforcement purpose, is identified below and incorporated by reference herein. Acceptance or use of said number for such purpose constitutes constructive or implied consent to said agreement by all those so using said number:*
>
> *Injury Defense Franchise and Agreement, Form #06.027; https://sedm.org/Forms/06-AvoidingFranch/InjuryDefenseFranchise.pdf.*
>
> *This provision is repeated in Section 0 in the attached form entitled Why It is Illegal for Me to Request or Use a Taxpayer Identification Number, Form #04.205. The reason for this provision is that everyone who asks for such number refers to them as "MINE" or "MY" or "YOUR", meaning that it is MY absolutely owned PRIVATE property. Therefore I am simply documenting the fact that it is my absolutely owned private property as a private human not affiliated with the government. All private property can be used as a basis to place conditions on its use or else it isn't mine. That's what "ownership" implies in a legal sense. Congress does the same thing with ITS property under Article 4, Section 3, Clause 2, and I am simply carrying out exactly the authority THEY claim over THEIR property in the same manner as them.*
>
> *2. All correspondence relating to this submission should be conducted electronically using the email address provided. Government sourced correspondence must include the work address and full name and signature of the sender in scanned PDF form. No printed correspondence sent via postal mail will be accepted. Submitter hereby waives HIPAA privacy protections for the purpose of correspondence with the Veterans Administration about eligibility for VA health benefit.*
>
> *3. The content of this form is rendered false, fraudulent, and perjurious if it is not accompanied by the following attachment and all forms incorporated by reference, and ESPECIALLY if this form is used as legal evidence in a court proceeding:*
>
> *Why It is Illegal for Me to Request or Use a Taxpayer Identification Number, Form #04.205; https://sedm.org/Forms/04-Tax/2-Withholding/WhyTINIllegal.pdf.*
>
> *4. The information disclosed on this form is provided ONLY for the INTERNAL use of the Veterans Administration. Any disclosure to any agency, person, or government outside of the VA shall constitute a HIPAA*

violation and a commercial use subject to the terms of the following document incorporated herein by reference: Privacy Agreement, Form #06.014; http://sedm.org/Forms/06-AvoidingFranch/PrivacyAgreement.pdf.

5. Submitter declares under penalty of perjury that supplying anything identified as a "Social Security Number" on this form is a product of illegal duress and criminal activity. I was told by the acceptance agent that they could not and would not process the application without such a number, and therefore the presence of any such number on this form is a product of illegal duress and is legal evidence of the following crimes if it is INTERPRETED as a statutory number rather than a PRIVATELY issued number that is my property with legal strings attached:

5.1 Illegal compulsion to use an SSN. 42 U.S.C. §408(a)(8).

5.2 Identity theft under 18 U.S.C. §912. See: Government Identity Theft, Form #05.046; https://sedm.org/Forms/05-MemLaw/GovernmentIdentityTheft.pdf.

5.3 Involuntary Servitude in violation of the Thirteenth Amendment and peonage under 18 U.S.C. §1581 and slavery under 18 U.S.C. §1583.

5.3 Extortion by officers or employees of the United States, 18 U.S.C. §872.

5.4 Acceptance or solicitation to obtain appointive public office 18 U.S.C. §211. The "benefits" are a bribe to entice me to misrepresent my status as an officer of the United States. Only said officers can lawfully use or possess public property, and a STATUTORY Social Security Number is public property as identified in 20 C.F.R. §422.103(d).

This submission shall therefore constitute a formal criminal complaint IN ADVANCE in the event that the term "Social Security Number" is INTERPRETED by the Recipient or anyone working in any government as a STATUTORY number or is used for any commercial or civil or criminal enforcement use or advantage by any government. It shall also constitute an implied agreement and stipulation by the recipient to TREAT it as satisfying all the above criteria and everything on this form as truthful and accurate. Any attempt to refuse to report or prosecute said crime is stipulated by the Submitter and the Recipient to be misprision of felony in violation of 18 U.S.C. §4 and accessory after the fact in violation of 18 U.S.C. §3.

21.2 Using all zeros

Yet another approach to avoid using the "government's" numbers is to either use all zeros. The following Social Security publication indicates on pages 16 and 29 that if the subject of the W-2 report does not have an SSN, then the number "000-00-0000" can be used:

Social Security Publication 42-007: Specifications for Filing Forms W-2 Electronically
http://sedm.org/Forms/04-Tax/0-CorrErrInfoRtns/FormW2/R07efw2.pdf

21.3 Defining "Social Security Number" with your own definition

Another useful approach is to use the same number as they use, but to give it a new name so that they can't use it as an SSN or TIN and can only use it as an account number. This prevents them from being able to presume that you are a "taxpayer" or that the number is THEIR number. The following authorities support this approach.

1. 26 C.F.R. §301.6109-1(g)(1)(i) authorizes anyone to send a request to the IRS and the Social Security Administration which allows the status of THEIR number to be changed into the equivalent of a "Nontaxpayer Identification Number" or "NIN" for short that belongs to a nonresident alien not engaged in a "trade or business".

    "...A person may establish a different status for the number by providing proof of foreign status with the Internal Revenue Service...Upon accepting an individual as a nonresident alien individual, the Internal Revenue Service will assign this status to the individual's social security number...
    [26 C.F.R. §301.6109-1(g)(1)(i)]

2. We have found no IRS publication that identifies EXACTLY what would satisfy the requirement for "proof" mentioned above, but we believe that either of the following two forms would suffice:
    2.1. *IRS Form W-8BEN*, Form #04.202
        http://sedm.org/Forms/FormIndex.htm
    2.2. *Affidavit of Citizenship, Domicile, and Tax Status*, Form #02.001

http://sedm.org/Forms/FormIndex.htm

3. Every correspondence you send the IRS should include proof of your "foreign status" such as that in the previous step, and a brief explanation of any numbers included in the correspondence. By "Foreign status", they mean that you are a "nonresident alien" as defined in 26 U.S.C. §7701(b)(1)(B) with no "trade or business" earnings, and all of whose estate is a "foreign estate" as defined in 26 U.S.C. §7701(a)(31). The correspondence should say that the number, if it is included:
    3.1. Is NOT "Social Security Number" or "Taxpayer Identification Number".
    3.2. Is a PRIVATELY ISSUED number called a "Nontaxpayer Identification Number" whose use is privileged, copyrighted, and licensed. That number happens to match the same number in IRS systems but is NOT an SSN or TIN.
    3.3. Belongs to a "nonresident alien" not engaged in a "trade or business" as defined in 26 C.F.R. §1.871-1(b)(i).

The ONLY occasion where we would take the above approach of inventing our own number is ONLY if we are sending in corrected information returns. We would not use it in any correspondence or tax returns we send to the IRS because they are handled by individual people, whereas the Information Returns are processed and scanned by computer, and the computers won't automatically fix the erroneous information returns unless they can do numeric matching. This approach of using a SUBSTITUTE NIN would be used, for instance, in submitting any of the following Forms:

1. *Correcting Erroneous Information Returns*, Form #04.001
   http://sedm.org/Forms/FormIndex.htm
2. *Corrected Information Return Attachment Letter*, Form #04.002
   http://sedm.org/Forms/FormIndex.htm
3. *Correcting Erroneous IRS Form 1042's*, Form #04.003
   http://sedm.org/Forms/FormIndex.htm
4. *Correcting Erroneous IRS Form 1098's*, Form #04.004
   http://sedm.org/Forms/FormIndex.htm
5. *Correcting Erroneous IRS Form 1099's*, Form #04.005
   http://sedm.org/Forms/FormIndex.htm
6. *Correcting Erroneous IRS Form W-2's*, Form #04.006
   http://sedm.org/Forms/FormIndex.htm

21.4 Useful forms

One form useful in removing the false presumption that you are a Social Security franchise participant who has a Social Security Number is the following form, which the SEDM Member Agreement, Form #01.001 mandates that all members must attach to every standard government form they submit that has not been amended to remove false and prejudicial presumptions about their status:

| *Tax Form Attachment*, Form #04.201 |
| http://sedm.org/Forms/FormIndex.htm |

Other than in the above specific circumstances, we suggest ALWAYS doing the following when either responding to federal or state collection correspondence or sending in a tax return:

1. Making a copy of the original notice you receive on the collection correspondence.
2. Blacking out any identifying numbers in thick black felt tip pen and writing next to it "WRONG!"
3. Not putting any identifying number in your responsive correspondence but instead emphasizing that you "have" no number and cannot lawfully possess "public property" such as federal identifying numbers as a "private person". 20 C.F.R. §422.103(d) says that the number and the card are the property of the Social Security Administration and NOT you. Therefore, it constitutes theft and embezzlement, and abuse of public property to use it as a "private person" who is NOT a "public officer" and who refuses to act as one.
4. Demand that the government IMMEDIATELY destroy ALL records about you, and especially information returns and identifying numbers. This is a requirement of the Privacy Act, 5 U.S.C. §552a(b), which says that the government *cannot* disclose or maintain any records about you without your consent. Tell them they DON'T have your consent and therefore MUST destroy and redact all records about you. If they violate this request, they are also violating your Fourth Amendment right to privacy, which it was the purpose of the Privacy Act to protect in the first place.

5. Include our Wrong Party Notice that contains a Copyright License Notice with each correspondence to put them into a "privileged" state if they use anything you give them similar to the below. This will cause them to have to pay a penalty every time they make demands on your time in responding without addressing any of the legal issues you raise:

> *Wrong Party Notice*, Form #07.105
> http://sedm.org/Forms/FormIndex.htm

22 Banking and Financial Industry Policy and Guidance on Use of SSN's and TINs

The banking industry maintains a website called "Bankers Online". On their website, they feature a pamphlet for use by bank personnel regarding the use of TINs by customers who do not wish to have or use them. Below are links to this important document:

- Other copy: http://sedm.org/Forms/04-Tax/1-Procedure/AboutSSNs/constructivenotice.pdf

If a bank pressures or compels you to provide a TIN when you want to open an account, you should ask them for the regulation that authorizes them to compel use of such a number. Chances are, they will cite 31 C.F.R. §1020.220, which says in pertinent part:

> Title 31: Money and Finance: Treasury
> Subpart B—Regulations Relating to Money and Finance
> Chapter X-Financial Crimes Enforcement Network, Department of the Treasury
> PART 1020 - RULES FOR BANKS (§§ 1020.100 - 1020.670)
> Subpart B - Programs (§§ 1020.200 - 1020.220)
> §1020.220 Customer Identification Programs for banks, savings associations, credit unions, and certain non-Federally regulated banks.
>
> *(a) Customer Identification Program: minimum requirements -*
>
> *(1) In general. A* bank *must implement a written* Customer *Identification Program (CIP) appropriate for its size and type of business that, at a minimum, includes each of the requirements of paragraphs (a)(1) through (5) of this section. If a* bank *is required to have an anti-money laundering compliance program under the regulations implementing* 31 U.S.C. 5318(h), 12 U.S.C. 1818(s), *or* 12 U.S.C. 1786(q)(1), *then the CIP must be a part of the anti-money laundering compliance program. Until such time as credit unions, private banks, and trust companies without a Federal functional regulator are subject to such a program, their CIPs must be approved by their boards of directors.*
>
> *(2) Identity verification procedures. The CIP must include risk-based procedures for verifying the identity of each* customer *to the extent reasonable and practicable. The procedures must enable the* bank *to form a reasonable belief that it knows the true identity of each* customer. *These procedures must be based on the* bank*'s assessment of the relevant risks, including those presented by the various types of* accounts *maintained by the* bank, *the various methods of opening* accounts *provided by the* bank, *the various types of identifying information available, and the* bank*'s size, location, and* customer *base. At a minimum, these procedures must contain the elements described in this paragraph (a)(2).*
>
> *(i) Customer information required -*
>
> *(A) In general. The CIP must contain procedures for opening an* account *that specify the identifying information that will be obtained from each* customer. *Except as permitted by paragraphs (a)(2)(i)(B) and (C) of this section, the* bank *must obtain, at a minimum, the following information from the* customer *prior to opening an account:*
>
> *(1) Name;*
>
> *(2) Date of birth, for an individual;*
>
> *(3) Address, which shall be:*
>
> *(i) For an individual, a residential or business street address;*
>
> *(ii) For an individual who does not have a residential or business street address, an Army Post Office (APO) or Fleet Post Office (FPO) box number, or the residential or business street address of next of kin or of another contact individual; or*

(iii) For a person other than an individual (such as a corporation, partnership, or trust), a principal place of business, local office, or other physical location; and

(4) Identification number, which shall be:

(i) For a U.S. person, a taxpayer identification number; or

(ii) For a non-U.S. person, one or more of the following: A taxpayer identification number; passport number and country of issuance; alien identification card number; or number and country of issuance of any other government-issued document evidencing nationality or residence and bearing a photograph or similar safeguard.

Note to paragraph (A)(2)(I)(A)(4)(ii):

When opening an account for a foreign business or enterprise that does not have an identification number, the bank must request alternative government-issued documentation certifying the existence of the business or enterprise.

(B) Exception for persons applying for a taxpayer identification number. Instead of obtaining a taxpayer identification number from a customer prior to opening the account, the CIP may include procedures for opening an account for a customer that has applied for, but has not received, a taxpayer identification number. In this case, the CIP must include procedures to confirm that the application was filed before the customer opens the account and to obtain the taxpayer identification number within a reasonable period of time after the account is opened.

(C) Credit card accounts. In connection with a customer who opens a credit card account, a bank may obtain the identifying information about a customer required under paragraph (a)(2)(i)(A) by acquiring it from a third-party source prior to extending credit to the customer.

(ii) Customer verification. The CIP must contain procedures for verifying the identity of the customer, using information obtained in accordance with paragraph (a)(2)(i) of this section, within a reasonable time after the account is opened. The procedures must describe when the bank will use documents, non-documentary methods, or a combination of both methods as described in this paragraph (a)(2)(ii).

(A) Verification through documents. For a bank relying on documents, the CIP must contain procedures that set forth the documents that the bank will use. These documents may include:

(1) For an individual, unexpired government-issued identification evidencing nationality or residence and bearing a photograph or similar safeguard, such as a driver's license or passport; and

(2) For a person other than an individual (such as a corporation, partnership, or trust), documents showing the existence of the entity, such as certified articles of incorporation, a government-issued business license, a partnership agreement, or trust instrument.

(B) Verification through non-documentary methods. For a bank relying on non-documentary methods, the CIP must contain procedures that describe the non-documentary methods the bank will use.

(1) These methods may include contacting a customer; independently verifying the customer's identity through the comparison of information provided by the customer with information obtained from a consumer reporting agency, public database, or other source; checking references with other financial institutions; and obtaining a financial statement.

(2) The bank's non-documentary procedures must address situations where an individual is unable to present an unexpired government-issued identification document that bears a photograph or similar safeguard; the bank is not familiar with the documents presented; the account is opened without obtaining documents; the customer opens the account without appearing in person at the bank; and where the bank is otherwise presented with circumstances that increase the risk that the bank will be unable to verify the true identity of a customer through documents.

(C) Additional verification for certain customers. The CIP must address situations where, based on the bank's risk assessment of a new account opened by a customer that is not an individual, the bank will obtain information about individuals with authority or control over such account, including signatories, in order to verify the customer's identity. This verification method applies only when the bank cannot verify the customer's true identity using the verification methods described in paragraphs (a)(2)(ii)(A) and (B) of this section.

(iii) Lack of verification. The CIP must include procedures for responding to circumstances in which the bank cannot form a reasonable belief that it knows the true identity of a customer. These procedures should describe:

(A) When the bank should not open an account;

(B) The terms under which a customer may use an account while the bank attempts to verify the customer's identity;

(C) When the bank should close an account, after attempts to verify a customer's identity have failed; and

(D) When the bank should file a Suspicious Activity Report in accordance with applicable law and regulation.

(3) Recordkeeping. The CIP must include procedures for making and maintaining a record of all information obtained under the procedures implementing paragraph (a) of this section.

(i) Required records. At a minimum, the record must include:

(A) All identifying information about a customer obtained under paragraph (a)(2)(i) of this section;

(B) A description of any document that was relied on under paragraph (a)(2)(ii)(A) of this section noting the type of document, any identification number contained in the document, the place of issuance and, if any, the date of issuance and expiration date;

(C) A description of the methods and the results of any measures undertaken to verify the identity of the customer under paragraph (a)(2)(ii)(B) or (C) of this section; and

(D) A description of the resolution of any substantive discrepancy discovered when verifying the identifying information obtained.

(ii) Retention of records. The bank must retain the information in paragraph (a)(3)(i)(A) of this section for five years after the date the account is closed or, in the case of credit card accounts, five years after the account is closed or becomes dormant. The bank must retain the information in paragraphs (a)(3)(i)(B), (C), and (D) of this section for five years after the record is made.

(4) Comparison with government lists. The CIP must include procedures for determining whether the customer appears on any list of known or suspected terrorists or terrorist organizations issued by any Federal government agency and designated as such by Treasury in consultation with the Federal functional regulators. The procedures must require the bank to make such a determination within a reasonable period of time after the account is opened, or earlier, if required by another Federal law or regulation or Federal directive issued in connection with the applicable list. The procedures must also require the bank to follow all Federal directives issued in connection with such lists.

(5)

(i) Customer notice. The CIP must include procedures for providing bank customers with adequate notice that the bank is requesting information to verify their identities.

(ii) Adequate notice. Notice is adequate if the bank generally describes the identification requirements of this section and provides the notice in a manner reasonably designed to ensure that a customer is able to view the notice, or is otherwise given notice, before opening an account. For example, depending upon the manner in which the account is opened, a bank may post a notice in the lobby or on its Web site, include the notice on its account applications, or use any other form of written or oral notice.

(iii) Sample notice. If appropriate, a bank may use the following sample language to provide notice to its customers:

Important Information About Procedures for Opening a New Account

To help the government fight the funding of terrorism and money laundering activities, Federal law requires all financial institutions to obtain, verify, and record information that identifies each person who opens an account.

What this means for you: When you open an account, *we will ask for your name, address, date of birth, and other information that will allow us to identify you. We may also ask to see your driver's license or other identifying documents.*

(6) Reliance on another financial institution. The CIP may include procedures specifying when a bank *will rely on the performance by another* financial institution *(including an affiliate) of any procedures of the* bank*'s CIP, with respect to any* customer *of the* bank *that is opening, or has opened, an* account *or has established a similar formal banking or business relationship with the other* financial institution *to provide or engage in services, dealings, or other financial transactions, provided that:*

> *(i) Such reliance is reasonable under the circumstances;*
>
> *(ii) The other* financial institution *is subject to a rule implementing* 31 U.S.C. 5318(h) *and is regulated by a Federal functional regulator; and*
>
> *(iii) The other* financial institution *enters into a contract requiring it to certify annually to the* bank *that it has implemented its anti-money laundering program, and that it will perform (or its agent will perform) the specified requirements of the* bank*'s CIP.*

(b) Exemptions. The appropriate Federal functional regulator, with the concurrence of the Secretary, may, by order or regulation, exempt any bank *or type of* account *from the requirements of this section. The Federal functional regulator and the Secretary shall consider whether the exemption is consistent with the purposes of the* Bank Secrecy Act *and with safe and sound banking, and may consider other appropriate factors. The Secretary will make these determinations for any* bank *or type of* account *that is not subject to the authority of a Federal functional regulator.*

(c) Other requirements unaffected. Nothing in this section relieves a bank *of its obligation to comply with any other provision in this chapter, including provisions concerning information that must be obtained, verified, or maintained in connection with any* account *or transaction.*

For the purposes of the above, the following terms are also defined in the regulation above:

> *Title 31: Money and Finance: Treasury*
> Subpart B—Regulations Relating to Money and Finance
> Chapter X-Financial Crimes Enforcement Network, Department of the Treasury
> PART 1020 - RULES FOR BANKS (§§ 1020.100 - 1020.670)
> Subpart A - General Definitions
> §1010.100   General definitions
>
> *When used in this chapter and in forms prescribed under this chapter, where not otherwise distinctly expressed or manifestly incompatible with the intent thereof, terms shall have the meanings ascribed in this subpart. Terms applicable to a particular type of* financial institution *or specific part* or *subpart of this chapter are located in that part or subpart. Terms may have different meanings in different parts or subparts.*
>
> *(iii) U.S. person.*
>
> *(1) A* United States *citizen; or (2) A* person *other than an individual (such as a corporation, partnership or trust), that is established or organized under the laws of a* State *or the* United States. *Non-U.S.* person *means a* person *that is not a U.S.* person.

A "U.S. person", is defined in 26 U.S.C. §7701(a)(30) as a "citizen", "resident", estate, trust, or federal (domestic) corporation:

> TITLE 26 > Subtitle F > CHAPTER 79 > *Sec. 7701.*
> Sec. 7701. - Definitions
>
> *(a) When used in this title, where not otherwise distinctly expressed or manifestly incompatible with the intent thereof—*
>
> *(30)* United States *person*
>
> *The term "United States person" means -*
> *(A) a* citizen *or* resident *of the United States,*
> *(B) a domestic partnership,*
> *(C) a domestic* corporation,
> *(D) any estate (other than a foreign estate, within the meaning of paragraph (31)), and*
> *(E) any trust if -*

> (i) a court within the United States is able to exercise primary supervision over the administration of the trust, and
> (ii) one or more United States persons have the authority to control all substantial decisions of the trust.

All of the above have in common a domicile within the "United States", which is defined in 26 U.S.C. §7701(a)(9) and (a)(10) as the District of Columbia. See our article below for further details:

> *Why Domicile and Becoming a "Taxpayer" Require Your Consent*, Form #05.002
> http://sedm.org/Forms/FormIndex.htm

Therefore, persons born in and domiciled within states of the Union are STATUTORY "non-resident non-persons" and Constitutional but not Statutory "citizens" pursuant to 8 U.S.C. §1101(a)(21) who are not required to have or to provide a TIN for opening a bank account. See also:

1. *Non-Resident Non-Person Position*, Form #05.020:
   http://sedm.org/Forms/FormIndex.htm
2. *Why You are a Political Citizen but Civil Non-Citizen, National, and Nonresident Alien*, Form #05.006
   http://sedm.org/Forms/FormIndex.htm

23 How to respond to requests for SSNs or TINs

If you do not think that your compensation from federal "employment" or "public office" is sufficient and do not choose to act as a Social Security "Trustee" and federal "employee", and especially not in the context of your private life, then you can follow the instructions in each of the following subsections. In addition to the responses below, you can also use the completed version of the *Resignation of Compelled Social Security Trustee, Form #06.002* form mentioned in the previous section as proof of the illegality of using a Social Security Number.

23.1 Avoiding confrontations in responding to requests for SSN/TIN from business associates

It is important to avoid conflict in your dealings with your business associates in responding to requests for an SSN/TIN. If you fail at this skill, you could find yourself starving to death on the street. The following sections address how to minimize conflicts in responding to such questions.

23.1.1 Legal constraints for requesting an SSN/TIN

1. STATUTORY SSNs/TINs are government property. 20 C.F.R. §422.103(d).
    1.1. It functions as what the Federal Trade Commission (F.T.C.) classifies as a "franchise mark".
    1.2. If they ask you for "YOUR Social Security Number" they effectively are asking: "Are you a public officer on official business, and if so, please present your LICENSE NUMBER to act in such a capacity".
2. Only PUBLIC OFFICERS on official business can use PUBLIC property. A public officer, after all, is legally defined as someone in charge of the PROPERTY of the public.
3. If they ask you for "YOUR Social Security Number" they are advertising to you that the version of it they are asking for is the one you absolutely own and can use to control THEM with.
    3.1. If it is YOUR absolutely owned PRIVATE property, you have a right to deny them the use of it and control EVERY aspect of how they use it and even deny them the ability to use it for reporting purposes.
    3.2. If it is the GOVERNMENT'S property, then it's not YOUR property, but Uncle's property, in which case you CANNOT use or benefit from public property while you are acting in a PRIVATE capacity. That would be theft and conversion.
4. Whether the term "SSN" or "TIN" is PUBLIC or PRIVATE property is determined by who DEFINES what the term means during the process of completing a government form or application.
    4.1. He who writes the RULES or the DEFINITIONS always wins.
    4.2. You as the person filling out the form are the only one who can DEFINE what the terms mean, because you are the only one filling out the form as a witness. It's a crime to threaten or tamper with such a witness.
    4.3. The government CANNOT define the terms on the form, because the courts have repeatedly held that YOU CANNOT TRUST anything the government administratively says or prints or publishes as legal evidence of ANYTHING. See Form #05.007.

4.4. You can ALWAYS win by defining the terms on the form to turn the form from a GOVERNMENT OFFER into a GOVERNMENT ACCEPTANCE OF YOUR OFFER. This is covered in:
> *Path to Freedom*, Form #09.015, Sections 5.5-5.7
> https://sedm.org/Forms/FormIndex.htm

For details on the above, see:
> *Avoiding Traps in Government Forms Course*, Form #12.023
> https://sedm.org/LibertyU/AvoidingTrapsGovForms.pdf

5. It is a crime to compel the use of SSNs in 42 U.S.C. §408(a)(8) for those who BELIEVE they are subject to federal law, which people in the states of the Union are NOT, INCLUDING your business associates.
   5.1. To overcome the burden of proof that it is a crime, your business partner must produce a statute and not regulation mandating the use of the number.
   5.2. If they cannot produce the statute, then they are committing this crime.
6. Those asking for a number therefore have a DUTY and burden of proof to:
   6.1. Produce the statute MANDATING the use of said number for someone with YOUR DECLARED CIVIL STATUS. Not the REGULATION, but the STATUTE. There is no such statute, by the way. It's all in the regulations, which is proof that the mandate only applies within the Department of the Treasury to EMPLOYEES who work for the Secretary of the Treasury. We prove this in Form #08.024.
   6.2. Prove that both YOU and THEY are SUBJECT to the statute they are enforcing.
   If they cannot satisfy this burden of proof, then use cannot be compelled. They cannot claim they have a policy to do so and still violate the law above in doing so. Such a policy is a CRIMINAL act, in fact, if no authority is provided for mandating use.
7. Whether an SSN/TIN is required is determined by the CIVIL STATUS that one claims in their interactions with their business associates:
   7.1. "U.S. Person" (Form W-9): Those claiming STATUTORY "U.S. person" status under 26 U.S.C. §7701(a)(30) are required to use an SSN/TIN. 26 C.F.R. §301.6109-1(a). These fictions are also referred to as "U.S. persons" under 26 C.F.R. §1.1441-1. Because the OBLIGATION to produce a number is found in REGULATIONS and NOT the statute, then the only lawful TARGET of said mandate are employees of the Secretary of the Treasury in the Department of the Treasury. The U.S. Supreme Court has held that regulations may not mandate anything that the statutes they implement do NOT. We explain this in Form #08.024.
   7.2. "Foreign Person" (Form W-8): Those claiming "nonresident alien" status are only required to use an SSN/TIN if they are engaged in a STATUTORY "trade or business"/public office franchise. 26 C.F.R. §301.6109-1(b). These people are referred to as "foreign persons" under 26 C.F.R. §1.1441-1. Because the OBLIGATION to produce a number is found in REGULATIONS and NOT the statute, then the only lawful TARGET of said mandate are employees of the Secretary of the Treasury in the Department of the Treasury. The U.S. Supreme Court has held that regulations may not mandate anything that the statutes they implement do NOT. We explain this in Form #08.024
   7.3. "Employee" (Form W-4): Those claiming this civil status on a Form W-4 effectively VOLUNTEER to be treated AS IF they are a GOVERNMENT EMPLOYEE whose earnings are GOVERNMENT PROPERTY pursuant to 26 U.S.C. §3402(p). NEVER USE THIS FORM!
8. Your business associates may not COMPEL you to claim any specific civil status from the list above, and certainly not as a "withholding agent":
   8.1. Anyone who claims the authority to use civil statutory law indirectly is claiming that you are a government public officer. A "public officer", after all, is anyone who can be the lawful target of government civil enforcement or civil statutory obligations.

> "The term office' has no legal or technical meaning attached to it, distinct from its ordinary acceptations. **An office is a public charge or employment; but, as every employment is not an office, it is sometimes difficult to distinguish between employments which are and those which are not offices…. A public officer is one who has some duty to perform concerning the public; and he is not the less a public officer when his duty is confined to narrow limits, because it is the duty, and the nature of that duty, which makes him a public officer, and not the extent of his authority.' 7 Bac. Abr. 280; Carth. 479…. Where an employment or duty is a continuing [***65] one, which is defined by rules prescribed by law and not by contract, such a charge or employment is an office, and the person who performs it is an officer…. "**
> [Ricker's Petition, 66 N.H. 207 (1890)]

   8.2. In acting as a "withholding agent" or "employer" subject to IRS enforcement, they are an instrumentality of the government and as such, may not violate your First Amendment rights.
   8.3. All they can do is ASK YOU to provide evidence of your status on the appropriate form signed under penalty of perjury.

8.4. They cannot compel you to fill out a specific withholding form. If they do, they again are violating your First Amendment right as a government instrumentality. If they compel or threaten you to change your withholding form or provide a number that your status doesn't require, you need to gather evidence of that so you can prosecute them later.
9. Even the requirement for backup withholding pertaining to "nonresident aliens" pertains to "EMPLOYEES". It is found in 26 U.S.C. §3406 under Internal Revenue Code, Subtitle C, which is "Employment Taxes".
    9.1. See:
        https://www.law.cornell.edu/uscode/text/26/subtitle-C
    9.2. Therefore, "nonresident alien" is a valid EMPLOYMENT status for those who don't want to be STATUTORY "employees" and fill out a Form W-4.
    9.3. The fact that their payroll or accounting software or payroll service bureau does NOT permit "nonresident alien" status is NOT YOUR problem. It's a software problem that you can't be made to suffer for or even be DISCRIMINATED against for.
10. Your business associates, even if they HAVE statutory "EMPLOYEES", who are all public officers of the national government, does not mean that they ALSO cannot function in a PRIVATE capacity for their business dealings.
    10.1. You are a Merchant (U.C.C. §2-104(1)) selling PRIVATE property, which is your labor.
    10.2. Your business associate is the Buyer (U.C.C. §2-103(l)(a)) buying your PRIVATE property on YOUR terms as the owner of the property.
    10.3. It is an interference with your inalienable right to contract and associate for any third party, including the government, to dictate the terms of your PRIVATE business dealings, contracts, and associations with others.
11. Your business associate only acts in a PUBLIC and CIVIL STATUTORY capacity to the extent that they are LAWFULLY acting as a STATUTORY "withholding agent" or "employer" IN RELATION TO YOU.
    11.1. They don't HAVE to act as a STATUTORY "EMPLOYER" in relation to you, and especially if they are merely PROCURING property as they would ANY OTHER VENDOR.
    11.2. If you don't want your business associates to treat you as a STATUTORY "employee", then negotiate a PRIVATE contract with them whereby you invoice them periodically for the sale of unspecified PRIVATE property on a monthly basis. Ensure that the property is not classified as CIVIL STATUTORY "wages". You as the Merchant and ABSOLUTE OWNER of the PRIVATE property (labor) have a right to determine the CIVIL STATUS of the property, and to exclude any and all others from using or benefitting from the use of the property. Otherwise, it isn't yours, in which case you can't be the "taxpayer" either. Ownership and responsibility always go together.
    11.3. If nothing else, the Bible says that the ENTIRE HEAVEN and the EARTH belong to the Lord. Deut. 10:14. Thus, they are RENTING OUT God's property for their beneficial use. You are a trustee over that property under the Bible Delegation of Authority Order, Form #13.007. The Bible is a trust indenture. That property is RELIGIOUS property. It is a CRIME to damage or destroy or convert RELIGIOUS property by making it or its owner or even its controller into the government/Caesar instead of God. 18 U.S.C. §247 and 18 U.S.C. §654. Where is separation of church (Private) and state (Public) when you REALLY need it? More on this subject in Form #12.025.
    11.4. For sample forms you can use to negotiate a contract for the sale of PRIVATE property with a PRIVATE company not acting as a STATUTORY "employer", see:

> *Federal and State Tax Withholding Options for Private Employers*, Form #09.001
> https://sedm.org/Forms/FormIndex.htm

23.1.2 Best strategy

1. It is important to avoid an argument with your business associates, or they may in effect terminate their business relationship. The best method of doing so is the Socratic method, by which you as a series of factual questions of their legal counsel with witnesses present.
2. You should never ask a question that you don't already know the answer to and have researched the answer to in advance. You can use what you know about the CORRECT answer to:
    2.1. Pattern questions that follow their answer.
    2.2. Remind them that they are violating the law as you understand it and ask them to explain why they do not think they are doing so.
3. It is always best for interactions relating to withholding to be IN WRITING signed by both parties. That way there is an evidentiary trail you can use later in court. Your business associate may have a legal department, and you can be sure that the main purpose for their presence in the company is **risk reduction**. They do this by preventing the

production of legal evidence of their own wrongdoing, which is clearly the case if they won't allow you to submit what you know and can prove with evidence is the correct withholding paperwork.
- 3.1. Avoid in-person discussions or phone discussions that don't have witnesses.
- 3.2. If they insist on a meeting, record it and/or bring your own witnesses.

23.1.3 Socratic questions in response to the request for "the number"

1. What do you intend to use the number for?
2. What specific statute obligates me to provide the specific type of number you are requesting? If there is no statute, do you realize that it is a crime to compel the use of Social Security Numbers?
3. What makes you think that a regulation can impose an obligation if the statute it implements DOES NOT?
4. Are you conditioning your willingness to do business with me upon me providing such a number?
5. Do you intend to do any of the following if I don't provide you with a number? (signs of illegal duress):
   - 5.1. Not hire me?
   - 5.2. Fire me?
   - 5.3. Terminate our business relationship?
   - 5.4. Not promote me?
   - 5.5. Discipline or punish me if I already work with you?
   - 5.6. Terminate or not commence our business relationship?
6. Will you accept a properly submitted Form W-8 identifying me as a "foreign person" NOT SUBJECT to withholding or reporting and exempt from the requirement to furnish an identifying number?
   - 6.1. If not, upon what legal authority do you rely in doing so?
   - 6.2. If not, if there is no legal authority, do you realize that you are compelling me to commit perjury on withholding forms by either submitting a form I know doesn't pertain to me or filling out one that does pertain to me but is not completed truthfully or accurately with the law as I understand it?
7. Is there anything you find incorrect in the Form W-8 withholding paperwork that I submitted to you? Please be as specific as possible.
8. Do you know that the term "nonresident alien" isn't defined in the Internal Revenue Code? The I.R.C. says what it ISN'T and not what it is. 26 U.S.C. §7701(b)(1)(B).
9. What makes you think that I am THE STATUTORY "citizen" upon whom the tax is imposed in 26 C.F.R. §1.1-1(c)?
   - 9.1. Do you think this "citizen" includes people in a constitutional state?
   - 9.2. If so, what proof do you have?
10. Do you realize that:
    - 10.1. The civil status of "citizen", or ANY civil status including "person" is voluntary?
    - 10.2. I don't have to volunteer?
    - 10.3. If you compel me to assume the obligations of the status, you are engaging in slavery and human trafficking in violation of the Thirteenth Amendment?
11. Would you be willing to contract with me to deliver property on a regular basis and treat me as a supplier of religious property covered by a Form W-8.
12. What makes you think that the ONLY way you can interact with me is as a statutory "employer" who works for the government? A statutory "employer" is defined as someone with statutory "employees" in 26 U.S.C. §3402(d) and an "employee" in turn is defined as someone who works ONLY for the national government as a public officer. 26 U.S.C. §3401(c), which per the rules of statutory construction excludes private workers selling private labor for hire.

> "...the term [employee] includes officers and employees, *whether elected or appointed*, of the United States, a [federal] State, Territory, Puerto Rico or any political subdivision, thereof, or the District of Columbia, or any agency or instrumentality of any one or more of the foregoing. The term 'employee' also includes an *officer of a corporation*."
> *[26 C.F.R. §31.3401(c)-1 Employee]*

NOTE: I'm not suggesting that IDIOTS cannot volunteer to become uncompensated statutory "employees" of the national government by filling out a Form W-4 and thereby through legal ignorance EXPAND the above definition. I'm not such an IDIOT and for you to coerce me into becoming one is an assault on my dignity and self-ownership as a human being with constitutional rights.

23.2 Dealing with Requests by Withholding Agents for an SSN/TIN to "U.S. Persons" on a W-9

The text after the line below is text you can use in responding to a request by a "withholding agent" for an SSN or TIN in connection with the submission of IRS Form W-9:

_____

I allege that you as a withholding agent have the authority to REQUEST but not to COMPEL the use of an SSN or TIN. The reasons set forth are described herein.

The Privacy Act Notice reveals that in order to be legitimate, all forms must display an Office of Management and Budget (OMB) number placed in the upper right or left corner. Said number must be there because the IRS is required to submit to the OMB all forms which request information, along with the applicable statute and/or regulation that authorizes the collection of the information requested. Forms which do not have an OMB number – such as Form W-9, are deemed by the federal courts as "bootleg" forms, and lack enforcement authority so as to harmonize with the legal requirements for Form 1099 under I.R.C. §6041 and its regulations wherein the legal authority to demand information is limited to name and address only. While some persons are required to request a TIN for a 1099, no legal authority is granted to require or demand that the recipients provide a TIN; Payors are only authorized to request a TIN.

The above information is further confirmed in the Privacy Act Notice within the Form W-9 itself, on page 6. While said Notice could be misread as requiring the recipient to provide a TIN, it actually requires that a correct TIN be provided -- should the recipients wish to do so. Form W-9 does not require providing a number as it would conflict with the very purpose of the Privacy Act:

> *"Privacy Act Notice" (W-9)*
>
> *"Section 6109 of the Internal Revenue Code requires you to provide your correct TIN to persons who must file information returns with the IRS to report interest, dividends, and certain other income paid to you, mortgage interest you paid, the acquisition or abandonment of secured property, cancellation of debt, or contributions you made to an IRA or Archer MSA." ... further citation omitted.*
> *[IRS Form W-9, p. 6]*

Not only does the "Privacy Act Notice" establish that 26 U.S.C. Section 6109 is controlling, but also that its subsection (3) (shown below) is likewise controlling, and re-confirms that the Payor's obligation is NOT to "furnish a number" by demanding it from the recipient, but merely "shall request from such other person, ..., such identifying number as may be prescribed...":

> *"IRC § 6109. Identifying numbers*
>
> *(a)   Supplying of identifying numbers.--When required by regulations prescribed by the Secretary:*
>
> *(1) Inclusion in returns. Any person required under the authority of this title to make a return, statement, or other document shall include in such return, statement, or other document such identifying number as may be prescribed for securing proper identification of such person. ..."*
>
> *(2) Furnishing number to other persons. Any person with respect to whom a return, statement, or other document is required under the authority of this title to be made by another person or whose identifying number is required to be shown on a return of another person shall furnish to such other person such identifying number as may be prescribed for securing his proper identification.*
>
> *(3) Furnishing number of another person.--Any person required under the authority of this title to make a return, statement, or other document with respect to another person shall request from such other person, and shall include in any such return, statement, or other document, such identifying number as may be prescribed for securing proper identification of such other person." ... further citation omitted ...*

Section (3) above authorizes a statutory "withholding agent" to "request... such identifying number as may be prescribed", but implementing regulations are "prescribed" for Section 6109 in 26 C.F.R. §301.6109-1 which are limited to employees of the Treasury Department pursuant to 5 U.S.C. §301, and the 18 regulations referencing it have nothing to do with reporting of payments with which we are concerned. However, identifying numbers may be required of a person IF – and only IF --

the person is required to file a return on behalf of the recipients (i.e. foreign entities). Please review 26 C.F.R. §1.6041-6, which was previously shown on page 2.

Clearly, the lack of implementing regulations for I.R.C. §6109(a)(2) renders the laws and regulations compliant with the Privacy Act by requiring from recipients to furnish only their name and address upon demand. The list of regulations for I.R.C. §6109 relating to TINs reveals that the implementation of 26 U.S.C. §6109 varies from code section to code section.

While there may be concerns that IRS charges penalties for "incomplete" 1099 Forms pursuant to 26 U.S.C. §§6721 - 6723 which impose a maximum penalty of $50 for each failure to provide complete information, such charges are superseded by 26 U.S.C. §6724(a), which also conforms to the Privacy Act by placing "no penalty" on either Payee, or Payor, if proper documentation shows "that such failure is due to reasonable cause and not to willful neglect.":

> *26 U.S.C. §6724(a) - "No penalty shall be imposed under this part with respect to any failure if it is shown that such failure is due to reasonable cause and not to willful neglect."*

SUMMARY:

1. I.R.C. §6041 - requires that payments of $600 or more to be shown in a return, together with the name and address of the recipient, and requires that recipients provide their name and address upon demand;

2. 26 C.F.R. §1.6041-6 – a Form 1099 reporting shall include the name and address of the recipient;

3. I.R.C. §6109(a)(2) – conditions the request for numbers to "as may be prescribed", but the prescriptions are limited to treasury employees pursuant to 5 U.S.C. 301 and 26 C.F.R. 301.6109-1;

4. I.R.C. §6109(a)(3) - the person required to make a return shall request an identifying number – but that request is limited to treasury employees pursuant to the above treasury regulations;

5. Form W-9 is to Request a TIN, not to require it, and thus has no OMB number;

6. The Payor lacks legal authority to demand information beyond the name and address of the recipient or Payee, or any other information unless the party is a treasury employee;

7. The Payee who is not a Treasury employee has no legal obligation to provide a TIN to the Payor, but if a number is provided, there is a requirement that the number be correct;

8. The Payor who is paying a Treasury Employee may use Form W-9 to demand the name and address of the Payee;

9. A statement of reservation of right to privacy from the Payee is reasonable cause for the Payor to NOT include the Payee's TIN on a Form 1099.

Businesses that file numerous 1099s keep a record that a request for the TIN was made by using Form W-9. By following the law and the regulations scrupulously, the Payee's privacy is protected, and the Payor has proof of the request within the provisions of law.

This letter provides the name and address per your request, and constitutes documentary confirmation of our keeping within the Privacy Act provisions. It also provides the lawful reasonable cause for not entering a TIN on a 1099 Form as well as the relevant excerpts from Treasury Decision 8734 and 26 U.S. Code §7701(a)(30) regarding information reporting for purposes of withholding of tax on certain U.S. source income as entered in the record by the service provider.

The information provided herein is not legal advice, but a response to your Form W-9 request and an obvious statement to prevent litigation that may ensue if you share any other information with anyone without my prior written consent.

Thank you for your patronage.

23.3 Financial Institutions

When Financial Institutions ask you for a number, do the following:

1. Hand them an AMENDED IRS Form W-8BEN filled out according to the instructions in the following article:
   About IRS Form W-8BEN, Form #04.202
   http://sedm.org/Forms/FormIndex.htm
2. Attach to the W-8BEN the following form filled out according to the instructions at the beginning of the form.
   Affidavit of Citizenship, Domicile, and Tax Status, Form #02.001
   http://sedm.org/Forms/FormIndex.htm
3. Explain to them that Social Security Numbers are NOT required in the case of nonresident aliens not engaged in a "trade or business", as per 31 C.F.R. §1020.410(b)(3)(x) indicted at the beginning of the next section. This is also repeated on the Affidavit of Citizenship, Domicile, and Tax Status, Form #02.001. You should study this form carefully before you use it and look up all the laws yourself so you can calmly and boldly explain everything on it to the clerk accepting your application.
4. Explain to them that because you are NOT engaged in a "trade or business", it would be ILLEGAL and a civil tort for them to complete or submit any kind of information return on any of your accounts, including IRS Forms 1098 or 1099. You can use the information in the following two articles to prove this to them.
   4.1. *Correcting Erroneous IRS Form 1098's*, Form #04.004
        http://sedm.org/Forms/FormIndex.htm
   4.2. *Correcting Erroneous IRS Form 1099's*, Form #04.005
        http://sedm.org/Forms/FormIndex.htm

23.4 Private Employer Job or Contract Applications

When private employers ask you to provide a Social Security Number do the following:

1. You can show them the signed letter from the Social Security Administration admitting that you aren't required to have or use the number:
   Social Security Administration Letter, Exhibit #07.004
   http://sedm.org/Exhibits/ExhibitIndex.htm
2. You should first quote 42 U.S.C. §408, which says that it is illegal to compel anyone to disclose or use a Social Security Number.

   > *TITLE 42 - THE PUBLIC HEALTH AND WELFARE*
   > *CHAPTER 7 - SOCIAL SECURITY*
   > *SUBCHAPTER II - FEDERAL OLD-AGE, SURVIVORS, AND DISABILITY INSURANCE BENEFITS*
   > *Sec. 408. Penalties*
   >
   > *In general*
   > *Whoever -...*
   > *(8) discloses, uses, or compels the disclosure of the social security number of any person in violation of the laws of the United States; shall be guilty of a felony and upon conviction thereof shall be fined under title 18 or imprisoned for not more than five years, or both.*

3. You can print out and hand them a copy of the following:
   Reasonable Cause Regulations and Requirements for Missing and Incorrect Name/TINs, IRS Publication 1586
   http://sedm.org/Forms/04-Tax/1-Procedure/AboutSSNs/IRSPub1586.pdf
4. You can tell them that it is illegal to use government property for a private purpose and that you are not there as a "public official" but a private person who cannot lawfully possess or use public property for a private purpose without committing theft and embezzlement. Explain that you do not consent to act as a voluntary federal "public official" or "employee" in order to make your possession of "public property" lawful. 20 C.F.R. §422.103(d) identifies the Social Security Number as government property, and to use this "public property" for a private purpose constitutes embezzlement and impersonating a federal employee, in violation of 18 U.S.C. §912.
5. You can tell them that you do not have a "Social Security Number" because you never participated voluntarily and never explicitly consented to participate. Then you can show them:
   5.1. The resignation document you sent in, if you sent it in at (Members are REQUIRED to do this):
   Resignation of Compelled Social Security Trustee, Form #06.002:

http://sedm.org/Forms/FormIndex.htm
- 5.2. Social Security Form 521 showing that you quit the social security program:
  http://famguardian.org/TaxFreedom/Instructions/3.17QuitSocialSecurity.htm
6. You tell them you are a "nonresident alien" and quote them 26 C.F.R. §1.872-2(f), which says you are not subject to taxation or withholding and give them a modified W-8BEN form. See:
   - 6.1. *About IRS Form W-8BEN*, Form #04.202:
     http://sedm.org/Forms/FormIndex.htm
   - 6.2. *Non-Resident Non-Person Position*, Form #05.020:
     http://sedm.org/Forms/FormIndex.htm
7. You can give them our free pamphlet Who are "Taxpayers" and who needs a "Taxpayer Identification Number"?, Form #05.013 and demand that they rebut the questions at the end. It's also a good idea to offer to sit down with anyone who is confronting you on this issue and educate them about the content of this pamphlet. The pamphlet is available at the link below as form #05.013:
   http://sedm.org/Forms/FormIndex.htm
8. You can download the free Federal and State Tax Withholding Options for Private Employers, Form #09.001 book and refer to sections 24.3.1 and 24.3.5 for further details. Section 27.12 also has a form you can use as a substitute for the W-9 form so that you can comply by submitting the form but still protect yourself and your privacy. Read this book carefully and it will answer most of your questions.

   Federal and State Tax Withholding Options for Private Employers, Form #09.001
   http://sedm.org/Forms/FormIndex.htm

9. If the person doing the compelling is not the owner of the organization, you can tell the person that you are going to sue them personally for recruiting you into slavery, in violation of the Thirteenth Amendment, 42 U.S.C. §1994, and 18 U.S.C. §1581.
10. You can show them the definition of "married" and "unmarried" individuals in 26 C.F.R. §1.1-1(a)(2)(ii), who are "aliens engaged in a 'trade or business'" and then explain that you are neither an "alien" or engaged in a "trade or business". See:

    The "Trade or Business" Scam, Form #05.001
    http://sedm.org/Forms/FormIndex.htm

11. If you are self-supporting and not an "employee" [federal instrumentality] but a private contractor, you can identify yourself as a "nonresident alien" and read them 26 U.S.C. §1402(b), which says that "nonresident aliens" do not earn "self employment income" and therefore need not report.

Whichever one or more of the above options you select:

1. Make sure you either have witnesses present or send everything registered overnight mail with return receipt. That way, you will have proof, if they decide to discriminate by either not hiring or firing you for basically refusing to violate the law or reward their ignorance with a surrender of your sovereign immunity under the Foreign Sovereign Immunities Act.
2. Warn them IN WRITING that because you are not engaged in a "trade or business", it is a CRIME and a CIVIL TORT for them to fill out and send in ANY information return, such as IRS Forms W-2 and 1099 and that any such document they might submit on you would be FRAUDULENT. FORMS 8 and 9 in sections 27.8 and 27.9 of the FREE Federal and State Tax Withholding Options for Private Employers, Form #09.001 book are very useful for this.
   - 2.1. 26 U.S.C. §7207: Fraudulent returns, statements, or other documents. This provision makes it a civil tort to knowingly file false information returns.
   - 2.2. 18 U.S.C. §912: Falsely impersonating an officer [PUBLIC OFFICER] or employee of the United States. A person engaged in a "trade or business" is defined as a "public officer" in 26 U.S.C. §7701(a)(26). It is a crime to claim that either you or anyone else is a "public officer" who in fact is not.
3. If the private employer wants to argue with you about whether it would be illegal to submit an information return then give them the following forms and ask them to rebut it with witnesses present or send it to them via certified mail with a proof of service in case they decide to fire or not hire you:
   - 3.1. *Demand for Verified Evidence of Trade or Business Activity: Information Return*, Form #04.007
     http://sedm.org/Forms/FormIndex.htm
   - 3.2. Demand that they rebut the questions at the end and anything within the pamphlet that is false
     The Trade or Business Scam, Form #05.001
     http://sedm.org/Forms/FormIndex.htm

4. If they fill out false information returns, such as IRS Forms W-2, 1042-S, 1098, or 1099, against you, make sure to correct them promptly after they are filed in order to avoid becoming the target of unlawful IRS collection activity in accordance with the following:
    4.1. *Income Tax Withholding and Reporting Course*, Form #12.004:
        http://sedm.org/Forms/FormIndex.htm
    4.2. *Correcting Erroneous Information Returns*, Form #04.001:
        http://sedm.org/Forms/FormIndex.htm
    4.3. *Corrected Information Return Attachment Letter*, Form #04.002:
        http://sedm.org/Forms/FormIndex.htm
    4.4. *Correcting Erroneous IRS Form 1042's*, Form #04.003:
        http://sedm.org/Forms/FormIndex.htm
    4.5. *Correcting Erroneous IRS Form 1098's*, Form #04.004:
        http://sedm.org/Forms/FormIndex.htm
    4.6. *Correcting Erroneous IRS Form 1099's*, Form #04.005:
        http://sedm.org/Forms/FormIndex.htm
    4.7. *Correcting Erroneous IRS Form W-2's*, Form #04.006:
        http://sedm.org/Forms/FormIndex.htm

23.5 Government applications for an account or benefit

1. Government application for an account or benefit. When the government asks for the number on an application for an account or benefit:
    1.1. Indicate "None".
    1.2. If they ask you whether you were ever issued such a number say "No". The reason you can say this is that the number is public property and can only be issued to public employees acting in their official capacity. Since you are not a public employee acting in your official capacity, then it wasn't issued to you, who are a private person.
    1.3. You do not choose to act as a "Trustee" or federal "employee" and you resigned your federal "employment" position.
    1.4. It is illegal for you to use public property for private gain unless on official duty as a public employee, and you are not on official duty.
2. Government notice. When the government sends you a notice and refers to you with such a number:
    2.1. It is not the correct number.
    2.2. The government should correct its records to reflect this fact and discontinue illegal collection actions against you, because you are no longer and never were a federal "employee".
    2.3. The employment compensation of the Trustee position is inadequate and you quit the position years ago and NEVER participated voluntarily. The compensation you want must ALSO include no federal tax liability and the federal government is unwilling to add this to the terms of the Trust Indenture document.

In addition to the above, you should also follow the guidelines contained in the following resource on our website within the Liberty University:

> *Developing Evidence of Citizenship and Sovereignty Course*, Form #12.002
> http://sedm.org/Forms/FormIndex.htm

When the IRS wants to request an identifying number, it asks for a "Social Security Number" on its forms. The IRS' own Internal Revenue Manual however, in Internal Revenue Manual (I.R.M.), Section 4.10.7.2.8, says that you can't rely on the accuracy of its forms and publications:

> "IRS Publications, issued by the National Office, explain the law in plain language for taxpayers and their advisors... While a good source of general information, publications should not be cited to sustain a position."
> [Internal Revenue Manual (I.R.M.), Section 4.10.7.2.8 (05-14-1999)]

Consequently, it would be unreasonable to conclude that an SSN as legally defined is really what they are asking for. If the IRS asked for a "Taxpayer Identification Number", however, they would have a lot fewer "taxpayers" because few people have TINs but most people apply for SSNs. Consequently, they falsify their forms to instead ask for the SSN instead of the TIN. Whenever you see the phrase "SSN", or "Social Security Number", you must conclude that they are really asking for a Taxpayer Identification Number. 26 C.F.R. §301.6109-1(d)(3) authorizes Taxpayer Identification Numbers to be issued by and used ONLY by "aliens", not "citizens". Since most Americans don't have TINs because they are not "aliens" or "residents" of the District of Columbia, then the safe way to answer such a question is to:

1. Line out "SSN" and write "TIN" above it.
2. In the box underneath write "None".
3. In the "Notes" section or blank area on the form, put:

> "Not authorized to use SSN in place of TIN. Please cite positive law if you disagree. In accordance with 5 U.S.C. §552a(b), you do not have my permission to use any identifying number in association with me and are COMMANDED to remove all such numbers from your records. All personal information about me is copyrighted and a trade secret and may not be maintained in ANY government information system or shared with any state revenue agency. Violation of the copyright will subject the violator to $1,000,000 for each occurrence."

If the IRS or a state revenue agency sends you a notice or form to fill out and an identifying number appears on the form or letter or correspondence, you should immediately respond to the notice by:

1. Lining in thick felt-tip pen all identifying numbers.
2. Writing next to this the following:

> "Invalid. Please remove this wrong number from my record. See attached 'Wrong Party Notice'."

3. Attaching the following form to your response, available below:

> *Wrong Party Notice*, Form #07.105
> http://sedm.org/Forms/FormIndex.htm

Then on the responsive letter, use language like what we showed you in this section to aver that the number is NOT "your" number. This will create doubt in the minds of the IRS or state revenue agency about whether they have the right number. When this doubt exists, they are far less likely to pursue illegal enforcement actions because they may be doing so against the WRONG target, which will subject them to personal liability for a tort. It will also increase the likelihood that all incorrect identifying numbers will be removed from any records they maintain about you. If they don't remove the invalid identifying number from their records, then you have a legal recourse for violation of copyright and of the Privacy Act.

If a financial institution or private employer asks you to complete and submit any government form that asks for a government identifying number, we highly recommend attaching the following form on our website per the instructions:

> *Why It is Illegal for Me to Request or Use a Taxpayer Identification Number*, Form #04.205
> http://sedm.org/Forms/FormIndex.htm

23.6 Dealing with "public servants" who demand a number at an audit or examination

Those who are invited into the company of IRS employees for an audit or "examination", or should we say a "proctology examination", will definitely be asked for "THEIR Social Security Number". This question, in fact, is usually the first question out of the mouth of the agent. It is very important to respond to such questions properly so as not to jeopardize your sovereignty by connecting you to:

1. Federal office, employment, or agency, and therefore federal jurisdiction.

> "The restrictions that the Constitution places upon the government in its capacity as lawmaker, i.e., as the regulator of private conduct, are not the same as the restrictions that it places upon the government in its capacity as employer. We have recognized this in many contexts, with respect to many different constitutional guarantees. Private citizens perhaps cannot be prevented from wearing long hair, but policemen can. Kelley v. Johnson, 425 U.S. 238, 247 (1976). Private citizens cannot have their property searched without probable cause, but in many circumstances government employees can. O'Connor v. Ortega, 480 U.S. 709, 723 (1987) (plurality opinion); id., at 732 (SCALIA, J., concurring in judgment). Private citizens cannot be punished for refusing to provide the government information that may incriminate them, but government employees can be dismissed when the incriminating information that they refuse to provide relates to the performance of their job. Gardner v. Broderick, [497 U.S. 62, 95] 392 U.S. 273, 277 -278 (1968). With regard to freedom of speech in particular: Private citizens cannot be punished for speech of merely private concern, but government employees can be fired for that reason. Connick v. Myers, 461 U.S. 138, 147 (1983). Private citizens cannot be punished for partisan political activity, but federal and state employees can be dismissed and otherwise punished for that reason. Public

Workers v. Mitchell, 330 U.S. 75, 101 (1947); Civil Service Comm'n v. Letter Carriers, 413 U.S. 548, 556 (1973); Broadrick v. Oklahoma, 413 U.S. 601, 616 -617 (1973)."
[Rutan v. Republican Party of Illinois, 497 U.S. 62 (1990)]

2. Federal benefit or commerce, which results in a surrender of sovereign immunity in satisfaction of 28 U.S.C. §1605(a)(2).

For details on the above, read section 9 of the following:

> *Non-Resident Non-Person Position*, Form #05.020
> http://sedm.org/Forms/FormIndex.htm

Below is an example script you can use when IRS agents ask for "YOUR Social Security Number" at an audit or examination:

IRS AGENT QUESTION:

What is YOUR Social Security Number?

YOUR ANSWER:

20 C.F.R. §422.103(d) says the "Social Security Number Card" but NOT the STATUTORY SSN belongs to the government. Since you didn't ask me for the card but the number, then you aren't asking me for government property you can place conditions on the use of. The only way the SSN could therefore be MY number as you call it is if I am the ABSOLUTE and PRIVATE owner of the number and the associated franchise it connects to and am appearing here today as a Merchant offering billable services to you under MY franchise contract. Thank you for inviting me here today to do business with you as a Merchant who makes all the rules and conditions under which I render services to you as the absolute owner and seller of myself and all of my property.

On the other hand, if you are going to use the SSN to connect me to YOUR Social Security franchise contract in Title 42 that only you own and control, then I don't HAVE THAT account number and there is no such thing, because:

My participation is clearly illegal, and an illegal act is not an official act you or I can lawfully participate in or use for profit.

My God forbids me to act as a Buyer of anything you own or control, to surrender constitutional or natural rights to you, or to allow you to make rules or laws that circumvent His holy laws. He is my ONLY CIVIL lawgiver according to the Bible.

Which of the two types of Social Security Numbers are you therefore asking me for today: PUBLIC STATUTORY number under your franchise contract or PRIVATE number under MY franchise contract? This will determine who is in charge of making the rules for use of the Number under these circumstances.

IRS AGENT QUESTION:

The only thing we can talk about here today are STATUTORY Social Security Numbers. The civil statutes enacted by Congress including the Social Security franchise in Title 42 are the source of our authority.

YOUR ANSWER:

Well then you are asking me to consent to participate in something that is clearly illegal and which I also have no delegated authority to do from My God as His full-time trustee. In which case, I don't HAVE a STATUTORY Social Security Number since participation is clearly ILLEGAL. Please destroy any records that I am eligible and stop using it for PUBLIC purposes or civil enforcement purposes outside the government. This is clearly criminal identity theft, which I have already notified you of on IRS Form 14039. [See our Form #14.020]. Further, I as a "nonresident alien" not engaged in a "trade or business" who consents to NOTHING you offer me and elects NOTHING am excluded by law from the requirement to furnish a Social Security Number per 26 C.F.R. §301.6109-1(b). So why do you even need such a number under the circumstances?

IRS AGENT QUESTION:

That's ridiculous. Everyone HAS a STATUTORY SSN. How else are we going to manage our relationship with you without one?

YOUR ANSWER:

When are you going to get it through your thick skull that I don't WANT ANY COMMERCIAL RELATIONSHIP with you and simply want to be CIVILLLY LEFT ALONE as justice itself requires. The fact that no one else realizes that or takes that approach and blindly uses SSNs to become government cattle on the government plantation doesn't mean I have to. Unlike the rest of the stupid cattle you "service" who volunteer to be cattle, I'm not your stupid whore who volunteers to work for free or donates my entire body to a public use without compensation. I as the exclusive and absolute owner of myself under the Thirteenth Amendment decide what my services to you or the use of my property are worth, not you, and they aren't free. The charge for my services to act as a federal "employee" or officer or trustee in possession of public property such as a STATUTORY SSN is documented in the following agreement:

> *Injury Defense Franchise and Agreement*, Form #06.027
> https://sedm.org/Forms/06-AvoidingFranch/InjuryDefenseFranchise.pdf

Will you agree in writing to the above agreement to act essentially as your federal coworker, because if you don't, then it's not MY number?

IRS AGENT QUESTION:

Don't play word games with me. It's YOUR number and we have a RIGHT to use it.

YOUR ANSWER:

Well good. Then if it's MY number and MY property, then I have EXCLUSIVE control and use over it and may LICENSE its use to you. That is what the word "property" implies. That means I, and not you, am the only one who may control or regulate its use under the following franchise:

> *Injury Defense Franchise and Agreement*, Form #06.027
> https://sedm.org/Forms/06-AvoidingFranch/InjuryDefenseFranchise.pdf

If it's MY property as you indicate, then your job as an alleged "government" is to protect me from abuses of MY property. If you don't want to do that job, you're not really a government, but a de facto government. If you can control and penalize me for misusing YOUR procedures and forms, which are YOUR property, then I am EQUALLY entitled to penalize you for misusing MY property. I can't be free unless I'm at least equal to you, according to Supreme Court:

> *No duty rests more imperatively upon the courts than the enforcement of those constitutional provisions intended to secure that equality of rights which is the foundation of free government."*
> *[Gulf, C. & S. F. R. Co. v. Ellis, 165 U.S. 150 (1897)]*

Are you willing to sign an agreement in writing to pay for the beneficial use of what you call MY property such as the NON-STATUTORY SSN, because if you aren't, you are depriving me of exclusive use and control over MY property and depriving me of the equal right to prevent abuses of my property, my identity, and my life??

IRS AGENT QUESTION:

OK, well it's OUR number. Sorry for deceiving you. Can you give us OUR number that WE assigned to you?

YOUR ANSWER:

I can find no statutory proof that the STATUTORY SSN ALONE absent the "Social Security Number CARD" is your property. Please provide evidence of same. And if it IS in fact YOUR property or PUBLIC property, why do you LIE to me by calling it MY property and MY number?

If the STATUTORY SSN is PUBLIC or GOVERNMENT property, then you can't allow me to use it as a private person, which is what I am appearing here today as. You can't lawfully issue public property such as an SSN to a private person or allow them to use it for a private purpose. That's criminal embezzlement. Therefore, the only way that PUBLIC property such as what you allege is a STATUTORY SSN could have been assigned to me is if I'm acting as a "public officer" or federal employee at this moment, and I am NOT. I am here as a private person and not a public employee who retains ONLY constitutional and not STATUTORY protections. Therefore, it couldn't have been lawfully issued to me.

Keep this up, and I'm going to file a criminal complaint with the U.S. Attorney for embezzlement in violation of 18 U.S.C. §641 and impersonating a public officer in violation of 18 U.S.C. §912 . I'm not here as a public officer and you are asking me to act like one without compensation that only I can determine and without demonstrated legal authority. Where is the compensation that I demand to act as a fiduciary and trustee over your STINKING number, which you claim is public property without proof? I remind you that the very purpose why governments are created is to PROTECT and maintain the separation between "public property" and "private property" in order to preserve my inalienable constitutional rights that you took an oath to support and defend. Why do you continue to insist on co-mingling and confusing them in order to STEAL my labor, property, and money without compensation in violation of the Fifth Amendment takings clause?

IRS AGENT QUESTION:

We have received third party reports relating to tax withholding or reporting that connect you to a STATUTORY SSN and indirectly, to a "trade or business" per 26 U.S.C. §6041(a). We therefore have reasonable cause to inquire of you about these reports and any possible income tax liability attached to the transactions they document.

YOUR ANSWER:

Third party information returns are classified by the courts as "lay legal opinions". That means none of the LABELS on the form can have any actionable effect and are therefore not necessarily statutory terms. 26 U.S.C. §6041(a) connects the FILER of the information return to a "trade or business" and a public office under 26 U.S.C. §7701(a)(26), and NOT the TARGET of the report. These reports also do NOT authorize the FILER to convert PRIVATE property to PUBLIC property and a PUBLIC office without the consent of the ABSOLUTE owner, which is me. Further, even the FILER is not lawfully engaged in a "trade or business" and public office as someone who was never lawfully appointed or elected to a public office and is not serving in the District of Columbia as required by 4 U.S.C. §72. So these reports are hereby declared to be false and also possibly FRAUDULENT under penalty of perjury. See:

> *Correcting Erroneous Information Returns*, Form #04.001
> https://sedm.org/Forms/04-Tax/0-CorrErrInfoRtns/CorrErrInfoRtns.pdf

The 1040NR return acknowledges that these information return reports do NOT necessarily connect me to such a public office by calling the earnings on the return "EFFECTIVELY connected" rather than merely "ACTUALLY connected". If I enter the amounts reported on these false information returns onto the 1040NR return, I am "in effect" and "effectively" donating the PRIVATE property they describe to a PUBLIC use, a PUBLIC purpose, and a PUBLIC office and thus subjecting them to income taxation and governmental control. I DO NOT consent to do that because all my earnings are EXCLUDED rather than EXEMPT from taxation as a nonresident alien not engaged in a "trade or business"/public office and whose earnings do not originate from the statutory geographical "United States" under 26 U.S.C. §871. See:

> *Excluded Earnings and People*, Form #14.019
> https://sedm.org/Forms/14-PropProtection/ExcludedEarningsAndPeople.pdf

I don't need your stinking exemptions or deductions on the 1040NR form if all my earnings are lawfully excluded under:

1. Earnings originate from outside:
   1.1. The STATUTORY "United States**" as defined in 26 U.S.C. §7701(a)(9) and (a)(10) (federal zone) and
   1.2. The U.S. government federal corporation as a privileged legal fiction.
   Thus, their earnings are expressly EXCLUDED rather than EXEMPTED from "gross income" under 26 U.S.C. §871 and are a "foreign estate" under 26 U.S.C. §7701(a)(31). See 26 U.S.C. §872 and 26 C.F.R. §1.872-2(f) and 26 C.F.R. §1.871-7(a)(4) and 26 U.S.C. §861(a)(3)(C)(i) for proof.

2. Earnings are expressly EXCLUDED rather than EXEMPTED from STATUTORY "wages" as defined in 26 U.S.C. §3401(a) because all services performed outside the STATUTORY "United States**" as defined in 26 U.S.C. §7701(a)(9) and (a)(10) (federal zone) and the CORPORATION "United States" as a legal fiction. Therefore, not subject to "wage" withholding of any kind for such services per:
    2.1. 26 C.F.R. §31.3401(a)(6)-1(b) in the case of income tax.
    2.2. 26 C.F.R. §31.3121(b)-3(c)(1) in the case of Social Security.
3. Expressly EXCLUDED rather than EXEMPTED from income tax reporting under:
    3.1. 26 C.F.R. §1.1441-1(b)(5)(i).
    3.2. 26 C.F.R. §1.1441-1(e)(1)(ii)(A)(1).
    3.3. 26 C.F.R. §1.6041-4(a)(1).
4. Expressly EXCLUDED rather than EXEMPTED from backup withholding because earnings are not reportable by 26 U.S.C. §3406 and 26 C.F.R. §31.3406(g)-1(e). Only "reportable payments" are subject to such withholding.

My earnings are excluded, by the way, because they are PRIVATE and the owner who is me never consented to convert them to PUBLIC. Stop engaging in sophistry to rope me into your servitude and pay money I don't owe. This is despicable!

IRS AGENT QUESTION:

Even if your participation in Social Security is illegal, everyone still uses Social Security Numbers at least for financial, banking, or lending purposes. If your participation is illegal, then how can you bank or get a loan?

YOUR ANSWER:

Your question presupposes that my activities in getting a loan or opening a financial account are PUBLIC activities using PUBLIC property and that I am therefore subject to taxation and regulation in doing so. I and not you get to decide when I am acting in a PRIVATE or PUBLIC capacity and to define the meaning of all terms that affect the enjoyment of my ABSOLUTELY OWNED PRIVATE PROPERTY and LABOR. YOU have NO AUTHORITY to write definitions affecting property that you have no ownership interest in, because doing so would be an interference with the absolute control over said property and therefore for a THEFT of property. I use ownership and control synonymously here. You even admit in IRM 4.10.7.2.8 that no one should trust any of your forms, which means no one should trust the WORDS or LABELS on the forms either, including but not limited to "Social Security Number", "Taxpayer", etc. If the forms and the labels on the forms are not ACTIONABLE or even factual, then my writing on the form even under penalty of perjury doesn't make them actionable either or connect them to a civil statutory context unless I expressly do so myself, which I DO NOT.

We have already established that the NUMBER is NOT public property under 20 C.F.R. §422.103(d), and that only the CARD is PUBLIC property. You have also essentially admitted that the NUMBER is MY absolutely owned property and therefore not YOURS or the GOVERNMENT'S or PUBLIC property by calling it "YOUR Social Security Number". And if it is "MY ABSOLUTELY OWNED PROPERTY" as you call it, then I have the right as the only lawful owner to control ANY and ALL commercial uses of it by ANYONE and EVERYONE, including banks or lenders and even YOU and every government. I exercise that control by specifying all the definitions affecting its use and the CONTEXT of those definitions: PUBLIC or PRIVATE. If I don't have a right to control my identity, my reputation, and the commercial use of information about me that might damage me through no act of my own, then you can turn the SSN into a vehicle for criminal identity theft. That appears to be what you are doing here and now. I remind you that you appear to be using this proceeding to IN FACT engage in criminal identity theft, and that you are trying to get my permission to allow you to abuse aspects of my identity and reputation for an unauthorized commercial use and for ILLEGAL tax enforcement purposes. By "illegal" I mean NON-CONSENSUAL purposes.

Calling myself a CIVIL STATUTORY "taxpayer", "person", "citizen", or "resident" are methods of manifesting consent to privileges and taxation, but I don't claim the "benefit" of ANY connection to ANY CIVIL statutory status within any government law or franchise, or a connection to any aspect of my identity to the CIVIL statutory protection of any government. The authority to do this is my First Amendment right to NOT civilly or legally associate and my right to NOT contract with you. Thus, I am exclusively PRIVATE in the context of this interaction, and you must leave me alone in the interests of JUSTICE, which is legally defined as "the right to be left alone". Since it costs you NOTHING to simply LEAVE ME ALONE, then you can't claim I owe you anything for it or that it is a privilege that I have to pay for in the form of "taxes". YES, a "taxpayer" is someone subject to a tax, but the decision to BECOME a "taxpayer" is voluntary. This is proven by:

1. *Why Domicile and Becoming a "Taxpayer" Require Your Consent*, Form #05.002;
   https://sedm.org/Forms/05-MemLaw/Domicile.pdf.
2. *How State Nationals Volunteer to Pay Income Tax*, Form #08.024
   https://sedm.org/Forms/08-PolicyDocs/HowYouVolForIncomeTax.pdf

Either I own my life and am in charge of it and everything that affects it through my own actions, or I'm a slave and a peon and you are a tyrant. It can't be both. Welcome to The Matrix, Neo.

IRS AGENT QUESTION:

Do we have permission to use YOUR number as private property for a commercial use to tax you with your permission?

YOUR ANSWER:

Absolutely not! My God forbids me to act as a Buyer or user of government property or services of any kind. Violating that edict constitutes treason and comes the most heinous curse in the Holy Bible in Deuteronomy 28:43-51. If you really are a legitimate government, you will do your ONLY real job of protecting private property, leaving it and me alone. The government's only job according to the Declaration of Independence is to protect PRIVATE property. The first step in delivering that PRIVATE property protection is to keep the property from being converted from PRIVATE to PUBLIC property or governmental control without the consent of the owner. It is your MAIN JOB to keep PUBLIC and PRIVATE separate at all times. See: *Separation Between Public and Private Course*, Form #12.025; https://sedm.org/LibertyU/SeparatingPublicPrivate.pdf . If you won't do YOUR ONLY job of maintaining that separation, then why the HELL would I want to hire you as a security guard to protect my PRIVATE property from anyone ELSE's theft? I remind you that income taxation is the institutionalized process of converting PRIVATE to PUBLIC in order to fund the government. That conversion MUST be consensual or we are all SLAVES and PEONS in violation of the Thirteenth Amendment. It is an oxymoron to implement tax SLAVERY to pay for FREEDOM from slavery. Are you crazy? What have you been smoking?

I don't want your CIVIL statutory protection and I have the right to reject its benefits in favor of the common law or private contracts. At the same time, I'm NOT saying you don't deserve to be paid for the protection you provide in the form of the criminal law, the common law, or the military. It would be irresponsible of me to object to NOT paying for that. A workman is always worthy of his hire, according to the Bible. HOWEVER, I must have the discretion to decide WHAT I want to hire you to protect at least in a CIVIL statutory context. If I don't have that degree of discretion and autonomy, then I'm a slave and government chattel. The scenario where I do have that protection I identify as "natural law". For a definition of "natural law", see:

> *Disclaimer*, Section 4.31: Natural law
> https://sedm.org/disclaimer.htm#4.31._Natural_law

Usually, after the above interchange, the IRS agent will realize he is digging a DEEP hole for himself and will abruptly end that sort of inquiry, and many times will also end his collection efforts. When you get him to admit on the record that he is committing crimes, he no longer has a plausible deniability defense if he ends up in front of a jury.

23.7 Submitting legal evidence as a non-resident indicating that "you" were never issued or applied for a "Social Security Number" or "Taxpayer Identification Number"

Those applying for government-issued ID such as driver's licenses or passports are often asked for "THEIR Social Security Number" and to provide legal evidence proving that they don't have one if they refuse to provide one. Below is an example of such a query:

Figure 4: Request for certification that you were never issued a Social Security Number

United States Department of State

San Diego Passport Agency
44132 Mercure Circle
PO Box 1136
Sterling, Virginia 20166-1136

September 26, 2018

RE:

Dear

Thank you for your recent passport application.

However, your Social Security Number was not provided on your passport application. Please provide your Social Security Number by clearly writing it in the spaces provided below.

_____-___-_____

If you have never been issued a Social Security Number, please submit a signed statement under penalty of perjury to that effect or use the following:

To whom it may concern,

I _____ (*print full name*) declare under penalty of perjury under the laws of the United States of America that the following is true and correct: I have never been issued a Social Security Number by the Social Security Administration.

Executed on: _____
(DATE)

Signature: _____
(Sign using full name as indicated on the passport application)

To assist with processing your application, we must receive the requested information <u>within **ninety (90) days of the date shown on this letter.**</u> If the information is not received or is insufficient to establish your entitlement to a U.S. passport, your application may be denied and your citizenship evidence will be returned. By law, the passport execution and application fees are non-refundable.

If you have any questions please contact the National Passport Information Center: 1-877-487-2778 (TTY/TDD: 1-888-874-7793).

For general passport information or to check the status of your passport application, please visit us on-line at travel.state.gov.

<u>**PLEASE RETURN A COPY OF THIS LETTER, ALONG WITH ALL REQUESTED INFORMATION TO THE ADDRESS LISTED ABOVE INCLUDING THE +4 ZIP CODE.**</u>

Sincerely,

Customer Service Department

More about how to respond to the above can be found in:

> *Getting a USA Passport as a "state national"*, Form #10.013, Section 9.6
> https://sedm.org/Forms/FormIndex.htm

We know that asking a PRIVATE human not representing a public office for "THEIR" Social Security Number is a deception, because if it really was "YOURS" (your property), then you could use it to control the government as a temporary loan of property to the government WITH CONDITIONS that YOU and not THEY specify. To even admit to being issued a STATUTORY Social Security Number or applying for one is to in effect admit that one is a public officer on official business, which is FRAUD, because private people can't possess, use, or benefit from public property. A public office is, in fact, legally defined as someone in charge of PUBLIC property.

> "**Public office**. The right, authority, and duty created and conferred by law, by which for a given period, either fixed by law or enduring at the pleasure of the creating power, an individual is invested with some portion of the sovereign functions of government for the benefit of the public. Walker v. Rich, 79 Cal.App. 139, 249 P. 56, 58. An agency for the state, the duties of which involve in their performance the exercise of some portion of the sovereign power, either great or small. Yaselli v. Goff, C.C.A., 12 F.2d. 396, 403, 56 A.L.R. 1239; Lacey v. State, 13 Ala.App. 212, 68 So. 706, 710; Curtin v. State, 61 Cal.App. 377, 214 P. 1030, 1035; Shelmadine v. City of Elkhart, 75 Ind.App. 493, 129 N.E. 878. State ex rel. Colorado River Commission v. Frohmiller, 46 Ariz. 413, 52 P.2d. 483, 486. **Where, by virtue of law, a person is clothed, not as an incidental or transient authority, but for such time as de- notes duration and continuance, with Independent power to control the property of the public**, or with public functions to be exercised in the supposed interest of the people, the service to be compensated by a stated yearly salary, and the occupant having a designation or title, the position so created is a public office. State v. Brennan, 49 Ohio.St. 33, 29 N.E. 593.
> [Black's Law Dictionary, Fourth Edition, p. 1235]

The property mentioned above in the context of Social Security, according to 20 C.F.R. §422.103(d) and the back of the Social Security Card itself, is the number and the card itself, which are the initial corpus of the Social Security trust established by those who lawfully and consensually participate. Note that this regulation is found in Title 20, which is "Employees' Benefits". If you weren't a statutory "employee" as defined in 5 U.S.C. §2105(a) BEFORE you made application for the card or the number, then you can't CREATE such an office by making such an application as a PRIVATE human and would be criminally impersonating a public officer in violation of 18 U.S.C. §912 to even try to do so. To even ADMIT that you made such application ILLEGALLY as a private human would be to admit that you committed such a crime. See the following for proof:

> *Government Instituted Slavery Using Franchises*, Form #05.030, Section 23
> https://sedm.org/Forms/FormIndex.htm

To COMPEL someone to MAKE such an admission would furthermore compel them to impersonate a public office AND to admit that they committed a crime in doing so in violation of the Fifth Amendment.

> TITLE 5 > PART III > Subpart A > CHAPTER 21 > § 2105
> § 2105. Employee
>
> (a) For the purpose of this title, "employee", except as otherwise provided by this section or when specifically modified, **means an officer and an individual who is**—

The above statute is the ONLY way from a civil perspective that a state domiciled party can be a statutory "individual" with a legislatively foreign domicile. Otherwise, they would be "non-residents" beyond the civil statutory control of the national government as a result of the Separation of Powers, as we prove in Form #05.018.

Similar legal and even ethical and moral problems plague the driver's license application process in California. Those owning private conveyances are told that they MUST provide a Social Security Number with their Driver's License application and that if they don't, they must furnish written proof from the Social Security Administration that they are NOT eligible to apply for Social Security. This ought to be a clue that the only place that driver's licenses can be issued is on federal territory that is the only place subject to the Social Security Act, based on the definitions of "State" in the Social Security Act itself at 42 U.S.C. §1301(a)(1). If you aren't domiciled on federal territory as a STATUTORY "U.S. citizen" or "U.S. resident", then the Social Security Act doesn't even apply, as we exhaustively prove in the following:

> *Why You Aren't Eligible for Social Security*, Form #06.001
> https://sedm.org/Forms/FormIndex.htm

Nevertheless, since the Social Security Administration is in the business of "marketing" to produce more "sponsors" so they can prolong the inevitable and certain collapse of their Socialist Ponzi Scheme, then:

1. They will say that EVERYONE is eligible for Social Security, including people who ARE NOT.
2. They will REFUSE to provide any legally admissible evidence upon which they base such a LEGAL DETERMINATION because guess what, there ISN'T any such evidence. It's all presumption. You should DEMAND such evidence signed under penalty of perjury. To fail to provide it is a violation of due process of law, in fact, because they are proceeding upon a mere PRESUMPTION that is not substantiated by FACTS and court-admissible evidence. All such presumptions that adversely affect or impair constitutionally protected rights are a violation of due process and a tort:

   > *(1) [8:4993]* **Conclusive presumptions affecting protected interests:**
   >
   > *A conclusive presumption may be defeated where its application would impair a party's constitutionally-protected liberty or property interests. In such cases, conclusive **presumptions have been held to violate a party's due process and equal protection rights.** [Vlandis v. Kline (1973) 412 U.S. 441, 449, 93 S.Ct. 2230, 2235; Cleveland Bed. of Ed. v. LaFleur (1974) 414 U.S. 632, 639-640, 94 S.Ct. 1208, 1215-presumption under Illinois law that unmarried fathers are unfit violates process]*
   > *[Federal Civil Trials and Evidence, Rutter Group, paragraph 8:4993, p. 8K-34]*

3. They can get away with this LIE because the courts have already put the people on notice that NO ONE in the government is accountable for telling the truth and that you can't rely on ANYTHING they say, including on any of their forms or their publications. See:
   3.1. *Legal Deception, Propaganda, and Fraud*, Form #05.014
        https://sedm.org/Forms/FormIndex.htm
   3.2. *Reasonable Belief About Income Tax Liability*, Form #05.007
        https://sedm.org/Forms/FormIndex.htm

If lying or deceiving people getting driver's licenses about their eligibility for Social Security is HIGHLY profitable, and if there is no downside, risk, or legal liability for LYING or DECEIVING, then you can be sure that they will institutionalize the LIE and tell EVERYONE they are eligible to increase their revenues unjustly. In the business world, this is called "marketing". If you wouldn't and shouldn't trust anything a private salesman would tell you, then you can't and shouldn't trust ANYTHING that anyone in the government tells you on ANY subject. Here is how we summarize this proverb:

> *"Never ask a barber if you need a haircut."*

There is ONE and ONLY ONE exception to the rule of never trusting ANYTHING that the government says or publishes, which is that if what they provide is signed under penalty of perjury, then it is reliable. That, in fact, is why EVERYHING you submit to them that has a commercial consequence must be signed under penalty of perjury. In practice, however, they NEVER sign anything under penalty of perjury, oftentimes not even during litigation relating to taxes in court! The IRS Form 4549 that is used to prove that a tax was due and owing as one element in a criminal tax prosecution is NEVER even signed and is NOT valid or admissible as evidence UNLESS it is signed under penalty of perjury as required by 26 U.S.C. §6065. We cover how to use this critical fact to derail ANY criminal tax prosecution in the following:

> *Why the Government Can't Lawfully Assess Human Beings with an Income Tax Liability Without Their Consent*, Form #05.011, Section 8.5
> https://sedm.org/Forms/FormIndex.htm

So the question then remains WHAT exactly can one submit as evidence in such a circumstance to PROVE that they either DO NOT HAVE one or are not ELIGIBLE to have a Social Security Number? The evidence must satisfy all the following conditions:

1. It can't come from anything the government says or publishes because NONE OF IT is trustworthy or admissible as evidence. See: *Legal Deception, Propaganda, and Fraud*, Form #05.014.

2. It must define key "words of art" on the form, and ESPECIALLY the word "you" in the instructions included with the form. When they tell "you" in the instructions that you have to do anything such as provide a number, they are making an UNCONSTITUTIONAL PRESUMPTION that the applicant is a public officer on official business who they can regulate and control. The purpose of asking for the number to begin with is to in effect CREATE or RECOGNIZE the existence of such an ILLEGAL public office and to produce evidence of your consent to fill said office. See *Presumption: Chief Weapon for Unlawfully Enlarging Federal Jurisdiction*, Form #05.017.
3. It must be signed under penalty of perjury so that it is useful as evidence in court. 26 U.S.C. §6065. The perjury statement must indicate your location as being OUTSIDE the "United States" as indicated in 28 U.S.C. §1746(1) so that you don't inadvertently misrepresent your location as being on federal territory.

> *28 U.S. Code § 1746 - Unsworn declarations under penalty of perjury*
>
> *Wherever, under any law of the United States or under any rule, regulation, order, or requirement made pursuant to law, any matter is required or permitted to be supported, evidenced, established, or proved by the sworn declaration, verification, certificate, statement, oath, or affidavit, in writing of the person making the same (other than a deposition, or an oath of office, or an oath required to be taken before a specified official other than a notary public), such matter may, with like force and effect, be supported, evidenced, established, or proved by the unsworn declaration, certificate, verification, or statement, in writing of such person which is subscribed by him, as true under penalty of perjury, and dated, in substantially the following form:*
>
> *(1) If executed without the United States: "I declare (or certify, verify, or state) under penalty of perjury under the laws of the United States of America that the foregoing is true and correct. Executed on (date).*
>
> *(Signature)".*
>
> *(2) If executed within the United States, its territories, possessions, or commonwealths: "I declare (or certify, verify, or state) under penalty of perjury that the foregoing is true and correct. Executed on (date).*
>
> *(Signature)".*
>
> *(Added Pub. L. 94–550, § 1(a), Oct. 18, 1976, 90 Stat. 2534.)*

4. It should not contain an admission that you ever violated any law. It is ILLEGAL and even criminal, for instance, to apply for or receive government "benefits" as a private human or to "elect" yourself into office by filling out any government form. 18 U.S.C. §912.

> **"To lay, with one hand, the power of the government on the property of the citizen, and with the other to bestow it upon favored individuals to aid private enterprises and build up private fortunes, is none the less a robbery because it is done under the forms of law and is called taxation. This is not legislation. It is a decree under legislative forms.**
>
> **Nor is it taxation. 'A tax,' says Webster's Dictionary, 'is a rate or sum of money assessed on the person or property of a citizen by government for the use of the nation or State.' 'Taxes are burdens or charges imposed by the Legislature upon persons or property to raise money for public purposes.'** Cooley, Const. Lim., 479.
>
> Coulter, J., in Northern Liberties v. St. John's Church, 13 Pa.St. 104 says, very forcibly, 'I think the common mind has everywhere taken in the understanding that **taxes are a public imposition, levied by authority of the government for the purposes of carrying on the government in all its machinery and operations—that they are imposed for a public purpose.**' See, also Pray v. Northern Liberties, 31 Pa.St. 69; Matter of Mayor of N.Y., 11 Johns., 77; Camden v. Allen, 2 Dutch., 398; Sharpless v. Mayor, supra; Hanson v. Vernon, 27 Ia., 47; Whiting v. Fond du Lac, supra."
> [Loan Association v. Topeka, 20 Wall. 655 (1874)]

> "A tax, in the general understanding of the term and as used in the constitution, signifies an exaction for the support of the government. The word has never thought to connote the expropriation of money from one group for the benefit of another."
> [U.S. v. Butler, 297 U.S. 1 (1936)]

5. It should warn the recipient that if they threaten to withhold service, punish you in any way, or order or threaten you to fill out the form in a specific way or with specific civil status indicated, then they are:
   5.1. Criminally tampering with a witness. Those signing perjury statements are witnesses. See 18 U.S.C. §1512.
   5.2. Practicing law on your behalf without your consent. You should NEVER consent to allow them to do this or to ANYTHING they want to do.

- 5.3. Making "legal determinations" about your status that they have no authority to do.
- 5.4. Soliciting a bribe from you intended to cause them to treat you AS IF you are a public officer. The tax withholdings are, in fact, the bribe. 18 U.S.C. §210.
- 5.5. Compelling you to contract or associate with the government in some way. Adopting a franchise license number is legal evidence that you are a franchisee. That is a crime and violates 22 U.S.C. §2721 in the case of passports:

> *22 U.S. Code § 2721 - Impermissible basis for denial of passports*
>
> *A passport may not be denied issuance, revoked, restricted, or otherwise limited because of any speech, activity, belief, affiliation, or membership, within or outside the United States, which, if held or conducted within the United States, would be protected by the first amendment to the Constitution of the United States.*
>
> *(Aug. 1, 1956, ch. 841, title I, § 49, as added Pub. L. 102–138, title I, § 113, Oct. 28, 1991, 105 Stat. 655.)*

6. It should not require you to violate your Fifth Amendment right to not incriminate yourself.
7. It should not connect you with any statute, franchise, civil status, statutory status, or public right. All such "benefits" are only available to those ALREADY in the government. You can't unilaterally "elect" or "appoint" yourself into public office by filling out any form. Neither can the recipient by accepting a form associating a public status with you CREATE any new public offices.
8. It should not call upon you to make what attorneys call a "legal conclusion" about your status, rights, or privileges. If even attorneys refuse to make such conclusions, then you can't either. During legal discovery, if you ask a question of an opposing counsel about the application of a statute to a specific situation, they will often make the following statement on the record:

> *"Objection, Your Honor. Calls for a legal conclusion".*

9. It should warn the recipient that nothing from the government is trustworthy or admissible as legal evidence, INCLUDING any document from the Social Security Administration stating that you are or are not eligible for Social Security.
10. It should prevent any possibility that equivocation could be used to confuse you, your status, or your actions as a PRIVATE human with any activity subject to any government civil statutes. Such civil statutes can and do regulate ONLY public conduct of PUBLIC officers on official business. Only private contracts, the Constitution, and the common law regulates or provides remedies for PRIVATE activity.
11. It should avoid "material" misrepresentations, which are false statements that have a damaging commercial consequence to the person you made the false statement to. The damage such false statements produce can form the basis for standing to sue. Generally, inaccurate statements that produce no demonstrated injury or standing are not "material" and cannot be prosecuted. Such inaccuracies, in fact, are the FOUNDATION of being a politician or a government employee generally. ALL politicians routinely lie or carelessly deceive because they are not accountable for the accuracy of their statements.

The above confluence of complicating factors is what we call a "perjury trap". They want you to think that you only have two choices, even though there are MORE than two. Legally ignorant people fall for this trap all the time but hopefully, you won't be one of them:

1. Provide an SSN and be enfranchised without your consent and injure your private rights thereby. . .OR
2. Make yourself susceptible to a prosecution for criminal perjury under 18 U.S.C. §1001 and 18 U.S.C. §1621 because you at least APPEAR to have lied on the application, even if you didn't.

If you don't know the difference between PRIVATE or PUBLIC or how to keep them separate and non-overlapping, then you are a sitting duck for the above perjury trap. That difference is explained below:

> *Separation Between Public and Private Course*, Form #12.025
> https://sedm.org/Forms/FormIndex.htm

Below are some examples of how we dealt with providing evidence proving that we are not eligible for an have never applied for a LAWFULLY issued number:

1. Recommended short language:

"I certify under penalty of perjury from without the statutory 'United States' (federal territory not under the exclusive jurisdiction of any constitutional state) pursuant to 28 U.S.C. §1746(1) the following facts:

1. I am not in possession, use, custody, or control of any government identifying number, including but not limited to a STATUTORY Social Security Number (20 C.F.R. §422.103) or STATUTORY Taxpayer Identification Number (26 U.S.C. §6109).

2. I am not eligible, and never HAVE been eligible to apply for or receive a statutory Social Security Number. The government has already defaulted and agreed with me on this fact in criminal complaints previously sent to them and not rebutted. No government can make this determination for me because no government can lawfully interfere with the management of my body and my absolutely owned private property without violating the Constitution. Even if they attempted to do so, it would be knowingly and willfully untrustworthy, because the courts have repeatedly held that government employees are NOT responsible for telling the truth and that what they say, write, or publish is INADMISSIBLE as evidence. A certification from the Social Security Administration that I am not eligible would therefore be MEANINGLESS, would not be admissible as evidence of anything in any court, and would be a clear violation of due process of law if used as a basis for making or enforcing any conclusive presumption or impair any of my constitutionally protected rights. All such statements would also be plagued by a criminal conflict of financial interest in violation of 18 U.S.C. §208. For proof that you can't trust anything that any government worker says, writes, or publishes on their forms or website see: Legal Deception, Propaganda, and Fraud, Form #05.014; https://sedm.org/Forms/05-MemLaw/LegalDecPropFraud.pdf.

3. Since I now know that I am not eligible for any government "benefit" and indicating otherwise would be criminal FRAUD, for you to COMPEL me to provide any evidence demonstrating otherwise, including a government identifying number, would constitute compelling me to incriminate myself, which the Fifth Amendment forbids you to do if you really ARE a government subject to the constitution. Therefore, by demanding that I PROVE that a private human like me not acting as a statutory "person" doesn't have an SSN or that I ever applied for one in itself violates the Fifth Amendment. It is what lawyers call a "perjury trap" to FORCE me to admit something that I do not need to admit in order to commercially benefit YOU. See the following for legally admissible proof that those born and domiciled in states of the Union are NOT eligible for social security if you don't believe me and rebut it within ten days or be found to AGREE and admit everything in it: Why You Aren't Eligible for Social Security, Form #06.001; https://sedm.org/Forms/06-AvoidingFranch/SSNotEligible.pdf. It therefore ought to be enough to merely tell you that I am ineligible, and to respond to this request by modifying any records that conflict with this submission. Anything more than that would be clearly unconstitutional.

"But let your 'Yes' be 'Yes,' and your 'No,' 'No.' For whatever is more than these is from the evil one."
[Jesus in Matt. 5:37, written by a FORMER tax collector]

4. I am submitting this application as a private human being protected ONLY by the Constitution and the common law. Any attempt to assign or enforce a statutory status such as "person", "individual", or "taxpayer" upon me shall constitute criminal identity theft, compelled association, and a violation of my religious beliefs. See Government Identity Theft, Form #05.046; https://sedm.org/Forms/05-MemLaw/GovernmentIdentityTheft.pdf.

5. I am not authorized to speak or act on behalf of any government in the context of this interaction. Hence, I am not acting in the capacity of a statutory "person" or "individual" under any government civil statute. I am also NOT the "you" referenced in the instructions of the form submitted in the context of any alleged "obligations", because you can't lawfully impose any duties upon non-consenting PRIVATE people such as myself without violating the Thirteenth Amendment prohibition against involuntary servitude because I don't consent or volunteer. Any attempt to impute or enforce the civil statutory status of "person", "individual", etc. is a violation of my constitutional right to not contract or associate civilly with any and every government under the First Amendment and causes the RECIPIENT to render this submission knowingly false in violation of 18 U.S.C. §1001 and 18 U.S.C. §1621.

6. I as a private human and non-attorney am not qualified or even obligated to make "legal determinations" or "legal conclusions" about my civil status or the applicability of any statute to my situation beyond that specified here or in relation to any statute not specifically mentioned herein. As attorneys would say: "Objection: Calls for a legal conclusion". I claim the SAME rights as attorneys in this regard. This includes knowing or obeying ANYTHING in any civil statute. Yes, "citizens" are presumed to know the law but I don't claim to BE a statutory "citizen" (8 U.S.C. §1401 or 26 C.F.R. §1.1-1(c)) subject to your authority and have the First Amendment right to NOT be one and to be ONLY a private human. See Why You are a Political Citizen but Civil Non-Citizen, National, and Nonresident Alien, Form #05.006; https://sedm.org/Forms/05-MemLaw/WhyANational.pdf. Your application process is flawed to FORCE ME into a position to make such determinations or learn or know any statutes that don't apply to a non-resident:

IDIOT. A person who has been without understanding from his nativity, and whom the law, therefore, presumes never likely to attain any. Shelf. Lun. 2. See Insanity. State v. Haner, 186 Iowa, 1259,173 N.W. 225; Jones v. Commonwealth, 154 Ky. 752,159 S.W. 568, 569.

> **IDIOTA.** *In the Civil Law. An unlearned, illiterate, or simple person. Calvin.* ***A private man; one not in office.***
>
> *In Common Law. An idiot or fool.*
> *[Black's Law Dictionary, Fourth Edition, p. 880]*

> "Idiot" is another word that has changed its meaning over the centuries, although not as dramatically as "nice" once it was imported into English. **The Greek "idiotes" meant simply "private individual" (from "idios," meaning "personal"), as opposed to a "public man," a politician (government agent mine) or other well-known individual. ("Idios" also gave us "idiom," one's own way of speaking, and "idiosyncrasy," one's personal quirks and habits.)**
>
> [The Word Detective: Idiot; Downloaded 1/30/2017; SOURCE: http://www.word-detective.com/2008/03/idiot/]

> "A private person cannot make constitutions or laws, nor can he with authority construe them, nor can he administer or execute [meaning OBEY or ENFORCE] them."
> [United States v. Harris, 106 U.S. 629, 1 S.Ct. 601, 27 L.Ed. 290 (1883)]

---

7. *Please DO NOT advise me or especially PUNISH ME about what to put or not put on the application to which the form relates.* It would be criminal witness tampering to do so, and especially if you threaten to punish or withhold the thing requested for a failure to perform any alleged obligation because it is an UNLAWFUL obligation. It would also result in you practicing law on my behalf, which I do not consent to allow you to do and which would also be a violation of your delegation of authority order. The ONLY thing I am willing to entertain that might change my testimony on the form is legally admissible evidence in affidavit form from a government worker signed under penalty of perjury containing only FACTS. Such a submission should be prepared by someone within the physical jurisdiction of the local courts in the event that the facts provided are FALSE. Otherwise, the courts have repeatedly held that all government forms, statements, and publications are UNTRUSTWORTHY, INCLUDING but not limited to anything and everything on the forms submitted herein.

8. *None of the terms used on this form or the instructions are defined or exist in any government civil or criminal statute.* They are useful ONLY in the PRIVATE or CONSTITUTIONAL context and not the PUBLIC or publici juris or STATUTORY contexts. Hence, no such statutes can or do regulate or control inaccuracies on this form or may form the basis for any kind of injury or standing to sue upon any government or upon the recipient. Any assertion otherwise constitutes purposeful availment of commerce with me and a waiver of official, judicial, and sovereign immunity under the Foreign Sovereign Immunities Act, 28 U.S.C. Chapter 97 and consent to be sued in STATE and not FEDERAL court.

9. *Any records in the possession of any government or the recipient that are in conflict with this submission are knowingly and willfully and even criminally false and fraudulent.* Such records must IMMEDIATELY be corrected. This submission shall constitute a formal request to correct all such records. It shall also shall constitute a criminal complaint if they are NOT corrected. See: 18 U.S.C. §1001, 18 U.S.C. §1003, 18 U.S.C. §1028, 18 U.S.C. §1030.

10. *This application does NOT constitute an "acceptance" under the Uniform Commercial Code (U.C.C.) of any kind toward any "benefit" offered by any government.* Such "benefit" includes the protection of any of the civil statutes or franchises enacted by the national congress or a state of the Union. The ONLY offer and acceptance involved in the context of this interaction is the offer of the TEMPORARY use of PRIVATE information about me to issue the identification requested. The only "Merchant" (U.C.C. §2-104(1)) in the context of this transaction is the affiant and the recipient of this form is the "Buyer" (U.C.C. §2-103(1)). For all purposes OTHER than this direct interaction AFTER the identification is issued, affiant shall be a civil statutory "non-resident" who shall NOT have or retain any civil statutory status, including but not limited to "citizen", "resident", "driver", "person", "individual", "taxpayer", etc. Any attempt by the Recipient or any government to impute or enforce such civil statuses shall constitute criminal identity theft and a waiver by those imputing or enforcing said statuses of official, judicial, and sovereign immunity under the Foreign Sovereign Immunities Act, 28 U.S.C. Chapter 97 and the Longarm Statutes of my State and an implied consent and agreement by the recipient and his/her employer to pay TEN TIMES the monetary value that could be derived from the enforcement of said statuses or the obligations attached thereto. Notice to the agent is notice to the principal.

11. *This application may not be used for any commercial purpose that would benefit any government, including but not limited to any administrative, tax, or statutory enforcement.* The ONLY legitimate purpose of any and every government is to benefit the beneficiaries of the public trust, which are the PRIVATE people protected by the Constitution and NOT to primarily benefit ITSELF. You cannot serve two masters: God and mammon. It is a violation of my religious beliefs to contract with, do business with, or be an officer or agent of any government

in the context of any government statute or anything resulting from this interaction other than that specified herein. Judges 2:1-4. Violation of my religious laws invites the CURSES of my God. Remedy is provided in the Religious Freedom Restoration Act (R.F.R.A.) in fulfillment of the First Amendment for any attempt to compel me to violate my sincerely held religious beliefs or practices, as documented in <u>Delegation of Authority Order from God to Christians</u>, Form #13.007; <u>https://sedm.org/Forms/13-SelfFamilyChurchGovnce/DelOfAuthority.pdf</u>.

12. Even if Affiant HAD consented to violate the Holy Bible by manifesting CONSENT to any government franchise or "benefit" the Declaration of Independence, which was enacted into law in 1 Stat. 1, declares that my constitutional rights are UNALIENABLE, which means that I am legally UNABLE to give them away or consent to any legal obligation that would impair them. Therefore, any presumption that I could have done so in fact and in law is not only a nullity, but cannot count as a lawful act or therefore ANY act at all cognizable in any court of law in relation to any REAL government. A so-called "government" that makes a profitable business or a franchise out of enticing people to surrender their constitutional rights by contracting with or legally associating with it is not government at all, but a de facto private corporation and the WHORE mentioned in the Bible book of Revelation.

'For among My [God's] people are found wicked [covetous public servant] men; <u>They lie in wait as one who sets snares; They set a trap; They catch men.</u> As a cage is full of birds, <u>So their houses are full of deceit.</u> Therefore they have become great and grown rich. They have grown fat, they are sleek; Yes, they surpass the deeds of the wicked; They do not plead the cause, The cause of the fatherless [for the innocent, widows, <u>or the nontaxpayer</u>]; Yet they prosper, And the right of the needy they do not defend. <u>Shall I not punish them for these things?</u>' says the Lord. 'Shall I not avenge Myself on such a nation as this?'

*"<u>An astonishing and horrible thing Has been committed in the land: The prophets prophesy falsely, And the priests [judges in franchise courts that worship government as a pagan deity] rule by their own power; And My people love to have it so. But what will you do in the end?</u>"
[<u>Jer. 5:26-31</u>, Bible, NKJV]*

The first function of any REAL government is to protect PRIVATE rights and PRIVATE property. That protection BEGINS with ensuring that such property is NEVER converted to PUBLIC property or PUBLIC rights, even WITH the consent of the owner. This keeps the government in the box and removes any temptation to trick people out of their property with franchises, "words of art", or "benefits". See <u>De Facto Government Scam</u>, Form #05.043; <u>https://sedm.org/Forms/05-MemLaw/DeFactoGov.pdf</u>.

13. It is a violation of the Sherman Anti-Trust Act to "bundle" any franchises such as Social Security with de jure constitutional functions such as passports in order to FORCE applicants into an adhesion contract that causes a surrender of any Constitutional right. It also violates the Unconstitutional Conditions Doctrine and results in criminal human trafficking. See <u>22 U.S.C. §2721</u>. I won't tolerate any attempt by you to "bundle" such services. Corporations such as Google are commonly sued for doing so, and you should be also if you continue to insist on such monopolistic and usurious practices. Google was fined $5 BILLION dollars by the EU for such bundling with their Android operating system.

14. For the purposes of this interaction, the term "Social Security Number", when used by any government for civil or criminal enforcement or commercial purposes to undermine the PRIVATE rights of the Affiant and Submitter, shall mean a license from the Affiant to the government or recipient under the terms of the following anti-franchise franchise: <u>Injury Defense Franchise and Agreement</u>, Form #06.027; <u>https://sedm.org/Forms/06-AvoidingFranch/InjuryDefenseFranchise.pdf</u>. I MUST define the term because I'm not allowed to trust anything the government says in its forms or publications, including its definitions, and I don't want to invite or allow anyone to make any presumptions that might impair my constitutional rights or civil status. Welcome to the Matrix, Neo.

_____
Signature

You can find an HTML version of the above on our website in that you can cut and paste and reuse in your own forms, so you don't have to retype it, below:

> *Language You Can Use in Identity Document Application to Prove You Don't Have an SSN and Aren't Eligible, and Never Applied for One*, SEDM
> https://sedm.org/language-you-can-use-in-identity-document-application-to-prove-you-dont-have-an-ssn-and-arent-eligible-and-never-applied-for-one/

2. *Why It is Illegal for Me to Request or Use a Taxpayer Identification Number*, Form #04.205
   https://sedm.org/Forms/FormIndex.htm
3. *USA Passport Application Attachment*, Form #06.007

https://sedm.org/Forms/FormIndex.htm

23.8 Proving to federal agencies that they are FORBIDDEN by the Privacy Act from compelling the use of an SSN

There are many occasions where you may be asked to PROVE to a federal agency that they are NOT PERMITTED to either maintain an SSN in your records or force you to disclose one in the context even of income taxation. By far the most prevalent occasion where this happens is with people from states of the Union who are either active duty military or discharged veterans dealing with military benefits or taxation. This section will focus exclusively on this group, all of whom typically deal directly or indirectly with any of the following:

1. Department of Defense (DOD).
2. Defense Finance Accounting Service (DFAS).
3. Veterans Administration (VA).

You can apply the concepts described in this section to ANY federal agency, because the concepts described apply to ALL federal agencies.

23.8.1 Forcing the agency to satisfy their burden or proof

Within the Department of Defense, the only UNIVERSAL id that is permitted is the DOD ID number. This was covered earlier in section 21.1. Most of the time this ID number alone is sufficient, but you will still encounter problems with specifying an SSN when dealing with DFAS. DFAS will ask for this when you apply for retirement benefits on the using the Form DD2656 entitled "Data for payment of Retired Personnel".

First of all, the Privacy Act specifies that federal agencies may only ask for an SSN when MANDATED by law:

> *Disclosure of Social Security Number*
>
> *Section 7 of Pub. L. 93–579 provided that:*
>
> *"(a)(1) It shall be unlawful for any Federal, State or local government agency to deny to any individual any right, benefit, or privilege provided by law because of such individual's refusal to disclose his social security account number. "*
>
> *(2) the [The] provisions of paragraph (1) of this subsection shall not apply with respect to— "*
>
> *(A) any disclosure which is required by Federal statute, or "*
>
> *(B) the disclosure of a social security number to any Federal, State, or local agency maintaining a system of records in existence and operating before January 1, 1975, if such disclosure was required under statute or regulation adopted prior to such date to verify the identity of an individual. "*
>
> *(b) Any Federal, State, or local government agency which requests an individual to disclose his social security account number shall inform that individual whether that disclosure is mandatory or voluntary, by what statutory or other authority such number is solicited, and what uses will be made of it."*
>
> *[SOURCE: 5 U.S.C. §552a Legislative Notes, https://www.law.cornell.edu/uscode/text/5/552a]*

The application of the above requirement of law is further described on the Department of Justice website at:

> *Disclosure of Social Security Numbers*, Department of Justice Office of Privacy and Civil Liberties
> https://www.justice.gov/opcl/overview-privacy-act-1974-2020-edition/ssn

The bottom line is that when a federal agency asks for the SSN they must satisfy the following two requirements:

1. They must specify whether its use is VOLUNTARY or MANDATORY.
2. They must tell you the SPECIFIC law that mandates providing it.

If they either don't provide the law mandating the use of the SSN as required by 5 U.S.C. §552a Legislative Notes, they can't ask for or keep it in their system of records. Even if they do provide the CIVIL statute mandating the use of the SSN, there is an additional burden of proof even beyond that, which is a providing proof that of how you became subject to the specific law they cite. Whether you are subject to the law they cite usually depends upon your CIVIL STATUTORY STATUS, which ONLY YOU can decide and acquire by an act of YOUR EXPRESS CONSENT.

Ultimately then, the federal agency must provide not only the law, but HOW you consented to the specific law they are citing by choosing a civil status that the law applies to such as CIVIL STATUTORY "U.S. person", "U.S. citizen", or "U.S. resident". All of these civil statuses are entirely voluntary and you can withdraw your consent to receive the "benefits" of these civil statuses at ANY TIME. We prove this in:

> *Your Exclusive Right to Declare or Establish Your Civil Status*, Form #13.008
> https://sedm.org/Forms/13-SelfFamilyChurchGovnce/RightToDeclStatus.pdf

We must ALWAYS remember in scenarios like this that:

1. Every CIVIL statutory status is a legislative creation of and PROPERTY of the government grantor. That means it is PUBLIC property.
2. Every CIVIL statutory status has both PRIVILEGES and OBLIGATIONS attached to it. These are two sides of the SAME coin.
3. If you ACCEPT, ASK FOR, or APPLY FOR the PRIVILEGES, BENEFITS, or PUBLIC RIGHTS of a CIVIL statutory status, then you implicitly ALSO accept the OBLIGATIONS that go with it as well. In that sense, there is an IMPLIED "quid pro quo" obligation to pay for whatever you ask for. If this were not so, those doing so would be STEALING from whomever has to PAY to DELIVER the PRIVILEGES that apply to those who invoke the status. Nothing in life is free.
4. If you ASK for or APPLY for a CIVIL statutory status or the BENEFITS, PRIVILEGES, or PUBLIC rights that attach to the status, then you are asking to receive PUBLIC property.
5. Only those who are PUBLIC OFFICERS can accept or use PUBLIC property. Otherwise, a theft and conversion would be involved.

> "**Public office**. The right, authority, and duty created and conferred by law, by which for a given period, either fixed by law or enduring at the pleasure of the creating power, an individual is invested with some portion of the sovereign functions of government for the benefit of the public. Walker v. Rich, 79 Cal.App. 139, 249 P. 56, 58. An agency for the state, the duties of which involve in their performance the exercise of some portion of the sovereign power, either great or small. Yaselli v. Goff, C.C.A., 12 F.2d. 396, 403, 56 A.L.R. 1239; Lacey v. State, 13 Ala.App. 212, 68 So. 706, 710; Curtin v. State, 61 Cal.App. 377, 214 P. 1030, 1035; Shelmadine v. City of Elkhart, 75 Ind.App. 493, 129 N.E. 878. State ex rel. Colorado River Commission v. Frohmiller, 46 Ariz. 413, 52 P.2d. 483, 486. **Where, by virtue of law, a person is clothed, not as an incidental or transient authority, but for such time as de- notes duration and continuance, with Independent power to control the property of the public**, or with public functions to be exercised in the supposed interest of the people, the service to be compensated by a stated yearly salary, and the occupant having a designation or title, the position so created is a public office. State v. Brennan, 49 Ohio.St. 33, 29 N.E. 593.
> [Black's Law Dictionary, Fourth Edition, p. 1235]

Thus, by asking for or receiving the PUBLIC property, rights, privileges, or "benefits", you ultimately must implicitly agree to be TREATED effectively as a "public officer" subject to CIVIL legislative control of Congress.

With the above in mind, anyone who would consent, either implicitly or explicitly, to ANY CIVIL statutory status that the obligation to provide the SSN attaches to is a FOOL. Those who ask for the numbers typically don't know any of this. The correct way to respond to a request for an SSN is therefore to:

1. Ask whether the disclosure is VOLUNTARY or MANDTORY.
2. Ask for the specific LAW that mandates the use of the SSN.
3. Ask them to provide legally admissible evidence that you satisfy the criteria for ACQUIRING the civil status that the obligation attaches to. In most cases, that CIVIL STATUTORY STATUS is STATUTORY "U.S. person" (26 U.S.C. §7701(a)(30)), "U.S. citizen", or "U.S. resident" as indicated in the Privacy Act itself at 5 U.S.C. §553a(a)(2):

> *5 U.S. Code § 552a - Records maintained on individuals*

> *(a)DEFINITIONS.*
>
> *For purposes of this section—*
>
> *(2) the term "<u>individual</u>" means a citizen of the United States or an alien lawfully admitted for permanent residence;*

The "citizen of the United States" as used above is not directly defined, but it can only mean a human being DOMICILED on federal territory within the exclusive jurisdiction of Congress. The separation of powers doctrine forbids federal CIVIL jurisdiction of Congress within the exclusive jurisdiction of a Constitutional State.

23.8.2 Proving that the TAX LAWS at least DO NOT require the use of an SSN in your case

It is a requirement of membership that all of our members must be nonresident aliens. In the case of nonresident aliens filing retirement papers with DFAS, for instance, they are asked to file the Form DD2656. That form is the first form that MANDATES providing an SSN in your interactions with the DOD, which naturally leads to questions about why and how the SSN could be mandatory in such a scenario to someone who is a compliant member. Ultimately, the authorities in section 21.2prove that the DOD ID is mandatory for everything EXCEPT DFAS and tax issues. What, then, about "taxes" makes the SSN mandatory? The answers are found in 26 C.F.R. §301.6109-1:

1. SSN is mandatory for STATUTORY "U.S. citizens" and "U.S. persons". STATUTORY "U.S. citizens" are VOLUNTARY offices within the Secretary of the Treasury for tax purposes ONLY. See:
    1.1. 26 C.F.R. §301.6109-1(b)(1).
    1.2. 26 C.F.R. §1.1441-1(d).
    1.3. *How State Nationals Volunteer to Pay Income Tax*, Form #08.024
    https://sedm.org/Forms/08-PolicyDocs/HowYouVolForIncomeTax.pdf
2. A "nonresident alien" is a "foreign person". SSN is mandatory for "nonresident aliens" per 26 C.F.R. §301.6109-1(b)(2) ONLY if:
    2.1. A foreign person that has income effectively connected with the conduct of a U.S. trade or business at any time during the taxable year. "Effectively connected" MEANS private property DONATED to a public use, public purpose, or public office to procure the "benefits" of 26 U.S.C. 162 deductions from tax on the 1040NR form. See:
    > *How to File Returns*, Form #09.074, Section 9.12** (Member Subscriptions)
    > https://sedm.org/product/filing-returns-form-09-074/
    2.2. A foreign person that has a U.S. office or place of business or a U.S. fiscal or paying agent at any time during the taxable year. The "office or place of business" must be in the STATUTORY geographical "United States" defined in 26 U.S.C. §7701(a)(9) and (a)(10) and 26 C.F.R. §301.7701-7(b). Thus, it EXCLUDES any part of the GEOGRAPHICAL states of the Union.
    2.3. A nonresident alien treated as a resident under section 6013(g) or (h). This scenario is where a "nonresident alien" files on a 1040 return with a spouse who is a STATUTORY "U.S. person".
    2.4. A foreign person that makes a return of tax (including income, estate, and gift tax returns), an amended return, or a refund claim **under** this title but excluding information returns, statements, or documents. Note that a "return of tax" is NOT the same as a "tax return". If no tax is owed, there is no such thing as a "return of tax" and the party is not a "taxpayer", but a victim of theft if money was withheld involuntarily by the withholding agent defined in 26 U.S.C. §7701(a)(16).
    2.5. A foreign person that makes an election under §301.7701–3(c).
    2.6. A foreign person that furnishes a withholding certificate described in §1.1441–1(e)(2) or (3) of this chapter or §1.1441–5(c)(2)(iv) or (3)(iii) of this chapter to the extent required under §1.1441–1(e)(4)(vii) of this chapter.
    2.7. A foreign person whose taxpayer identifying number is required to be furnished on any return, statement, or other document as required by the income tax regulations under section 897 or 1445. This paragraph (b)(2)(vii) applies as of November 3, 2003.
    2.8. A foreign person that furnishes a withholding certificate described in §1.1446–1(c)(2) or (3) of this chapter or whose taxpayer identification number is required to be furnished on any return, statement, or other document as required by the income tax regulations under section 1446. This paragraph (b)(2)(viii) shall apply to partnership taxable years beginning after May 18, 2005, or such earlier time as the regulations under §§1.1446–1 through 1.1446–5 of this chapter apply by reason of an election under §1.1446–7 of this chapter.

An application for retired pay from the Defense Finance Accounting Service (DFAS) on Form DD2656 on the part of a compliant member who is a "nonresident alien" does NOT, by the way, fit into any of the categories listed in item 2 above WITHOUT your consent in some form. Only by CONSENT in the following forms:

1. You DONATE your earnings to a public office and public purpose by declaring exemptions and deductions under 26 U.S.C. §162 on the 1040NR return.
    1.1. These are PRIVILEGES and BENEFITS that have financial value and thus constitute consideration that forms the basis for an obligation on your party.
    1.2. Since ALL the earnings of most Americans physically present and domiciled within a constitutional state are "excluded" rather than "exempted" under 26 U.S.C. §872, these deductions are UNNECESSARY in most cases. See:
        > *Excluded Earnings and People*, Form #14.019
        > https://sedm.org/Forms/14-PropProtection/ExcludedEarningsAndPeople.pdf
2. You have to "return a tax" by virtue of having payments from the U.S. government and NOT anyplace within the statutory geographical "United States" under 26 U.S.C. §7701(a)(9) and (a)(10).
    2.1. Ordinarily, in order to even RECEIVE a payment from the U.S. government, you must be engaged in a privilege, and thus, incur the obligation to pay a tax. This is the case with Social Security, for instance, which is Taxable "gross income" by statute in 26 U.S.C. §861(a)(8).
    2.2. Even in the case of government payments, some are not taxable, such as those that are a product of selling "labor" in exchange for money under 26 U.S.C. §83, as in the case of those receiving retired pay. The entitlement to RECEIVE the retirement pay was earned with your labor, which cost money to produce and is therefore not "profit" in a constitutional or Sixteenth Amendment sense. See:
        > *Proof that Involuntary Income Taxes on Your Labor are Slavery*, Form #05.055** (Member Subscriptions)
        > https://sedm.org/product/proof-that-involuntary-income-taxes-on-your-labor-are-slavery-form-05-055/
3. You pursue privileged STATUTORY "resident" status by filing jointly with a privileged STATUTORY "U.S. person" spouse on a 1040 return. This is done by an "election" under 26 U.S.C. §6013(g) and (h).

All of the above circumstances are NOT known at the time of APPLYING for retirement pay on Form DD2656. They don't even happen until AFTER you even RECEIVE the pay. So, there is NO WAY that the DFAS could satisfy the burden of proving that there is a STATUTORY requirement IN YOUR CASE AND WITHIN YOUR CIRCUMSTANCES as a "nonresident alien" to supply an SSN. As such, if they demand or insist on a Social Security Number or even continue to maintain a record of one against your consent, they are VIOLATING the Privacy Act of 1974 because there is no statute MANDATING said use or collection. In that scenario, the only thing they can ask for or enforce a REQUIREMENT for is a DOD ID Number and NEVER a Social Security number as we indicated earlier in section 21.1.

The only defense that DFAS can have at this point in insisting on an SSN is to PRESUME that you are a STATUTORY "U.S. person" (26 U.S.C. §7701(a)(30)) or "U.S. citizen" under 8 U.S.C. §1401 (someone born in a TERRITORY) and hope you don't CHALLENGE said presumption. You should NEVER let them get away with this presumption and INSIST that they PROVE you are one or even that they can FORCE you to "elect" to be one if you don't want to. Clearly, such an "election" cannot lawfully even be made if you truly are a "nonresident alien" born within a CONSTITUTIONAL state and domiciled there. In fact, there is no provision in the Internal Revenue Code or Treasury Regulations even AUTHORIZING such an "election" and such an election is NOT listed in 26 C.F.R. §301.6109-1(b) either a the origin of the requirement to have or use an SSN. In fact, all such ELECTIONS are a crime in violation of 18 U.S.C. §911:

> *18 U.S. Code § 911 - Citizen of the United States*
>
> *Whoever falsely and willfully represents himself to be a citizen of the United States shall be fined under this title or imprisoned not more than three years, or both.*
>
> *(June 25, 1948, ch. 645, 62 Stat. 742; Pub. L. 103–322, title XXXIII, § 330016(1)(H), Sept. 13, 1994, 108 Stat. 2147.)*

Like the entire Internal Revenue Code, the "citizen of the United States" above is a STATUTORY "citizen", not a CONSTITUTIONAL or Fourteenth Amendment citizen. STATUTORY and CONSTITUTIONAL "citizens of the United States" are mutually exclusive and non-overlapping, because EACH depends on a DIFFERENT geographical "United States" as we prove in:

> *Why the Fourteenth Amendment is NOT a Threat to Your Freedom*, Form #08.015
> https://sedm.org/Forms/08-PolicyDocs/FourteenthAmendNotProb.pdf

The STATUTORY "citizen of the United States" in 18 U.S.C. §911 above is a legislative creation of Congress and property of Congress and using that property without their consent is STEALING and hence a crime. HOWEVER, not that 18 U.S.C. 911 has WILLFULNESS as a prerequisite. If you don't' know what the difference between a STATUTORY "citizen of the United States" and a CONSTITUTIONAL or Fourteenth Amendment "citizen of the United States" are, then falsely claiming to be a STATUTORY "citizen of the United States" is NOT a crime, but merely a "mistake of law" that has DIRE financial consequences upon you and makes you into PERPETUAL surety to pay off an endless and ever-growing mountain of public debt. SHAME OF YOU if you don't understand citizenship as documented below in that case by using the following materials:

1. *Citizenship Status v. Tax Status*, Form #10.011
   https://sedm.org/Forms/10-Emancipation/CitizenshipStatusVTaxStatus/CitizenshipVTaxStatus.htm
2. *Citizenship and Sovereignty Course*, Form #12.002
   SLIDES: https://sedm.org/LibertyU/CitAndSovereignty.pdf
   VIDEO: http://www.youtube.com/watch?v=xMrSiiAqJAU
3. *Affidavit of Citizenship, Domicile, and Tax Status*, Form #02.001
   https://sedm.org/Forms/02-Affidavits/AffCitDomTax.pdf
4. *Why You are a Political Citizen but Civil Non-Citizen, National, and Nonresident Alien*, Form #05.006
   https://sedm.org/Forms/05-MemLaw/WhyANational.pdf

If you don't understand citizenship and domicile, you will INEVITABLY become a target of CRIMINAL IDENTITY THEFT by all the government tyrants who want to STEAL your money. Your legal ignorance is the main method of protecting them from the consequences of such IDENTITY THEFT. That identity theft is documented in the following form that members must file as part of our compliance process:

> *Identity Theft Affidavit*, Form #14.020
> https://sedm.org/Forms/14-PropProtection/Identity_Theft_Affidavit-f14039.pdf

At this point, you have defeated every opportunity that DFAS could use as an exculpatory defense in DEMANDING or MANDATING a Social Security Number. Since they can't meet their burden or proving its use is mandated by law in YOUR SPECIFIC CASE, and since you have notified them that you do not CONSENT to its use, they must withdraw any demand to REQUIRE it and destroy any records of it in their system if you don't WANT them using it or else they are guilty of violating the Privacy Act of 1974, 5 U.S.C. §552a(a)(1).

23.8.3 Conclusion and summary

1. DOD Instruction 1000.30 mandates the DOD ID within the Department of Defense.
    1.1. It authorizes DFAS to ask for the SSN only when required by law.
    1.2. Retirement paperwork Form DD108 and DD2656 as for the SSN
    1.3. All the authorities listed below explicitly say that a "nonresident alien" applicant such as myself am NOT required to have or use an SSN or TIN, so there is no requirement by law to have or use the SSN. See:
        1.3.1. 26 C.F.R. §301.6109-1(b)(2).
        1.3.2. 31 C.F.R. §1020.410(b)(3)(x).
        1.3.3. 31 C.F.R. §306.10.
        1.3.4. W-8BEN Inst. p. 1,2,4,5 (Cat. 25576H).
        1.3.5. W-8 Supp. Inst, p. 1,2,6 (Cat. 26698G).
        1.3.6. IRS Pub. 515 Inst. p. 7.
    1.4. The following withholding form proves that nonresident alien applicants are NOT required to supply an SSN, are not subject to reporting, and not subject to withholding. See:
        > *W-8SUB*, Form #04.231
        > https://sedm.org/Forms/04-Tax/2-Withholding/W-8SUB.pdf
2. It is not up to DFAS to make legal determinations about the civil status of the applicants, and especially whether they are "U.S. person" or "nonresident aliens":

2.1. Only the APPLICANT can determine their CIVIL and LEGAL status. This is a fulfillment of the First Amendment right of freedom to ASSOCIATE and DISASSOCIATE.
2.2. DFAS is OBLIGATED to ACCEPT and act as if the determinations of the APPLICANT about their civil status are accurate so long as the application forms submitted are signed under penalty of perjury by the ONLY witness, which is the APPLICANT.
3. Any attempt to unilaterally change that civil status from "nonresident alien" to STATUTORY "citizen of the United States" is:
    3.1. An act of criminally identity theft in violation of 18 U.S.C. §§911 and 912.
    3.2. An interference with the First Amendment right to associate or disassociate of the applicant. See:
    > *Your Exclusive Right to Declare or Establish Your Civil Status*, Form #13.008
    > https://sedm.org/Forms/13-SelfFamilyChurchGovnce/RightToDeclStatus.pdf
    3.3. Could result in criminal identity theft in violation of 18 U.S.C. §912.
    More on the above at:
    > *Identity Theft Affidavit*, Form #14.020
    > https://sedm.org/Forms/14-PropProtection/Identity_Theft_Affidavit-f14039.pdf
4. Any attempt to file information returns in contradiction to this status is a criminal offense under the Internal Revenue Code, 26 U.S.C. §7207. See:
    > *Form 1099CC*, Form #04.309
    > https://sedm.org/Forms/04-Tax/3-Reporting/Form1099-CC-Cust/Form1099-CC.pdf
5. The DOD SORN describes data that the DFAS retirement system collects below and include SSNs:
    > DFAS SORN, Defense Military Retiree and Annuity Pay System Records (January 07, 2009, 74 FR 696)
    > *https://dpcld.defense.gov/Privacy/SORNsIndex/DOD-wide-SORN-Article-View/Article/570196/t7347b/*
    5.1. Unfortunately, Defense Military Retiree and Annuity Pay System Records can only be searched through SSN rather than DOD ID. An agent on the DFAS support phone line personally admitted this.
    5.2. Even if you provide a DOD ID to the DFAS telephone representative, they can't locate the caller with it.
6. Retirees who refuse to disclose an SSN:
    6.1. Are FORBIDDEN from interacting electronically with DFAS through the MyPay System, because they are FORCED to enter their SSN instead of their DOD ID to access their retired pay records.
    6.2. Are FORBIDDEN from interacting telephonically with DFAS, because all agents answering the phone REFUSE to help them if they won't supply an SSN rather than the more proper DOD ID.
    The above are clearly DISCRIMINATION and unlawful and clear violation of the Privacy Act of 1974, 5 U.S.C. §552a(a)(1).
7. Social Security Justification Memos covering the following systems of records are therefore ILLEGALLY granted in VIOLATION of the Privacy Act of 1974, at least in the case of those who do not CONSENT to disclose an SSN, do not want such records maintained about them, and which no law expressly requires the use of SSNs for retirees who are nonresident aliens not engaged in any of the activities listed under 26 C.F.R. §301.6109-1(b)(2).
    > *Justification for the Continued Use of Social Security Numbers in Case Management System-DITPR #8679*, DFAS
    > https://media.defense.gov/2020/Feb/29/2002257235/-1/-1/0/CASE%20MANAGEMENT%20SYSTEM%20(CMS).PDF
8. The Privacy Impact Assessment (PIA) for the DFAS Case Management System says that DFAS tracks both DOD ID and SSN so there is NO EXCUSE why you CANNOT use the DOD ID RATHER than the SSN for ALL dealings with retirees. See:
    8.1. *Privacy Impact Assessments (PIA)*, DFAS
    https://www.dfas.mil/foia/privacyimpactassessments/
    8.2. *Privacy Impact Assessment (PIA)- Case Management System*-Contains the DOD ID Number, SSN
    https://www.dfas.mil/Portals/98/August%20Impact%20Assessements/20210723_CMS.pdf?ver=geHxrG0Y7XZbOTI_flE0xw==
    8.3. *Privacy Impact Assessment (PIA) -Defense Retiree and Annuitant Pay System (DRAS)*-Contains SSN. No mention of DOD ID. Information collected for retirees and annuitants includes name, social security number, military records, address, etc. Personally Identifiable Information (PII) data is received through a wide range of collection methods with the largest being interfaces with partners at Veterans Administration, Military Services, Internal Revenue Service (IRS), etc. PII data is also received from individuals during Retiree Seminars and during conversations with DFAS Call Center Customer Services Representatives. The RAPID (Retired Annuity Pay Information DRAS) system collects PII data from documents that are received from our customer base through the mail or via fax. Customers can send PII data to DFAS via Internet capabilities such as direct emails and forms on the DFAS Website.

https://media.defense.gov/2020/Feb/29/2002257205/-1/-1/0/DEFENSE%20RETIREE%20AND%20ANNUITANT%20PAY%20SYSTEM%20(DRAS)%202016.PDF

24 Rebutted False Arguments About Government Identifying Numbers

24.1 California DMV: We have a right to ask for Social Security Numbers as part of driver license applications

FALSE STATEMENT:

On the California Department of Motor Vehicles (DMV) website it makes the following statement:

> *Why Collect an SSN?*
>
> *The California Vehicle Code (CVC) requires the Department of Motor Vehicles (DMV) to collect your social security number (SSN). (CVC §§1653.5(a)(b), 12800(a), 12801) Federal law also allows any state to use a person's SSN for the purpose of establishing his/her identification. (42 U.S.C. §405(c)(2)(C)(i))*
> *[Social Security Number (FFDL 8); SOURCE: https://www.dmv.ca.gov/portal/dmv/detail/pubs/brochures/fast_facts/ffdl08]*

REBUTTAL:

4. It is illegal and unconstitutional to compel the surrender of any constitutional right in exchange for any state service such as a license of any kind. This prohibition includes compelling people to misrepresent their civil status or the location as being on federal territory when they are not there and cannot consent to be treated as IF they are there. Therefore, all statutes compelling the surrender of any constitutional right must be and in fact are "directory in nature" and of no practical force or effect upon a state domiciled party protected by the Constitution:

   > *"It has long been established that a State may not impose a penalty upon those who exercise a right guaranteed by the Constitution." Frost & Frost Trucking Co. v. Railroad Comm'n of California, 271 U.S. 583. "Constitutional rights would be of little value if they could be indirectly denied,' Smith v. Allwright, 321 U.S. 649, 644, or manipulated out of existence,' Gomillion v. Lightfoot, 364 U.S. 339, 345."*
   > *[Harman v. Forssenius, 380 U.S. 528 at 540, 85 S.Ct. 1177, 1185 (1965)]*

5. The U.S. Supreme Court has held that federal legislation doesn't apply to the internal affairs of states. The statute you cite is IRRELEVANT to those domiciled and present within a constitutional state and not present on federal territory:

   > *"It is no longer open to question that **the general government, unlike the states**, Hammer v. Dagenhart, 247 U.S. 251, 275, 38 S.Ct. 529, 3 A.L.R. 649, Ann.Cas.1918E 724, **possesses no inherent power in respect of the internal affairs of the states; and emphatically not with regard to legislation.** "*
   > *[Carter v. Carter Coal Co., 298 U.S. 238, 56 S.Ct. 855 (1936)]*

6. The California Vehicle Code only applies where constitutional rights don't exist, which is on federal territory within the exterior limits of the state not protected by the Constitution or the Bill of Rights. These areas are called "federal enclaves". See the following for a study by Congress on the nature of federal jurisdiction within these areas:
   Jurisdiction Over Federal Areas Within the States, U.S. Attorney General
   http://constitution.famguardian.org/juris/fjur/fed_jur.htm

7. The California Revenue and Taxation Code acknowledges that federal areas are the ONLY place it applies to with the following definitions relating to income tax and sales tax:

   > *California Revenue and Taxation Code*
   > *Division 2: Other Taxes*
   > *Part 10: Personal Income Tax*
   >
   > *17018. "State" includes the District of Columbia, and the possessions of the United States.*

   > *California Revenue and Taxation Code*
   > *Division 2: Other Taxes*
   > *Part 1: Sales and Use Taxes*

> 6017. "In this State" or "in the State" means within the exterior limits of the State of California and includes all territory within these limits owned by or ceded to the United States of America.

8. Congress cannot establish a "trade or business" within a CONSTITUTIONAL state in order to tax it, according to the U.S. Supreme Court:

    > *"Congress cannot authorize a trade or business within a State in order to tax it."*
    > [License Tax Cases, 72 U.S. 462, 18 L.Ed. 497, 5 Wall. 462, 2 A.F.T.R. 2224 (1866)]

9. The I.R.C. Subtitle A income tax is an excise tax upon a "trade or business", which is defined in 26 U.S.C. §7701(a)(26) as "the functions of a public office". Consequently, it cannot be offered or enforced within the exclusive jurisdiction of a constitutional state of the Union. See and rebut:

    > *The "Trade or Business" Scam*, Form #05.001
    > FORMS PAGE: https://sedm.org/Forms/FormIndex.htm
    > DIRECT LINK: https://sedm.org/Forms/05-MemLaw/TradeOrBusScam.pdf

10. The statute cited as 42 U.S.C. §405(c)(2)(C)(i) applies to federal territory ONLY within the exterior limit of the state. The definition of "State" found in the Social Security Act at 42 U.S.C. 1301(a)(1) includes only federal territory and NOT any state of the Union:

    > Social Security Act
    > SEC. 1101. [42 U.S.C. 1301] (a) When used in this Act—
    >
    > *(1) The term 'State', except where otherwise provided, includes the District of Columbia and the Commonwealth of Puerto Rico, and when used in titles IV, V, VII, XI, XIX, and XXI includes the Virgin Islands and Guam. Such term when used in titles III, IX, and XII also includes the Virgin Islands. Such term when used in title V and in part B of this title also includes American Samoa, the Northern Mariana Islands, and the Trust Territory of the Pacific Islands. Such term when used in titles XIX and XXI also includes the Northern Mariana Islands and American Samoa. In the case of Puerto Rico, the Virgin Islands, and Guam, titles I, X, and XIV, and title XVI (as in effect without regard to the amendment made by section 301 of the Social Security Amendments of 1972[3]) shall continue to apply, and the term 'State' when used in such titles (but not in title XVI as in effect pursuant to such amendment after December 31, 1973) includes Puerto Rico, the Virgin Islands, and Guam. Such term when used in title XX also includes the Virgin Islands, Guam, American Samoa, and the Northern Mariana Islands. Such term when used in title IV also includes American Samoa."*
    > [Social Security Act as of 2005, Section 1101]

11. The CONSTITUTIONAL state of California, acting in its sovereign capacity, CANNOT lawfully impersonate a federal territory for the purposes of STEALING people's money under the color, but without the actual authority, of law. It does this by claiming that it is a "State" under any act of Congress, INCLUDING that found in Title 42 of the U.S. Code. Doing so constitutes CRIMINAL identity theft, as documented in:

    > *Government Identity Theft*, Form #05.046
    > FORMS PAGE: https://sedm.org/Forms/FormIndex.htm
    > DIRECT LINK: https://sedm.org/Forms/05-MemLaw/GovernmentIdentityTheft.pdf

12. When acting upon federal enclaves, states of the Union are AGENTS and OFFICERS of the national government, according to the Founding Fathers.

    > *"It is true, that the Confederacy is to possess, and may exercise, the power of collecting internal as well as external taxes throughout the States; but it is probable that this power will not be resorted to, except for supplemental purposes of revenue; that an option will then be given to the States to supply their quotas by previous collections of their own; and that the eventual collection, under the immediate authority of the Union,* **will generally be made by the officers, and according to the rules, appointed by the several States. Indeed it is extremely probable, that in other instances, particularly in the organization of the judicial power, the officers of the States will be clothed with the correspondent authority of the Union.** "
    >
    > *"Should it happen, however, that separate collectors of internal revenue should be appointed under the federal government, the influence of the whole number would not bear a comparison with that of the multitude of State officers in the opposite scale. "*

> *"Within every district to which a federal collector would be allotted, there would not be less than thirty or forty, or even more, officers of different descriptions, and many of them persons of character and weight, whose influence would lie on the side of the State.* ***The powers delegated by the proposed Constitution to the federal government are few and defined. Those which are to remain in the State governments are numerous and indefinite. The former will be exercised principally on external objects, as war, peace, negotiation, and foreign commerce; with which last the power of taxation will, for the most part, be connected. The powers reserved to the several States will extend to all the objects which, in the ordinary course of affairs, concern the lives, liberties, and properties of the people, and the internal order, improvement, and prosperity of the State. The operations of the federal government will be most extensive and important in times of war and danger; those of the State governments, in times of peace and security. As the former periods will probably bear a small proportion to the latter, the State governments will here enjoy another advantage over the federal government. The more adequate, indeed, the federal powers may be rendered to the national defense, the less frequent will be those scenes of danger which might favor their ascendancy over the governments of the particular States.****"*
> [Federalist Paper No 45 (Jan. 1788), James Madison]

13. Land under the exclusive jurisdiction of the national government is not within the "United States" as geographically defined in the Internal Revenue Code, and, by implication, the California Revenue and Taxation Code and the Vehicle Code. Hence, any attempt to PRESUME that "drivers" applying for licenses need such a license or can be taxed or regulated in conducting commerce outside of these places.

    > TITLE 26 > Subtitle F > CHAPTER 79 > Sec. 7701. [Internal Revenue Code]
    > Sec. 7701. - Definitions
    >
    > *(a) When used in this title, where not otherwise distinctly expressed or manifestly incompatible with the intent thereof—*
    >
    > *(9) United States*
    >
    > *The term "United States" when used in a geographical sense includes only the States and the District of Columbia.*
    >
    > *(10) State*
    >
    > *The term "State" shall be construed to include the District of Columbia, where such construction is necessary to carry out provisions of this title.*
    >
    > _____
    >
    > TITLE 4 - FLAG AND SEAL, SEAT OF GOVERNMENT, AND THE STATES
    > CHAPTER 4 - **THE STATES**
    > Sec. 110. Same; definitions
    >
    > *(d) The term "State" includes any Territory or possession of the United States.*

14. The CONSTITUTIONAL state of California CANNOT act as a "State" as defined in the Buck Act, 4 U.S.C. §110(d) because it is not included in the definition and this would be a violation of the separation of powers. See:
    > *Government Conspiracy to Destroy the Separation of Powers*, Form #05.023
    > FORMS PAGE: https://sedm.org/Forms/FormIndex.htm
    > DIRECT LINK: https://sedm.org/Forms/05-MemLaw/SeparationOfPowers.pdf
15. It is CONSTRUCTIVE FRAUD and a conspiracy against rights to identify the Constitutional state of California, which is legislatively "foreign" in relation to the national government, as the "State" one is making application to when applying for a STATE license of any kind.
16. Any attempt to enforce the Vehicle Code, the Revenue and Taxation Code, or the income tax by California to places OUTSIDE of federal enclaves therefore constitutes and is stipulated by the recipient to constitute:
    16.1. A waiver of official, judicial, and sovereign immunity under 28 U.S.C. §1605(a).
    16.2. Makes California a "foreign state" in relation to the national government operating extraterritorially.
    16.3. Creates a criminal financial conflict of interest in the state, by incentivizing them to falsely claim that they can act as a federal territory or federal corporation in relation to the CONSTITUTIONAL citizens physically present OUTSIDE of federal enclaves.
17. It is ILLEGAL for a state citizen to apply for or use Social Security as exhaustively described in:
    > *Why You Aren't Eligible for Social Security*, Form #06.001
    > FORMS PAGE: https://sedm.org/Forms/FormIndex.htm
    > DIRECT LINK: https://sedm.org/Forms/06-AvoidingFranch/SSNotEligible.pdf

18. It is ILLEGAL for a state citizen to apply for or use a Social Security Number or Taxpayer Identification Number as exhaustively described in:

> *Why It is Illegal for Me to Request or Use a Taxpayer Identification Number*, Form #04.205
> FORMS PAGE: https://sedm.org/Forms/FormIndex.htm
> DIRECT LINK: https://sedm.org/Forms/04-Tax/2-Withholding/WhyTINIllegal.pdf

The recipient, which is the CONSTITUTIONAL and not STATUTORY state of California, has ten days to rebut the above evidence or be found to agree and be in estoppel in pais.

Furthermore, a failure to rebut constitutes an admission that by denying a constitutional right, they are in possession and have STOLEN private property and PRIVATE rights protected by the Bill of Rights and the Fourteenth Amendment. As such, they are subject to the following conditions of the loan of such property. This agreement establishes a franchise not unlike the "trade or business" franchise to defend the applicant against usurpations. It is patterned after the government's similar use of loans of government property to establish obligations in the form of a franchise. I have an equal right to establish government obligations in the same way they try to do to me, and to do it as a defense against government's attempts to do the same to me:

> *Injury Defense Franchise and Agreement*, Form #06.027
> FORMS PAGE: https://sedm.org/Forms/FormIndex.htm
> DIRECT LINK: https://sedm.org/Forms/06-AvoidingFranch/InjuryDefenseFranchise.pdf

25 Summary and Conclusions

We will now summarize all of the conclusions of fact and conclusions of law derived from the evidence provided in this document:

1. Government-issued identifying numbers include:
    1.1. Social Security Numbers (SSN) issued by the Social Security Administration under the authority of 20 C.F.R. §422.104. Issued only to "U.S. persons" defined in 26 U.S.C. §7701(a)(30) with a domicile on federal territory.
    1.2. Taxpayer Identification Numbers. Issued by the IRS pursuant to 26 U.S.C. §6109. Can be issued only to "U.S. persons" as defined in 26 U.S.C. §7701(a)(30) who have a domicile on federal territory.
        1.2.1. Employer Identification Numbers (EIN) obtained using IRS Form SS-4.
        1.2.2. Taxpayer Identification Numbers obtained using IRS Form W-9.
    1.3. Individual Taxpayer Identification Numbers (ITIN) obtained using IRS Form W-7. ITINs can only be issued to aliens pursuant to 26 C.F.R. §301.6109-1(d)(3).
2. SSNs and TINs are made interchangeable for the purposes of income taxes pursuant to the following authorities:
    2.1. 26 U.S.C. §6109(a) (at the end) authorizes the substitution of an SSN for a TIN, but neither MANDATES it nor states the circumstances under which it is appropriate.
    2.2. 26 C.F.R. §301.7701-11.
    2.3. 26 U.S.C. §6011(b).
3. Only persons with a domicile on federal territory that is no part of a state of the Union are eligible to be issued Taxpayer Identification Numbers or Social Security Numbers. 20 C.F.R. §422.104 and 26 U.S.C. §6109. Persons domiciled outside of federal territory such as in a state of the Union are NOT eligible for federally issued identifying numbers.
4. The possession or use of the Social Security Card or Social Security Number causes a surrender of constitutional rights and conveys to the government the authority to penalize the abuses of these forms of public property and the activities of the "trustees", fiduciaries, and "public officers" who are in custody of them:
    4.1. The back of the Social Security Card itself admits this:

> "Improper use of this card or number by anyone is punishable by fine, imprisonment or both."
> [SOURCE: http://sedm.org/Forms/Discovery/BPDFOIA.pdf]

   4.2. The U.S. Supreme Court has said that anyone who receives a government benefit waives their rights and their standing in court to sue the government for violations of rights caused by the administration of government franchises:

> "The Government urges that **the Power Company is estopped to question the validity of the Act creating the Tennessee Valley Authority**, and hence that the stockholders, suing in the right of the corporation, cannot [297

> U.S. 323] maintain this suit. ..... *The principle is invoked that one who accepts the benefit of a statute cannot be heard to question its constitutionality. Great Falls Manufacturing Co. v. Attorney General, 124 U.S. 581; Wall v. Parrot Silver & Copper Co., 244 U.S. 407; St. Louis Casting Co. v. Prendergast Construction Co., 260 U.S. 469."*
> [Ashwander v. Tennessee Valley Auth., 297 U.S. 288 (1936)]

5. All identifying numbers issued by the government are property of their Creator, which is the government, and not to the person holding or using them. See:
    5.1. 20 C.F.R. §422.103(d).
    5.2. The Social Security Card itself, which says:

    > "This card belongs to the Social Security Administration and you must return it if we ask for it."

    5.3. The SSA Form SS-5 application is entitled "Application for a Social Security Card". It does not say "Application for Social Security Benefits". You are applying to become a custodian and fiduciary over public property, and strings attach to that application.
    5.4. Any person in possession or use of a Social Security Card or Number is a trustee and fiduciary over public property in their temporary custody and control. Anything they attach the card or the number to become "private property donated to a public use to procure the benefits of a franchise".
6. Anyone who asks you for "Your Social Security Number" is asking TWO questions:
    6.1. Are you a public officer and government trustee on official business at this meeting?
    6.2. If so, what is your license number to act in that capacity?
    If you provided a number in response to the above question, you answered "Yes" to the first question and then provided your license number.
7. Government-issued identifying numbers act as de facto license numbers for persons engaged in government franchises. Such franchises include:
    7.1. Social Security. Also called Old Age Survivors Disability Insurance (OASDI).
    7.2. Medicare.
    7.3. Unemployment Insurance. Also called FICA.
8. The U.S. Supreme Court held in the License Tax Cases that Congress cannot establish a licensed or privileged activity in a state of the Union in order to tax it. This includes all the above forms of federal franchises.

    > "Thus, Congress having power to regulate commerce with foreign nations, and among the several States, and with the Indian tribes, may, without doubt, provide for **granting** coasting **licenses**, licenses to pilots, licenses to trade with the Indians, and any other **licenses** necessary or proper for the exercise of that great and extensive power; and the same observation is applicable to every other power of Congress, to the exercise of which the granting of licenses may be incident. All such licenses confer authority, and give rights to the licensee.
    >
    > But very different considerations apply to the **internal commerce** or **domestic trade** of the **States**. Over this commerce and trade Congress has **no power of regulation nor any direct control**. This power belongs **exclusively** to the States. **No interference by Congress with the business of citizens transacted within a State is warranted by the Constitution, except such as is strictly incidental to the exercise of powers clearly granted to the legislature**. The power to authorize a business within a State is plainly repugnant to the exclusive power of the State over the same subject. It is true that the power of Congress to tax is a very extensive power. It is given in the Constitution, with only one exception and only two qualifications. Congress cannot tax exports, and it must impose direct taxes by the rule of apportionment, and indirect taxes by the rule of uniformity. Thus limited, and thus only, it reaches every subject, and may be exercised at discretion. But, it reaches only existing subjects. **Congress cannot authorize [e.g. "license"] a trade or business within a State in order to tax it.**"
    > [License Tax Cases, 72 U.S. 462, 18 L.Ed. 497, 5 Wall. 462, 2 A.F.T.R. 2224 (1866)]

    8.1. Consequently, the ONLY place that such government franchises can lawfully be offered is on federal territory. This is consistent with the definition of "State" within the Social Security Act and all the other acts. For further details, see sections 5 through 5.5 of the following:
    > *Government Instituted Slavery Using Franchises*, Form #05.030
    > http://sedm.org/Forms/FormIndex.htm

    8.2. *Why You Aren't Eligible for Social Security*, Form #06.001
    http://sedm.org/Forms/FormIndex.htm
9. Anyone who obtains or uses a government-issued identifying number who does NOT have a domicile on federal territory at the time of its issuance is:
    9.1. Impersonating an employee or officer of the government in criminal violation of 18 U.S.C. §912.
    9.2. Impersonating a statutory "U.S. citizen" in criminal violation of 18 U.S.C. §911.

9.3. Defrauding the U.S. government in criminal violation of 42 U.S.C. §408.
10. Government-issued identifying numbers are used to track those in receipt of government "benefits". This is confirmed by the instructions for IRS Form 1042s, which list all the circumstances under which such numbers must be provided. Note that all of the situations described relate to financial benefits of one kind or another:

> Box 14, Recipient's U.S. Taxpayer Identification Number (TIN)
>
> **You must obtain a U.S. taxpayer identification number (TIN) for:**
>
> - *Any recipient whose income is effectively connected with the conduct of a trade or business in the United States.*
>   *Note. For these recipients, exemption code 01 should be entered in box 6.*
> - *Any foreign person claiming a reduced rate of, or exemption from, tax under a tax treaty between a foreign country and the United States, unless the income is an unexpected payment (as described in Regulations section 1.1441-6(g)) or consists of dividends and interest from stocks and debt obligations that are actively traded; dividends from any redeemable security issued by an investment company registered under the Investment Company Act of 1940 (mutual fund); dividends, interest, or royalties from units of beneficial interest in a unit investment trust that are (or were, upon issuance) publicly offered and are registered with the Securities and Exchange Commission under the Securities Act of 1933; and amounts paid with respect to loans of any of the above securities.*
> - *Any nonresident alien individual claiming exemption from tax under section 871(f) for certain annuities received under qualified plans.*
> - *A foreign organization claiming an exemption from tax solely because of its status as a tax-exempt organization under section 501(c) or as a private foundation.*
> - *Any QI.*
> - *Any WP or WT.*
> - *Any nonresident alien individual claiming exemption from withholding on compensation for independent personal services [services connected with a "trade or business"].*
> - *Any foreign grantor trust with five or fewer grantors.*
> - *Any branch of a foreign bank or foreign insurance company that is treated as a U.S. person.*
>
> *If a foreign person provides a TIN on a Form W-8, but is not required to do so, the withholding agent must include the TIN on Form 1042-S.*
>
> [IRS Form 1042s Instructions, Year 2006, p. 14]

11. The government cannot lawfully spend any of its revenues on a private purpose. Consequently, it is ILLEGAL to offer any kind of federal benefit to a person who is NOT ALREADY an officer or employee of the government BEFORE they signed the application such as the SSA Form SS-5:
    11.1. 5 U.S.C. §552a(a)(13) defines "federal personnel" as all those entitled to receive government retirement benefits including Social Security.

    > TITLE 5 > PART I > CHAPTER 5 > SUBCHAPTER II > § 552a
    > § 552a. Records maintained on individuals
    >
    > (a) Definitions.— For purposes of this section—
    >
    > **(13)** the term "Federal personnel" means officers and employees of the Government of the United States, members of the uniformed services (including members of the Reserve Components), <u>**individuals entitled to receive immediate or deferred retirement benefits under any retirement program of the Government of the United States (including survivor benefits)**</u>.

    11.2. The term "employee" is defined in the I.R.C. as including only government workers and not those in private industry. Consequently, all those who sign and submit IRS Form W-4 effectively become "temps" or "Kelly Girls" on temporary loan by Uncle Sam to their private employers:

    > 26 C.F.R. §31.3401(c)-1 Employee:
    >
    > "...the term [employee] includes officers and employees, <u>whether elected or appointed</u>, of the United States, a **[federal] State, Territory, Puerto Rico or any political subdivision, thereof, or the District of Columbia, or any agency or instrumentality of any one or more of the foregoing**. The term 'employee' also includes an <u>**officer of a corporation**</u>."

8 Federal Register, Tuesday, September 7, 1943, §404.104, pg. 12267

> **Employee**: "The term employee **specifically includes** officers and employees **whether elected or appointed**, of the United States, a state, territory, or political subdivision thereof or the District of Columbia or any agency or instrumentality of any one or more of the foregoing."

11.3. The U.S. Supreme Court held that the power to tax cannot be used to transfer wealth among PRIVATE human beings. Therefore, the only "individuals" within the I.R.C. Subtitle A franchise agreement are public officers and employees and instrumentalities of the government:

> *To lay, with one hand, the power of the government on the property of the citizen, and with the other to bestow it upon favored individuals to aid private enterprises and build up private fortunes, is none the less a robbery because it is done under the forms of law and is called taxation. This is not legislation. It is a decree under legislative forms.*
>
> *Nor is it taxation. 'A tax,' says Webster's Dictionary, 'is a rate or sum of money assessed on the person or property of a citizen by government for the use of the nation or State.' 'Taxes are burdens or charges imposed by the Legislature upon persons or property to raise money for public purposes.' Cooley, Const. Lim., 479.*
>
> *Coulter, J., in Northern Liberties v. St. John's Church, 13 Pa.St. 104 says, very forcibly, 'I think the common mind has everywhere taken in the understanding that **taxes are a public imposition, levied by authority of the government for the purposes of carrying on the government in all its machinery and operations—that they are imposed for a public purpose.**' See, also Pray v. Northern Liberties, 31 Pa.St. 69; Matter of Mayor of N.Y., 11 Johns., 77; Camden v. Allen, 2 Dutch., 398; Sharpless v. Mayor, supra; Hanson v. Vernon, 27 Ia., 47; Whiting v. Fond du Lac, supra."*
> [*Loan Association v. Topeka, 20 Wall. 655 (1874)*]

> "A tax, in the general understanding of the term and as used in the constitution, signifies an exaction for the support of the government. The word has never thought to connote the expropriation of money from one group for the benefit of another."
> [*U.S. v. Butler, 297 U.S. 1 (1936)*]

For exhaustive proof of the above, see:

> *Why Your Government is Either a Thief or You are a "Public Officer" for Income Tax Purposes*, Form #05.008
> http://sedm.org/Forms/FormIndex.htm

12. Any time IRS insists on using a Social Security Number as a Taxpayer Identification Number, then they are:
    12.1. Making a presumption that you are a "U.S. person" domiciled on federal territory.
    12.2. Making a presumption that you are engaged in excise taxable franchises such as a "trade or business".
    In the vast majority of cases, it is a FALSE presumption that violates due process of law and injures constitutionally protected rights.
13. If you are neither an "alien", nor are domiciled on federal territory because you are domiciled in a state of the Union, then you can't lawfully:
    13.1. Have or use any government identifying number.
    13.2. Participate in any government franchise, including Social Security, Medicare, Unemployment insurance, Driver's Licenses, Marriage Licenses, etc. See:
    > *Government Instituted Slavery Using Franchises*, Form #05.030
    > http://sedm.org/Forms/FormIndex.htm
    13.3. Be subject to federal statutory law. See:
    > *Why Statutory Civil Law is Law for Government and Not Private Persons*, Form #05.037
    > http://sedm.org/Forms/FormIndex.htm
14. If the government uses an identifying number to refer to you and you do not rebut it, then:
    14.1. You have agreed to accept a "public office" within the government.
    14.2. If you didn't already work for the government, the office you occupy is entirely without compensation.
    14.3. You have misrepresented your status as a person domiciled on federal territory or engaged in federal franchises such as a "trade or business".
15. The only law that creates an obligation to supply a number is at 26 C.F.R. §301.6109-1(b).

> *26 C.F.R. §301.6109-1(b)*
>
> *(b) Requirement to furnish one's own number—*

> (1) U.S. persons.
>
> *Every **U.S. person** who makes under this title a return, statement, or other document must furnish **its** own taxpayer identifying number as required by the forms and the accompanying instructions.*

The above requirement says the number must be disclosed IF THE SUBMITTER HAS ONE. It does not impose a requirement to apply for or have a number. The above requirement only applies to federal employees and not private human beings per 5 U.S.C. §301. If it applied to the "taxpayer" and not the IRS employee, then it would be under Part 1 instead of Part 301 of Title 26 of the Code of Federal Regulations.

16. The only penalty prescribed in the Internal Revenue Code for failure to use or disclose an identifying number is that found in 26 U.S.C. §6721(a) and 26 C.F.R. §1.6721-1(a)(1), which collectively impose a penalty of $50 for the filing of an information return that does not contain all the information required on the form.
17. If you want to withdraw an unlawful application to participate in Social Security made using SSA Form SS-5, then we suggest using the following form on our website:

> *Resignation of Compelled Social Security Trustee*, Form #06.002
> http://sedm.org/Forms/FormIndex.htm

26 Resources for Further Study and Rebuttal

If you would like to study the subjects covered in this short pamphlet in further detail, may we recommend the following authoritative sources, and also welcome you to rebut any part of this pamphlet after you have read it and studied the subject carefully yourself just as we have:

1. *Property and Privacy Protection Topic*, Section 7: Numerical Identification and Automated Tracking (OFFSITE LINK) – Family Guardian Fellowship
   http://famguardian.org/Subjects/PropertyPrivacy/PropertyPrivacy.htm#NUMERICAL_IDENTIFICATION_AND_AUTOMATED_TRACKING:
2. *Why It is Illegal for Me to Request or Use a Taxpayer Identification Number*, Form #04.205 -Use this form in the case of employers and financial institutions who are trying to compel you to procure or use a government issued identifying number.
   http://sedm.org/Forms/FormIndex.htm
3. *Government Instituted Slavery Using Franchises*, Form #05.030 - Documents the primary mechanism abused by the government to destroy the constitutional rights and sovereignty of the people.
   http://sedm.org/Forms/FormIndex.htm
4. SEDM Liberty University- Free educational materials for regaining your sovereignty as an entrepreneur or private person
   http://sedm.org/LibertyU/LibertyU.htm
5. Family Guardian Website, Taxation page- Free website
   http://famguardian.org/Subjects/Taxes/taxes.htm
6. *Great IRS Hoax*, Form #11.302. See section 5.4.17
   http://famguardian.org/Publications/GreatIRSHoax/GreatIRSHoax.htm
7. *Sovereignty Forms and Instructions Online*, Form #10.004- Free references and tools to help those who want to escape federal slavery
   http://famguardian.org/TaxFreedom/FormsInstr.htm
8. *Who are "Taxpayers" and who needs a "Taxpayer Identification Number"?*, Form #05.013- Free downloadable pamphlet
   http://sedm.org/LibertyU/LibertyU.htm (see item 4.2)
9. *Social Security: Mark of the Beast*, Form #11.407- Free book by Steven Miller
   http://famguardian.org/Publications/SocialSecurity/TOC.htm
10. Social Security: Idolatry and Slavery- Mercy Seat Christian Church
    http://famguardian.org/Subjects/Taxes/Articles/Christian/SocialSecurity-Idolatry.htm
11. Social Security Act, Title 42, Chapter 7- United States Code
    https://www.law.cornell.edu/uscode/text/42/chapter-7
12. Social Security Act- Social Security Administration
    http://www.ssa.gov/OP_Home/ssact/comp-toc.htm
13. Social Security Regulations- Social Security Administration
    http://www.ssa.gov/OP_Home/cfr20/cfrdoc.htm
14. Social Security Program Policy Documents-Social Security Administration

http://www.ssa.gov/OP_Home/
15. Legal Information Institute: Social Security- Cornell University
https://www.law.cornell.edu/socsec/
16. *666 and the Mark of the Beast*-Amazing Facts
http://www.amazingfacts.org/media-library/media/e/364/t/666-and-the-mark-of-the-beast
17. *Satan's Mark and God's Seal*-Amazing Facts
http://www.amazingfacts.org/media-library/media/e/14118/t/satans-mark---gods-seal
18. *The Mark of the Beast*-Amazing Facts
http://www.amazingfacts.org/media-library/media/e/419/t/the-mark-of-the-beast
19. *The Mark of the Beast*-Amazing Facts
http://www.amazingfacts.org/media-library/study-guide/e/4997/t/the-mark-of-the-beast

27 Questions that Readers, Grand Jurors, and Petit Jurors Should be Asking the Government

27.1 Interrogatories

This section contains questions you can ask clerks who are demanding Social Security Numbers on government forms or applications. Read the items below the following line to the clerk.

___

I need help in correctly filling out your application because you have told me that the prior application is ineffectual or that you can't give me what I am requesting on the application. Therefore, I must have made an error and I seek to prevent making or repeating an error while also ensuring that I do not knowingly commit a crime or perjury during the application process by misrepresenting my status:

1. Please provide your identification in case a legal dispute arises over this violation of my constitutional rights and private property rights. [Write the information below from government ID provided]

   ANSWER:_____

2. The U.S. Supreme Court in Bowen v. Roy, 476 U.S. 693 (1986) indicated that Social Security Number use could only be compelled in the case of those seeking government "benefits". Do you or your employer allege that this application involves a request for a benefit?

   ANSWER:_____

3. By what authority does the government issue PUBLIC property such as a Social Security Card and number to PRIVATE people who remain private AFTER receiving the property?

   > *"A tax, in the general understanding of the term and as used in the constitution, signifies an exaction for the support of the government. The word has never thought to connote the expropriation of money [or property] from one group for the benefit of another."*
   > *[U.S. v. Butler, 297 U.S. 1 (1936)]*

   ANSWER:_____

4. If it is in fact "MY" number and my property, then why don't I have the same right to exclude you from using it or storing it or even REQUESTING it? Isn't the essence of ownership the right to EXCLUDE others from using or benefitting from the property?

   > **"PROPERTY**. Rightful dominion over external objects; ownership; the **unrestricted and exclusive right to a thing; the right to dispose of the substance of a thing in every legal way, to possess it, to use it and to exclude every one else from interfering with it. Mackeld. Rom. Law, § 265.**
   > [Black's Law Dictionary, Second Edition, p. 955]

> *"In this case, we hold that the "right to exclude," so universally held to be a fundamental element of the property right,[11] falls within this category of interests that the Government cannot take without compensation."*
> [Kaiser Aetna v. United States, 444 U.S. 164 (1979)]

    ANSWER:_____

5. Do you or your employer have any evidence in your possession that I am appearing here today as a statutory "employee" of the U.S. government?

    ANSWER:_____

6. Are you aware that all the regulations governing the issuance of Social Security Numbers are found in Title 20 of the C.F.R. and entitled "Employees' benefits".

    ANSWER:_____

7. Do you have any evidence that proves the "Employees" mentioned in Title 5 of the U.S. Code or Title 20 of the C.F.R. include private humans protected by the constitution?

    ANSWER:_____

8. Do you or your employer allege that the use of Social Security Numbers is a "benefit"?

    ANSWER:_____

9. Do you or your employer allege that I am a statutory federal "employee" as defined in 5 U.S.C. §2105(a) or will be treated as such?

    ANSWER:_____

10. Do you have any reason to believe that I am here to REQUEST a "benefit" as a statutory "employee" of the national government?

    ANSWER:_____

11. Are you aware that it is a crime to impersonate an agent or officer of the national government?

    ANSWER:_____

12. Are you aware that all franchises involve the exercise of privilege, which is always attached to an office in the government?

> *"FRANCHISE. **A special privilege conferred by government on individual or corporation, and which does not belong to citizens of country generally of common right.** Elliott v. City of Eugene, 135 Or. 108, 294 P. 358, 360. **In England it is defined to be a royal privilege in the hands of a subject.** "*
> [Black's Law Dictionary, Fourth Edition, pp. 786-787]

_____

> *privilege \ˈpriv-lij, ˈpri-və-\ noun*
>
> [Middle English, from Anglo-French, from Latin privilegium law for or against a private person, from privus private + leg-, lex law] 12th century: a right or immunity granted as a peculiar benefit, advantage, or favor: prerogative especially: such a **right or immunity attached specifically to a position or an office**
> [Mish, F. C. (2003). Preface. Merriam-Websters collegiate dictionary. (Eleventh ed.). Springfield, MA: Merriam-Webster, Inc.]

    ANSWER:_____

13. Are you aware that the Federal Trade Commission identifies Social Security Numbers (SSNs) as a "franchise mark"?

> "...a commercial business arrangement is a "franchise" if it satisfies three definitional elements. Specifically, the franchisor must:
>
> (1) promise to provide a trademark or other commercial symbol;
> (2) promise to exercise significant control or provide significant assistance in the operation of the business; and
> (3) require a minimum payment of at least $500 during the first six months of operations."
> [FTC Franchise Rule Compliance Guide, May 2008, p. 1;
> SOURCE: http://business.ftc.gov/documents/bus70-franchise-rule-compliance-guide]

> "A franchise entails the right to operate a business that is "identified or associated with the franchisor's trademark, or to offer, sell, or distribute goods, services, or commodities that are identified or associated with the franchisor's trademark." The term "trademark" is intended to be read broadly to cover not only trademarks, but any service mark, trade name, or other advertising or commercial symbol. This is generally referred to as the "trademark" or "mark" element.
>
> **_The franchisor [the government] need not own the mark itself, but at the very least must have the right to license the use of the mark to others. Indeed, the right to use the franchisor's mark in the operation of the business - either by selling goods or performing services identified with the mark or by using the mark, in whole or in part, in the business' name - is an integral part of franchising. In fact, a supplier can avoid Rule coverage of a particular distribution arrangement by expressly prohibiting the distributor from using its mark."_**
> [FTC Franchise Rule Compliance Guide, May 2008;
> SOURCE: http://business.ftc.gov/documents/bus70-franchise-rule-compliance-guide]

ANSWER:_____

14. Are you aware that "employees" of the national government are franchisees of the national government, and the activity that is enfranchised is a public office described in 5 U.S.C. §2105 and mentioned above?

    ANSWER:_____

15. Are you aware that the regulations at 20 C.F.R. §422.103(d) identify the Social Security Number and accompanying card as property of the Social Security Administration and NOT me?

    > *Title 20: Employees' Benefits*
    > *PART 422—ORGANIZATION AND PROCEDURES*
    > *Subpart B—General Procedures*
    > *§ 422.103 Social security numbers.*
    >
    > *(d) Social security number cards. A person who is assigned a social security number will receive a social security number card from SSA within a reasonable time after the number has been assigned. (See §422.104 regarding the assignment of social security number cards to aliens.)* **Social security number cards are the property of SSA and must be returned upon request.**

    ANSWER:_____

16. How can I have or own that which belongs to the government and not me?

    ANSWER:_____

17. How can it be "MY" number if it belongs to the government?

    ANSWER:_____

18. How can you truthfully call it "MY" number without lying in the instructions if in fact it belongs to the government?

    ANSWER:_____

19. When you say it is "MY number" are you implying that its not the same number described in 20 C.F.R. §422.103(d) or any OTHER government statute?

ANSWER:_____

20. If the number requested on the application is the SAME number as that described in 20 C.F.R. §422.103(d) and all other government statutes, then by continuing to insist that it is "MY number" don't you have to PRESUME that I'm working for the U.S. government owner as an agent or officer in order to truthfully say that it is "MY" number?

    ANSWER:_____

21. When you say "You" or "Your" either in person or on your forms, what legal person do you specifically mean by "you" or "your"?:

    21.1. A government officer or agent in possession or use of public property such as the Social Security Number (SSN) or what the Federal Trade Commission calls a franchise mark?

    ANSWER:_____

    21.2. A private non-resident human not able to possess, use, or claim the "benefit" of public property, rights, statutes, or franchise marks such as statutory Social Security Numbers?

    NOTE: It can't simultaneously be BOTH. It can only be ONE or the OTHER. The reason I need to know is because I must know exactly who you are PRESUMING that I am in interacting with you as. In court this is called an identity hearing. To impersonate a public officer is a crime under 18 U.S.C. §912 and I am simply trying to avoid even the APPEARANCE that I am committing such a crime.

    ANSWER:_____

22. How can an SSN simultaneously have TWO absolute or exclusive owners, you and me?

    ANSWER:_____

23. If in fact the number belongs to the government as the true "owner", then aren't they and not me the ONLY party responsible for the legal liabilities resulting from the use of said number? Isn't the OWNER of property always the only party responsible for the damage that property causes to others?

    ANSWER:_____

24. Do you, as the only true and absolute government owner of the card and number agree to accept all civil and legal liabilities for the use of said number you are asking me for?

    ANSWER:_____

25. Do you have any evidence in your possession that the U.S. government has the authority to use the application process to CREATE new federal statutory "employees" out of PRIVATE people like me who don't consent to BECOME statutory "employees" or receive the "benefits" thereof or of any government franchise?

    ANSWER:_____

26. Do you have any evidence in your possession that the U.S. government has the authority to use loans of government property to CREATE new federal statutory "employees" out of PRIVATE people who don't consent to BECOME said "employees" or receive the "benefits" thereof?

    ANSWER:_____

27. If you can make me into an employee merely by loaning me PRIVILEGES under a franchise, why can't I turn information about me in to a loan with conditions that I specify under the concept of equal protection and equal treatment?

ANSWER:_____

28. How can I as a private human not appearing as a public officer use a Social Security Number without creating the false appearance that I am conspiring with you to impersonate a public officer under 18 U.S.C. §912?

> *TITLE 18 > PART 1 > CHAPTER 43 > § 912*
> *§ 912. Officer or employee of the United States*
>
> *Whoever falsely assumes or pretends to be an officer or employee acting under the authority of the United States or any department, agency or officer thereof, and acts as such, or in such pretended character demands or obtains any money, paper, document, or thing of value, shall be fined under this title or imprisoned not more than three years, or both.*

ANSWER:_____

29. Is there a way for you to change your records to indicate that a Social Security Number is unlawfully fraudulently issued and to remove it from your records?

ANSWER:_____

30. If you don't have a method to indicate in your records that the number indicated in your records is false and even fraudulent, then aren't you an accessory after the fact and committing misprision of felony in knowingly maintaining such fraudulent records under 18 U.S.C. §1002, 18 U.S.C. §3, and 18 U.S.C. §4?

ANSWER:_____

27.2 Admissions

These questions are provided for readers, Grand Jurors, and Petit Jurors to present to the government or anyone else who would challenge the facts and law appearing in this pamphlet, most of whom work for the government or stand to gain financially from perpetuating the fraud. If you find yourself in receipt of this pamphlet, you are demanded to answer the questions within 10 days. Pursuant to Federal Rule of Civil Procedure 8(b)(6), failure to deny within 10 days constitutes an admission to each question. Pursuant to 26 U.S.C. §6065, all of your answers must be signed under penalty of perjury. We are not interested in agency policy, but only sources of reasonable belief identified in the pamphlet below:

> *Reasonable Belief About Income Tax Liability*, Form #05.007
> http://sedm.org/Forms/FormIndex.htm

Your answers will become evidence in future litigation, should that be necessary in order to protect the rights of the person against whom you are attempting to unlawfully enforce federal law.

1. Admit that Social Security Numbers and Social Security Cards are the property of the U.S. government and not the person in possession of them:

   > *Title 20: Employees' Benefits*
   > *PART 422—ORGANIZATION AND PROCEDURES*
   > *Subpart B—General Procedures*
   > *§ 422.103 Social security numbers.*
   >
   > *(d) Social security number cards. A person who is assigned a social security number will receive a social security number card from SSA within a reasonable time after the number has been assigned. (See §422.104 regarding the assignment of social security number cards to aliens.)* **Social security number cards are the property of SSA and must be returned upon request.**

2. Admit that because Social Security Numbers and Social Security Cards are the property of the U.S. government, then they constitute property devoted to a "public purpose" or "public uses":

   > "**Public purpose**. *In the law of taxation, eminent domain, etc., this is a term of classification to distinguish the objects for which, according to settled usage, the government is to provide, from those which, by the like usage,*

> *are left to private interest, inclination, or liberality. <u>The constitutional requirement that the purpose of any tax, police regulation, or particular exertion of the power of eminent domain shall be the convenience, safety, or welfare of the entire community and not the welfare of a specific individual or class of persons [such as, for instance, federal benefit recipients as individuals].</u> "Public purpose" that will justify expenditure of public money generally means such an activity as will serve as benefit to community as a body and which at same time is directly related function of government. Pack v. Southwestern Bell Tel. & Tel. Co., 215 Tenn. 503, 387 S.W.2d. 789, 794.*
>
> *The term is synonymous with governmental purpose. As employed to denote the objects for which taxes may be levied, it has no relation to the urgency of the public need or to the extent of the public benefit which is to follow; <u>the essential requisite being that a public service or use shall affect the inhabitants as a community, and not merely as individuals.</u> A public purpose or public business has for its objective the promotion of the public health, safety, morals, general welfare, security, prosperity, and contentment of all the inhabitants or residents within a given political division, as, for example, a state, the sovereign powers of which are exercised to promote such public purpose or public business."*
> [Black's Law Dictionary, Sixth Edition, p. 1231, Emphasis added]

   YOUR ANSWER:_____

3. Admit that only public "employees" on official duty can possess, use, or control property devoted to a "public use".

   YOUR ANSWER:_____

4. Admit that it is illegal to use public property for a *private* purpose:

   > TITLE 18 > PART I > CHAPTER 11 > § 208
   > § 208. Acts affecting a personal financial interest
   >
   > *(a) Except as permitted by subsection (b) hereof, <u>whoever, being an officer or employee of the executive branch of the United States Government, or of any independent agency of the United States</u>, a Federal Reserve bank director, officer, or employee, or an officer or employee of the District of Columbia, including a special Government employee, <u>participates personally and substantially as a Government officer or employee, through decision, approval, disapproval, recommendation, the rendering of advice, investigation, or otherwise, in a judicial or other proceeding, application, request for a ruling or other determination, contract, claim, controversy, charge, accusation, arrest, or other particular matter in which, to his knowledge, he, his spouse, minor child, general partner, organization in which he is serving as officer, director, trustee, general partner or employee, or any person or organization with whom he is negotiating or has any arrangement concerning prospective employment, has a financial [or personal/private] interest</u>—*
   >
   > *Shall be subject to the penalties set forth in section 216 of this title.*

   YOUR ANSWER:_____

5. Admit that the number assigned by the Social Security Administration called a Social Security Number is created, owned, reissued, and controlled exclusively by the Social Security Administration.

   YOUR ANSWER:_____

6. Admit that the Social Security Number is primarily used to control you, and that you have no control or ownership over how the government uses or discloses it.

   YOUR ANSWER:_____

7. Admit that it is impossible to "have" a number. A number is information and you can know information but you can't own it unless it is copyrighted.

   YOUR ANSWER:_____

8. Admit that claiming a number or participating in Social Security guarantees NOTHING, according to the Supreme Court.

   > *"We must conclude that <u>a person covered by the Act has not such a right in benefit payments</u>... This is not to say, however, that Congress may exercise its power to modify the statutory scheme free of all constitutional restraint."*
   > [Flemming v. Nestor, 363 U.S. 603 (1960)]

> *"The Social Security system may be accurately described as a form of social insurance, enacted pursuant to Congress' power to "spend money in aid of the `general welfare,'" Helvering v. Davis, supra, at 640, whereby persons gainfully employed, and those who employ them, are taxed to permit the payment of benefits to the retired and disabled, and their dependents. Plainly the expectation is that many members of the present productive work force will in turn become beneficiaries rather than supporters of the program. But each worker's benefits, though flowing from the contributions he made to the [363 U.S. 603, 610] national economy while actively employed, are not dependent on the degree to which he was called upon to support the system by taxation. **It is apparent that the noncontractual interest of an employee covered by the Act cannot be soundly analogized to that of the holder of an annuity, whose right to benefits is bottomed on his contractual premium payments**.*"
> *[Flemming v. Nestor, 363 U.S. 603, 610, 80 S.Ct. 1367 (1960)]*

YOUR ANSWER:_____

9. Admit that without a guaranteed benefit, anyone using a number cannot claim any legally enforceable right or entitlement or "property".

YOUR ANSWER:_____

10. Admit that the Social Security Act is found on the Social Security website at the following address:

    https://www.ssa.gov/OP_Home/ssact/ssact.htm

YOUR ANSWER:_____

11. Admit that the Social Security Act is also found in the U.S. Code, Title 42, Chapter 7 available on the web at the address below:

    https://www.law.cornell.edu/uscode/text/42/chapter-7

YOUR ANSWER:_____

12. Admit that only "U.S. citizens" and "lawful permanent residents" may apply for the Social Security program. See website above and 20 C.F.R. §422.104(a).

YOUR ANSWER:_____

13. Admit that the term "United States" is defined in the current Social Security Act, Section 1101(a)(2) as follows:

    > *SEC. 1101. [42 U.S.C. §1301] (a) When used in this Act—*
    >
    > *"(2) The term "United States" when used in a geographical sense means, except where otherwise provided, the States."*
    >
    > *[Social Security Act as of 2005, Section 1101]*

YOUR ANSWER:_____

14. Admit that the term "State" is defined in the current Social Security Act, Section 1101(a)(1) as follows:

    > *SEC. 1101. [42 U.S.C. §1301] (a) When used in this Act—*
    >
    > *(1) The term 'State', except where otherwise provided, includes the District of Columbia and the Commonwealth of Puerto Rico, and when used in titles IV, V, VII, XI, XIX, and XXI includes the Virgin Islands and Guam. Such term when used in titles III, IX, and XII also includes the Virgin Islands. Such term when used in title V and in part B of this title also includes American Samoa, the Northern Mariana Islands, and the Trust Territory of the Pacific Islands. Such term when used in titles XIX and XXI also includes the Northern Mariana Islands and American Samoa. In the case of Puerto Rico, the Virgin Islands, and Guam, titles I, X, and XIV, and title XVI (as in effect without regard to the amendment made by section 301 of the Social Security Amendments of 1972[3])*

shall continue to apply, and the term 'State' when used in such titles (but not in title XVI as in effect pursuant to such amendment after December 31, 1973) includes Puerto Rico, the Virgin Islands, and Guam. Such term when used in title XX also includes the Virgin Islands, Guam, American Samoa, and the Northern Mariana Islands. Such term when used in title IV also includes American Samoa."
[Social Security Act as of 2005, Section 1101]

YOUR ANSWER:_____

15. Admit that states of the Union are *not* included in the above definition of either "State" or "United States".

    YOUR ANSWER:_____

16. Admit that under the rules of statutory construction, that which is not explicitly included is excluded by implication:

    *"**Expressio unius est exclusio alterius**. A maxim of statutory interpretation meaning that **the expression of one thing is the exclusion of another.** Burgin v. Forbes, 293 Ky. 456, 169 S.W.2d. 321, 325; Newblock v. Bowles, 170 Okl. 487, 40 P.2d. 1097, 1100. Mention of one thing implies exclusion of another. **When certain persons or things are specified in a law, contract, or will, an intention to exclude all others from its operation may be inferred.** Under this maxim, if statute specifies one exception to a general rule or assumes to specify the effects of a certain provision, other exceptions or effects are excluded."*
    [Black's Law Dictionary, Sixth Edition, p. 581]

    YOUR ANSWER:_____

17. Admit that the federal government has no legislative jurisdiction within states of the Union according to the U.S. Supreme Court:

    *"It is no longer open to question that **the general government, unlike the states**, Hammer v. Dagenhart, 247 U.S. 251, 275, 38 S.Ct. 529, 3 A.L.R. 649, Ann.Cas.1918E 724, **possesses no inherent power in respect of the internal affairs of the states; and emphatically not with regard to legislation.**"*
    [Carter v. Carter Coal Co., 298 U.S. 238, 56 S.Ct. 855 (1936)]

    _____

    *"The difficulties arising out of our dual form of government and the opportunities for differing opinions concerning the relative rights of state and national governments are many; **but for a very long time this court has steadfastly adhered to the doctrine that the taxing power of Congress does not extend to the states or their political subdivisions**. The same basic reasoning which leads to that conclusion, we think, requires like limitation upon the power which springs from the bankruptcy clause. United States v. Butler, supra."*
    [Ashton v. Cameron County Water Improvement District No. 1, 298 U.S. 513; 56 S.Ct. 892 (1936)]

    YOUR ANSWER:_____

18. Admit that the Social Security Act qualifies as "legislation" as indicated in the above cites.

    YOUR ANSWER:_____

19. Admit that participation in Social Security is voluntary for people who live outside of the District of Columbia and the territories and possessions of the "United States" as defined above because it does not and cannot apply to them absent their informed, explicit, written consent.

    YOUR ANSWER:_____

20. Admit that it is ILLEGAL for the Social Security Administration to approve an application from a person who is not a "U.S. citizen" under 8 U.S.C. §1401 or lawful "permanent resident".

    Title 20: Employees' Benefits
    PART 422—ORGANIZATION AND PROCEDURES
    Subpart B—General Procedures
    § 422.104   Who can be assigned a social security number.

(a) Persons eligible for SSN assignment. We can assign you a social security number if you meet the evidence requirements in §422.107 and you are:

(1) A United States citizen; or

(2) An alien lawfully admitted to the United States for permanent residence or under other authority of law permitting you to work in the United States (§422.105 describes how we determine if a nonimmigrant alien is permitted to work in the United States); or

(3) An alien who cannot provide evidence of alien status showing lawful admission to the U.S., or an alien with evidence of lawful admission but without authority to work in the U.S., if the evidence described in §422.107(e) does not exist, but only for a valid nonwork reason. We consider you to have a valid nonwork reason if:

(i) You need a social security number to satisfy a Federal statute or regulation that requires you to have a social security number in order to receive a Federally-funded benefit to which you have otherwise established entitlement and you reside either in or outside the U.S.; or

(ii) You need a social security number to satisfy a State or local law that requires you to have a social security number in order to receive public assistance benefits to which you have otherwise established entitlement, and you are legally in the United States.

YOUR ANSWER:_____

21. Admit that an illegal or unconstitutional act does not constitute an "act" of a government, but simply the act of a private human being masquerading as a public officer:

> "... *the maxim that the King can do no wrong has no place in our system of government; yet it is also true, in respect to the State itself, that whatever wrong is attempted in its name is imputable to its government and not to the State, for, as it can speak and act only by law, whatever it does say and do must be lawful. That which therefore is unlawful because made so by the supreme law, the Constitution of the United States, is not the word or deed of the State, but is the mere wrong and trespass of those individual persons who falsely spread and act in its name.*"

> "This distinction is essential to the idea of constitutional government. To deny it or blot it out obliterates the line of demarcation that separates constitutional government from absolutism, free self- government based on the sovereignty of the people from that despotism, whether of the one or the many, which enables the agent of the state to declare and decree that he is the state; to say 'L'Etat, c'est moi.' Of what avail are written constitutions, whose bills of right, for the security of individual liberty, have been written too often with the blood of martyrs shed upon the battle-field and the scaffold, if their limitations and restraints upon power may be overpassed with impunity by the very agencies created and appointed to guard, defend, and enforce them; and that, too, with the sacred authority of law, not only compelling obedience, but entitled to respect? And how else can these principles of individual liberty and right be maintained, if, when violated, the judicial tribunals are forbidden to visit penalties upon individual offenders, who are the instruments of wrong, whenever they interpose the shield of the state? **The doctrine is not to be tolerated.** The whole frame and scheme of the political institutions of this country, state and federal, protest against it. Their continued existence is not compatible with it. It is the doctrine of absolutism, pure, simple, and naked, and of communism which is its twin, the double progeny of the same evil birth."
> [U.S. Supreme Court in *Poindexter v. Greenhow, 114 U.S. 270, 5 S.Ct. 903 (1885)*]

YOUR ANSWER:_____

22. Admit that an illegal or unconstitutional act is an "act" of a private party that certainly cannot be recognized as an act of any kind on the part of a legitimate government.

> "An unconstitutional act is not a law; it confers no rights; it imposes no duties; it affords no protection; it creates no office; it is in legal contemplation, as inoperative as though it had never been passed."
> [Norton v. Shelby County, 118 U.S. 425 (1885)]

YOUR ANSWER:_____

23. Admit that an illegally issued Social Security Number is not a Social Security Number, but simply an illegal act that cannot be recognized and certainly not benefited from by anyone exercising a lawful, constitutional function of government.

YOUR ANSWER:_____

24. Admit that persons born in states of the Union are "nationals" under 8 U.S.C. §1101(a)(21) but not "citizens" under 8 U.S.C. §1401. If you disagree, please rebut:

    Why You are a "national", "state national", and Constitutional but not Statutory Citizen, Form #05.016
    http://sedm.org/Forms/05-MemLaw/WhyANational.pdf

    YOUR ANSWER:_____

25. Admit that applicant has stated under penalty of perjury that he is neither a statutory "U.S. citizen" as defined in 8 U.S.C. §1401 nor a "lawful nor a permanent resident".

    YOUR ANSWER:_____

26. Admit that applicant has provided to you a copy of his U.S. passport, proving that he is a "national" as defined in 8 U.S.C. §1101(a)(21).

    > "...the only means by which an American can lawfully leave the country or return to it - absent a Presidentially granted exception - is with a passport... As a travel control document, **a passport is both proof of identity and proof of allegiance to the United States.** Even under a travel control statute, however, a passport remains in a sense a document by which the Government vouches for the bearer and for his conduct."
    > [Haig v. Agee, 453 U.S. 280 (1981)]

    YOUR ANSWER:_____

27. Admit that those who either never applied for Social Security or whose application was made by others who they never authorized cannot be obligated to participate and that any number that might have been assigned under such circumstance is illegally obtained and invalid because issued without consent.

    YOUR ANSWER:_____

28. Admit that it is a federal crime to compel the use or disclosure of Social Security Numbers.

    > TITLE 42 - THE PUBLIC HEALTH AND WELFARE
    > CHAPTER 7 - SOCIAL SECURITY
    > SUBCHAPTER II - FEDERAL OLD-AGE, SURVIVORS, AND DISABILITY INSURANCE BENEFITS
    > Sec. 408. Penalties
    >
    > (a) In general
    > Whoever -...
    >
    > (8) discloses, uses, or compels the disclosure of the social security number of any person in violation of the laws of the United States; shall be guilty of a felony and upon conviction thereof shall be fined under title 18 or imprisoned for not more than five years, or both.

    YOUR ANSWER:_____

Affirmation:

I declare under penalty of perjury as required under 26 U.S.C. §6065 that the answers provided by me to the foregoing questions are true, correct, and complete to the best of my knowledge and ability, so help me God. I also declare that these answers are completely consistent with each other and with my understanding of the Constitution of the United States, Internal Revenue Code, Treasury Regulations, the Internal Revenue Manual, and the rulings of the Supreme Court but not necessarily lower federal courts.

Name (print):_____

Signature:_____

Date:_____

Witness name (print):_____

Witness Signature:_____

Witness Date:_____